The Son of God

The Son of God

Three Views of the Identity of Jesus

A Trinitarian View by
Charles Lee Irons

An Arian View by
Danny André Dixon

A Socinian View by
Dustin R. Smith

Foreword by
James F. McGrath

WIPF & STOCK · Eugene, Oregon

THE SON OF GOD
Three Views of the Identity of Jesus

Copyright © 2015 Charles Lee Irons, Danny André Dixon, and Dustin R. Smith. All rights reserved. Except for brief quotations in critical publications or reviews, no part of this book may be reproduced in any manner without prior written permission from the publisher. Write: Permissions, Wipf and Stock Publishers, 199 W. 8th Ave., Suite 3, Eugene, OR 97401.

Wipf & Stock
An Imprint of Wipf and Stock Publishers
199 W. 8th Ave., Suite 3
Eugene, OR 97401

www.wipfandstock.com

ISBN 13: 978-1-4982-2426-0

Manufactured in the U.S.A.

CONTENTS

Foreword by James F. McGrath | vii
On the Labels | xiii
English Versions of the Bible | xvi
List of Abbreviations | xvii

PART ONE

A Trinitarian View: Jesus, the Divine Son of God (Irons) | 3
An Arian Response to a Trinitarian View (Dixon) | 23
A Socinian Response to a Trinitarian View (Smith) | 36
A Trinitarian Reply (Irons) | 47

PART TWO

An Arian View: Jesus, the Life-Given Son of God (Dixon) | 65
A Trinitarian Response to an Arian View (Irons) | 84
A Socinian Response to an Arian View (Smith) | 96
An Arian Reply (Dixon) | 107

PART THREE

A Socinian View: Jesus, the Human Son of God (Smith) | 127
A Trinitarian Response to a Socinian View (Irons) | 146
An Arian Response to a Socinian View (Dixon) | 157
A Socinian Reply (Smith) | 165

Bibliography | 181
Index of Ancient Sources | 189
Index of Authors | 204
Index of Subjects | 207

FOREWORD

THE STUDY OF NEW Testament Christology—the depiction(s) of Jesus articulated by the authors of the New Testament—has never ceased to be of interest. But if it may not be true to say that there has been *more* interest in the subject in recent years, the past several decades have at the very least witnessed a burst of *creativity* in the field, with significant new and interesting proposals being offered by a range of scholars. This work has been stimulated in turn by an increased amount of attention to ancient Jewish sources, sparked by the publication of the Dead Sea Scrolls and other ancient literature that was previously neglected or unknown. This has allowed scholars to get a sense as never before of the Jewish context within which Jesus and his earliest followers reflected on who he was.

The New Testament sources are full of affirmations of the sort that one also finds in non-Christian Jewish sources: "Jesus answered, 'The first [commandment] is, "Hear, O Israel: the Lord our God, the Lord is one"'" (Mark 12:29), "there is no God but one" (1 Cor 8:4), "there is one God" (1 Tim 2:5), "the only true God" (John 17:3), "You believe that there is one God. Good!" (Jas 2:19). And yet Christians have typically coupled such references to the one God with references to Christ as "one Lord," "one Mediator," "the one whom [the only true God] sent." Much of the first few Christian centuries were spent trying to work out how these statements were best to be understood, and what their implications might be. The present day has seen not only an increasing awareness of the ancient Jewish context of the New Testament, but also the fact that views which were in the past dismissed as clear heresies were—whether one judges them to be right or wrong—sincere attempts to make sense of the range of New Testament evidence.

FOREWORD

So much has been written on New Testament Christology in recent years and decades, that it is simply impossible to summarize it all in a preface and do it justice. Fortunately, the pages of this book will survey and engage the key issues, highlighting key points of disagreement among scholars in the process. But it may nevertheless be worth listing here a few of the important points about which there is ongoing debate:

- Did the earliest Christians think of Jesus as a human being singled out and sent by God, or as a preexistent angelic or other celestial figure subordinate to God, or as the incarnation of one who was fully God?
- Did different early Christian authors have different views of Jesus, corresponding to those listed above?
- Was there a development in early Christology, from the view of Jesus as a special human being to the view of Jesus as a preexistent celestial figure, or was the latter view held from the very beginning?
- Did Christians, in formulating their view of Jesus, include him within the nature, or the identity, of the one God, or did they view him as distinct from the one God, however closely related to him?
- In viewing Jesus as they did, did the earliest Christians depart from Jewish monotheism as it existed in their time?

On the pages that follow, you will find most of these points engaged directly; and where any are not addressed explicitly, reading the scholarly literature that is cited will bring you into contact with discussions of the remaining issues. These are points about which there is ongoing vigorous disagreement among scholars, and this disagreement, however much it has progressed, mirrors debates which have been going on for nearly 2,000 years. And yet many Christians may not even be aware either of the diversity of views held among Christians, or of the scholarship that brings historical knowledge to bear on these questions.

There has been a delightful trend in recent years towards the production of multi-author volumes offering three (or in some cases four or even five) different views on a particular subject. In the present volume, three views of Jesus are presented. Each of these views is attested in very ancient Christian sources (often in the process of the one being denounced by a proponent of another view). Each view is one that significant numbers of scholars are convinced is reflected in at least some of the writings of the New Testament. The authors who have contributed to this volume each

FOREWORD

seeks not only to engage with this New Testament scholarship, but also to formulate a convincing portrait of Jesus on that basis.

Scholarship is a conversation, and the wider public often has only the vaguest sense of how central interaction between viewpoints is to the scholarly endeavor. On the one hand, every scholar seeks to break new ground, to come up with new ideas and interpretations. It is a requirement as part of our jobs, since we are expected to publish, and no scholarly periodical is likely to publish an article which simply says things that have been said before. On the other hand, the scholarly community evaluates our new proposals, looking at them with critical scrutiny. Only rarely do our new proposals overturn a prevailing consensus. And that is as it should be. Both these two poles are conversational in character. The individual scholar interacts with the scholarly community through the literature that has been published previously, trying to see just a little bit further standing on our shoulders. And then the scholarly community responds in turn with feedback and evaluation, and with acceptance or rebuttal.

I still recall a friend who was, like me at the time, both a Christian and a PhD student, saying that the process of trying to earn a doctorate pushes you towards heresy. The truth has supposedly already been established, and so new ideas can only represent departures from them. This viewpoint is not uncommon, and is a reason why ordinary people in churches often view scholars and scholarship with suspicion.

However, it ought to be clear in our internet age, if it was not clear well before that, that the notion of the "truth established once for all" has never reflected the reality. Churches use Bibles the contents of which differ. And churches which share the exact same Bible, and the exact same view of the Bible as without error, may disagree radically on what the Bible means. Christians have always been engaging in conversations which involved not only the Jewish Scriptures and the life and teaching of Jesus, but the world around them. Some have claimed to be doing otherwise, but the claims do not reflect the reality. Tertullian famously asked "What has Athens to do with Jerusalem?"—suggesting that there is a huge gulf between biblical religion and Greek philosophy. And yet it seems clear that Tertullian's thinking—for instance, in applying the term "Trinity" (threeness) to God—was indebted to his background in Stoic philosophy. We cannot ignore the ancient context of the Biblical texts, nor can we ignore the context within which we interpret them. And when we do both those things, we come to

FOREWORD

see just how it is possible for people with the same shared Scriptures and the same shared Jesus to nonetheless have drawn different conclusions.

More than a century ago, an editorial in the periodical *The Biblical World* addressed this very point:

> The duty of Christian thinkers in the present generation is to address themselves consciously and earnestly to the task never indeed abandoned, but long held in check by the doctrine of an authoritative canon of Scripture or an authoritative church, and to seek from all the sources at our disposal to frame for our day such a statement of truths in the realm of religion as will on the one hand satisfy in the fullest possible measure the data at our disposal and on the other hand meet as fully as possible the needs of our day . . . . In this process the true greatness of Jesus and the finality of his fundamental thought will not be lost, but only transferred from postulate to assured result of investigation. But no period and no experience, certainly not that of our own day, will be without its possible contribution, and our effort will be not to return to the position of any past age, even that of the dawn of Christianity, but with fullest loyalty to the achievements of the past to push on as far as possible toward the larger light and fuller truth.[1]

The situation has not changed, but this dialogical nature of theology seems no more generally recognized among Christian laypeople than it was in the past. And that is unfortunate.

Most of the volumes that have been published offering multiple viewpoints on a topic have done so within the framework of a shared set of assumptions, typically that of conservative Evangelicalism. Some of the views included might seem radical within that context, but often they appear quite narrowly clustered when viewed from another perspective. Occasionally such volumes include, in the interest of "fairness" or perhaps of sensationalism, a viewpoint that is considered fringe not merely by Evangelicals but by all academics. The present volume is different from such other volumes in important ways. On the one hand, the contributors share a commitment to interpreting the Bible diligently and accurately, and allowing the evidence from the Bible to shape their views. On the other hand, the three christological viewpoints which the authors represent are only relatively rarely found within the same church setting. Trinitarianism, Arianism, and Socinianism are typically not found within the same denomination, much

---

1. "Truth 'Once for All Delivered,'" *The Biblical World* 35.4 (April 1910) 221–22.

FOREWORD

less within the same church, and more often than not, adherents to one of the viewpoints will regard the other views as anathema.

And so the fact that the authors are *friends* across such divides is an important message of the book, one which should not be missed. The content of their discussions is important, but so too is the fact that people with a shared desire to follow Jesus and to be faithful to Scripture can understand who Jesus is in different ways. In the past, those with the authority to do so who held one of these viewpoints might have excommunicated or expelled the others. In some circles, that might still happen today. And yet if we think about the emperor Constantine, he brought Christians together at the Council of Nicaea to seek unity, and oversaw the condemnation of Arius—and yet he would later be baptized by a bishop who adhered to the same viewpoint as Arius. Christians who listened carefully to the various sides could find arguments from both to be compelling, and could find it difficult to choose between them.

Christianity has always been diverse, and has long been plagued by a tendency toward reciprocal condemnation and exclusion of others who have different opinions than our own, as we have proved time and again to be unable to apply the demand of Jesus that we love our enemies to those who are "enemies" only of our idea, but not necessarily of ourselves. The contributors exemplify something that scholars have long known, and which explains the approach to scholarship which I outlined towards the start of this preface. It is very easy for any one of us, no matter how great our expertise in a given area, to be wrong. If we are to get at the truth, our chances of achieving this are much greater if we seek it in community, a community that challenges us with a critical examination of our assumptions and claims, and presents us with alternative viewpoints which we in turn must evaluate. It is a delight to see three individuals with such different viewpoints committed to interacting with the best scholarship on New Testament Christology, and to engaging one another. I hope that readers will find themselves welcomed into the conversation, and that they in turn will not just learn about Christology, but about being Christians who disagree—sometimes adamantly and vociferously—yet without hating one another. For it seems to me that, if we figure out who Jesus is, and in the process ignore what he taught, we have missed the point. It is possible to be genuinely concerned—as the authors of this volume are—to mean the "right thing" when calling Jesus "Lord, Lord," and yet to recognize that this

FOREWORD

Lord, however his nature is understood, has called those who follow him to live in a certain way.

James F. McGrath, PhD
Clarence L. Goodwin Chair in New Testament Language & Literature
Department of Philosophy and Religion, Butler University
Indianapolis, Indiana

ON THE LABELS

CHARLES LEE IRONS ON THE "TRINITARIAN" LABEL

THE TRINITARIAN VIEW OF the identity of Jesus that I wish to defend is the historic position enshrined as church doctrine in the Nicene Creed. It is the position that Jesus is the divine Son of God. Jesus' identity as the Son of God implies his full ontological equality with the Father. Jesus did not become the Son; he always was the Son. There was never a time when the Father was without his Son. The Son, in his very person, not merely through his words, fully reveals the Father, which he could not do if he were a mere creature. Crucial to this understanding is a fundamental metaphysical presupposition that there are only two kinds of being: Creator and creature. Any existing being that has a beginning and a time when it did not exist is a creature. Any existing being that is described in Scripture as having created all things belongs on the Creator side of the Creator-creature distinction. Since the New Testament asserts that God created all things through the Son, the Son must be fully divine and not a creature. In addition to focusing on the Son's eternal preexistence, I also defend his full humanity. This yields a three-phase Christology: (1) eternal preexistence, (2) incarnation, and (3) exaltation. The eternally preexistent Son became man and was exalted to the right hand of God the Father in order to receive divine worship and to exercise divine sovereignty over all things, a worship and a sovereignty that are appropriate because of his ontological deity.

ON THE LABELS

DANNY ANDRÉ DIXON ON THE "ARIAN" LABEL

I have, with stipulations, agreed to allow the tag "An Arian View" to summarize my position. If my point of view is successful in its attempt to consistently make sense of the biblical data, then it would have been true many years *before* Arius's flash-in-the-pan appearance in history and his followers' crystalizing his perspectives. I do not quote Arius in presenting my argument, although at the end I generally grant that Arius and I would have points of agreement. I do not know if Arius himself ever said any of these things. His friends and enemies report in *their* writings what he purportedly taught and did. So one may believe as I do without ever having heard of Arius or perused even the skeletal pickings that exist of his reported creed.

In this discussion, I think I appropriately interpret biblical texts to say that as God miraculously caused Mary, a virgin, to conceive in a way that has never been known to happen among the brotherhood of men (Luke 1:34–35), so it is no difficult matter for him to miraculously cause a preexisting entity to take on a God-prepared body (Heb 10:5)—in effect, to become a human being like his brothers in every way without disrupting God's eternal perspective of what a man is supposed to be (Heb 2:17).

I conclude that Scripture says God gave life to his Son, a unique entity—though not an angel—in preexistent time (John 1:1–3), and God granted him things like creative power (Heb 1:12ff), an eternal throne, and a present seat of honor next to him in heaven (Heb 1:5–13). God has also given to his Anointed authority (Matt 9:5–8; 28:18ff) to bear Yahweh's name and titles; to forgive sins; to receive worship; and to perform miracles. Second-temple Jewish writings also see such marvels as being true of preexisting spiritual entities, who later became human. If "an Arian View" serves as a summary of these pre-Arian observations, then so be it.

DUSTIN R. SMITH ON THE "SOCINIAN" LABEL

Socinian Christology is the perspective which insists that the God revealed in Scripture is numerically one and that Jesus possessed no literal preexistence, having come into existence at his birth. This perspective is also known today as unitary monotheism or unitarianism (but not Unitarian Universalism).

ON THE LABELS

"Socinian" is a label which is simultaneously helpful and anachronistic. The designation began to be used in the early 1600s to describe the views of the Sozzini family, namely Lelio and his nephew Fausto. As a product of the Radical Reformation, these men were convinced that the trinitarian dogmas were problematic and in need of considerable overhaul. They were similarly unsatisfied with the Arian perspective on Christ, which adhered to literal preexistence but observed that Jesus was subordinated to God in a variety of passages. Lelio and Fausto Sozzini argued instead that Jesus' existence began in the womb of Mary, at the moment of the virginal conception. Their views spread into Poland, Holland, and England by the end of the 1600s. Socinian writings, such as the Racovian Catechism, were highly influential among such thinkers as John Locke, Isaac Newton, and John Milton. In sum, the designation "Socinian" appropriately describes the Christology of the Sozzini family. However, this term is anachronistic because those persuaded to embrace this Christology reckon that it was both held and taught by the historical Jesus, the twelve disciples, the Apostle Paul, etc. It is in this regard that the label "Socinian" is an anachronism. Nevertheless, for the sake of differentiating the Christology which I find within the Scriptures from those held by my dialogue partners, Socinian is an acceptable term.

ENGLISH VERSIONS OF THE BIBLE

Scripture quotations marked "ASV" are from the American Standard Version of the Bible, published in 1901 by Thomas Nelson & Sons. Public domain.

Scripture quotations marked "ESV" are from the ESV® Bible (The Holy Bible, English Standard Version®), copyright © 2001 by Crossway, a publishing ministry of Good News Publishers. Used by permission. All rights reserved.

Scripture quotations marked "KJV" are from the King James (or Authorized) Version of the Bible, completed in 1611. Public domain.

Scripture quotations marked "NASB" are from the New American Standard Bible®, copyright © 1960, 1962, 1963, 1968, 1971, 1972, 1973, 1975, 1977, 1995 by The Lockman Foundation. Used by permission.

Scripture quotations marked "NET Bible" are from the NET Bible® copyright ©1996–2006 by Biblical Studies Press, LLC. http://netbible.com. Used by permission. All rights reserved.

Scripture quotations marked "NIV" are from the Holy Bible, New International Version®, NIV®, copyright © 1973, 1978, 1984, 2011 by Biblica, Inc.™ Used by permission of Zondervan. All rights reserved worldwide. The "NIV" and "New International Version" are trademarks registered in the United States Patent and Trademark Office by Biblica, Inc.™

Scripture quotations marked "NKJV" are from the New King James Version®, copyright © 1982 by Thomas Nelson. Used by permission. All rights reserved.

Scripture quotations marked "NRSV" are from the New Revised Standard Version Bible, copyright © 1989 by the Division of Christian Education of the National Council of the Churches of Christ in the United States of America. Used by permission. All rights reserved.

Scripture quotations marked "RSV" are from the Revised Standard Version of the Bible, copyright 1952 (2nd edition, 1971) by the Division of Christian Education of the National Council of the Churches of Christ in the United States of America. Used by permission. All rights reserved.

Unless otherwise noted, Charles Lee Irons quotes Scripture from the ESV. Unless otherwise noted, Danny André Dixon quotes Scripture from the NIV (1984 edition). Unless otherwise noted, Dustin R. Smith quotes Scripture from the NASB (1995 edition).

ABBREVIATIONS

AB	The Anchor Bible
ABD	*The Anchor Bible Dictionary*, ed. D. N. Freedman
ABRL	Anchor Bible Reference Library
ANTC	Abingdon New Testament Commentaries
BDAG	Bauer, Danker, Arndt, and Gingrich, *A Greek-English Lexicon of the New Testament and Other Early Christian Literature*. 3rd ed.
BDB	Brown, Driver, and Briggs, *Hebrew and English Lexicon of the Old Testament*
BNTC	Black's New Testament Commentary
BSac	*Bibliotheca Sacra*
CBQ	*Catholic Biblical Quarterly*
DJG	IVP *Dictionary of Jesus and the Gospels*, ed. J. B. Green
DLNT	IVP *Dictionary of the Later New Testament*, ed. R. P. Martin and P. H. Davids
DPL	IVP *Dictionary of Paul and His Letters*, ed. G. F. Hawthorne and R. P. Martin
DSSR	*The Dead Sea Scrolls Reader*, 6 vols., ed. D. W. Parry and E. Tov
ET	English Translation
HBT	*Horizons in Biblical Theology*
ICC	International Critical Commentary

ABBREVIATIONS

ISBE	*International Standard Bible Encyclopedia*, ed. J. Orr et al
JBL	*Journal of Biblical Studies*
JSJ	*Journal for the Study of Judaism*
JSJSup	Journal for the Study of Judaism Supplement Series
JSNT	*Journal for the Study of the New Testament*
JSP	*Journal for the Study of the Pseudepigrapha*
JTS	*Journal of Theological Studies*
LXX	Septuagint
NICNT	New International Commentary on the New Testament
NIDB	*New Interpreter's Dictionary of the Bible*, ed. K. D. Sankefeld
NIDNTT	*New International Dictionary of New Testament Theology*, ed. C. Brown
NIDOTT	*New International Dictionary of Old Testament Theology*, ed. W. A. VanGemeren
NIGTC	New International Greek Testament Commentary
NovT	*Novum Testamentum*
NPNF2	Nicene and Post-Nicene Fathers, Second Series
NSBT	New Studies in Biblical Theology
NTD	Neue Testament Deutsch
NTS	New Testament Studies
ODCC	*Oxford Dictionary of the Christian Church*, ed. F. L. Cross and E. A. Livingstone
OTP	*Old Testament Pseudepigrapha*, 2 vols., ed. J. H. Charlesworth
PNTC	Pillar New Testament Commentary
RB	*Revue Biblique*
SNTSMS	Society for New Testament Studies Monograph Series
SVTP	Studia in Veteris Testamenti Pseudepigrapha
TCGNT	*Textual Commentary on the Greek New Testament*, by B. Metzger and B. Ehrman

ABBREVIATIONS

TDNT	*Theological Dictionary of the New Testament*, ed. G. Kittel
TDOT	*Theological Dictionary of the Old Testament*, ed. G. J. Botterweck et al
WBC	Word Biblical Commentary
WUNT	Wissenschaftliche Untersuchungen zum Neuen Testament
ZECNT	Zondervan Exegetical Commentary on the New Testament

Part One

A TRINITARIAN VIEW
Jesus, the Divine Son of God

CHARLES LEE IRONS

Ralph Waldo Emerson, the famous nineteenth-century New England Unitarian minister and father of transcendentalism, was a confessed non-Trinitarian. He dismissed the deity of Christ as the post-apostolic church's "noxious exaggeration about the person of Jesus."[1] My interlocutors, Dixon and Smith, while no doubt differing with Emerson on many points, presumably would agree with him here. In this essay, I take up the challenge of demonstrating that the deity of Christ is not an exaggeration, but the sober claim of Jesus himself and a core part of the apostolic proclamation.

THESIS AND DEFINITION

Before I attempt to sketch the biblical case for the deity of Christ, I need to explain more carefully what I mean by it. The terms "deity" or "divine" can be used in different senses. When the founder of Rome died, he was hailed as "the divine Romulus"[2], but the ancient Romans did not view Romulus as an eternally preexistent, divine being. He was regarded as an ordinary man who, because of his greatness as the founder of Rome, was taken up into heaven to join the pantheon of the gods after his death—a strictly

---

1. From his 1838 address to the Harvard Divinity School graduates. Emerson, *Nature*, 126.

2. Livy, *History of Rome*, 1.16; 5.24

postmortem affair called *apotheosis*. But this is not at all what the church means when it confesses the deity of Christ. Indeed, the church could not mean that without abandoning monotheism. Rather, the church confesses that Jesus Christ is eternally divine and belongs on the divine side of the Creator-creature distinction. He is not a man who became a god, but the Son of God who became man.

It is important to set the ontological deity of Christ within a broader web of doctrines defined with increasing precision by the church in the first four ecumenical councils. The following statement encapsulates the church's historic understanding of the person of Christ:

> The Son of God, the second person in the Trinity, being very and eternal God, of one substance and equal with the Father, did, when the fullness of time was come, take upon him man's nature, with all the essential properties, and common infirmities thereof, yet without sin (*The Westminster Confession of Faith* VIII.2).

The historic Christian doctrines of the Trinity and the incarnation are interconnected and inseparable. I will be focusing on just one (extremely important) part of the web. By "the ontological deity of Christ" I mean that his career has three stages. First, he is the eternally preexistent Son of God, possessing the same divine nature as the Father; there never was a time when he did not exist as the divine Son.[3] Second, he became man ("took upon him man's nature") when he was born of the Virgin Mary, and so in his earthly ministry he was the Son of God incarnate, both divine and human. Third, after he completed his redeeming work as the incarnate Son and Messiah, God exalted him at his right hand and gave him divine honor fitting for one who is eternally divine. I believe this is what the New Testament teaches, and that is what I will try to show in what follows.

JESUS IS THE SON OF GOD

The apostles confessed and proclaimed that Jesus is the Son of God. Next to "Christ" and "Lord," it is one of the most common christological titles in the New Testament. It occurs in various forms: "my Son," "the Son," "the Son of God," "his Son," and so on. Some variant of the title appears twenty-two times in Matthew, eleven times in Mark, fourteen times in Luke,

---

3. Contra Arius, who said "there was a time when he did not exist" and "before he was brought into being, he did not exist" (as quoted by Athanasius, *Against the Arians* 1.5 [*NPNF*2 4.308–9]). See Williams, *Arius*, 95–116.

A TRINITARIAN VIEW

twenty-seven times in John, seventeen times in Paul's epistles, twelve times in Hebrews, and twenty-four times in the epistles of John. The designation occurs in every New Testament author except James and Jude. We cannot examine all of these instances, but as seen in Table 1, there are five key moments in the earthly life of Jesus as recorded in the Synoptic Gospels where the declaration of Jesus' status as God's Son is made. Actually, only Matthew has the "Son of God" title in all five, but even Mark and Luke record these five events even if they use the explicit title less consistently.

Table 1. Five Significant "Son of God" Moments in the Synoptic Gospels[4]

	Matthew	Mark	Luke
The Baptism of Jesus	3:17	1:11	3:22
Peter's Confession	16:16	[8:29]	[9:20]
The Transfiguration of Jesus	17:5	9:7	9:35
Jesus before Caiaphas	26:62–66	14:61–64	22:67–71
The Centurion at the Crucifixion	27:54	15:39	[23:47]

Whether it is the voice of God the Father from heaven saying, "This is my beloved Son" at Jesus' baptism and transfiguration, or Peter confessing, "You are the Christ, the Son of the living God," or Jesus before the high priest Caiaphas being charged with blasphemy and condemned to death because he claimed to be the Son of God, or the centurion at the scene of the crucifixion confessing, "Truly this was the Son of God!"—in all five key moments, the declaration of Jesus' divine Sonship has the aura of being utterly significant and decisive.

But it was not limited to what others said of him. Jesus understood himself to be "the Son of God" as well. There are three passages in the Synoptic Gospels that make this extremely likely from a historical point of view. The first is the one where Jesus is reported as praying to the Father: "All things have been handed over to me by my Father, and no one knows the Son except the Father, and no one knows the Father except the Son and anyone to whom the Son chooses to reveal him" (Matt 11:27 || Luke 10:22).[5] The second is Jesus' implicit self-reference in the parable of the wicked tenants: "He had still one other, a beloved son. Finally he sent him to them, saying, 'They will respect my son'" (Mark 12:6 || Matt 21:37 || Luke

---

4. The three verses in brackets do not actually contain the "Son of God" title.

5. Unless otherwise indicated, all Scripture quotations are from the English Standard Version.

THE SON OF GOD

20:13). The third is the statement in the eschatological discourse of Jesus, "But concerning that day or that hour, no one knows, not even the angels in heaven, nor the Son, but only the Father" (Mark 13:32 || Matt 24:36). Even scholars who do not accept the authenticity of Jesus' more explicit claims to divine Sonship in the Gospel of John are prepared to accept the authenticity of these three sayings in the Synoptic Gospels.[6]

"SON OF GOD" MUCH MORE THAN "MESSIAH"

"Son of God" has a fair claim to being central to Jesus' identity, both in his own self-consciousness and in the apostolic proclamation concerning Jesus. But what does it mean? Does it mean that a man named Jesus was God's "Son" in a functional sense, i.e., that he was a merely human, Davidic messiah? This is a plausible interpretation of the title, given that it was part of the biblical (2 Sam 7:14; Ps 2:7; 89:26–27) and early Jewish (4Q174; 4Q246) expectation that the messiah would be called God's Son.[7] Many New Testament scholars interpret the "Son of God" title in that functional or messianic sense. But there are others who have mounted compelling arguments for taking "Son of God" as meaning something far more than that he is the hoped-for human king from the line of David. Let us review the most compelling arguments.

Distinction Between "Messiah" and "Son of God"

The "Son of God" title cannot be reduced to "Son of David" or "Messiah" because it is used to explain what kind of Messiah he is. The phrase "the Christ, the Son of God" occurs six times in the Gospels (Matt 16:16; 26:63; Mark 1:1; 14:61; John 11:27; 20:31). The way the two titles, "the Christ" and "the Son of God," are juxtaposed can be interpreted in different ways. It might mean that the two titles are synonyms. But another way of interpreting the juxtaposition is to take the second title as adding precision and definition to the first title. "The second title, 'the Son of God,' far from being a synonym for 'the Messiah,' indicates *what sort* of messianic expectation is in view: *not* the Messiah-Son-of-David, nor the Messiah as the son of any other human being, but rather the Messiah-Son-of-*God*."[8]

---

6. R. Brown, *Introduction to New Testament Christology*, 88–89.
7. On the Qumran "son of God" texts, see Fitzmyer, *Dead Sea Scrolls*, 41–72.
8. Marcus, "Mark 14:61," 130.

A TRINITARIAN VIEW

Further evidence that the two titles, "Son of God" and "Messiah," are not equivalent can be found in the account of the baptism of Jesus. At the beginning of his public ministry, immediately after being baptized by John, the voice from heaven declared: "You are my beloved Son; with you I am well pleased" (Mark 1:11; cp. Matt 3:17 || Luke 3:22). The baptism of Jesus is widely recognized as the moment when he was anointed by the Spirit in order to undertake his office as the Messiah. But according to the heavenly voice, he was already God's beloved Son and pleasing to the Father before he was chosen and appointed to be the Messiah. Therefore, "sonship and messianic status are not synonymous. Rather, sonship . . . is antecedent to messiahship."[9]

Jesus' Question to the Pharisees

Jesus himself said that his identity is not exhausted by calling him the son of David. He asked the Pharisees, "What do you think about the Christ? Whose son is he?" They responded that the Messiah is "the son of David." But Jesus asked, "How is it then that David calls him Lord," quoting Ps 110:1. "If then David calls him Lord, how is he his son?" (Matt 22:41–46 || Mark 12:35–37 || Luke 20:41–44). Matthew's version of the story cries out for the obvious answer. Yes, he is the son of David, but that cannot be all he is, for what ancestor calls his descendant "Lord"? In response to Jesus' rhetorical question ("Whose son is he?"), "there can be little doubt that Matthew and his readers would have supplied the answer, 'the Son of God,' and Mark may well have expected his readers to do the same."[10] On this reading the title "Son of God" must mean more than "son of David," otherwise Jesus' argument would make no sense.

Jesus' Calling God His "Father"

Jesus characteristically spoke of God as his "Father" in a way that no merely human messiah could have.[11] It is probable that Jesus used the Aramaic word *Abba* (Mark 14:36). The fact that Jesus addressed God as *Abba* made

9. Ladd, *Theology of the New Testament*, 163–64.
10. France, *Mark*, 484–85.
11. The New Testament depicts Jesus as speaking of God as "my/his Father" approximately fifty times (there are a couple of textual variants) and as directly addressing God as "Father" nineteen times.

THE SON OF GOD

an impression on the first disciples and the very Aramaic word was treasured by the early church. This form of divine address, having limited parallels in Judaism, captures the heart of Jesus' unique relationship to God.[12] Jesus' distinctive application of the term in prayer to God bespeaks a daring degree of filial intimacy with God indicative of his self-consciousness as God's unique Son. It is true that Jesus also taught his disciples to call God "Father." At first, this may seem to compromise the uniqueness of his relationship to the Father, but on further reflection it does not. He spoke of "my Father" and of "your Father" when speaking to the disciples, but never of "our Father" in a way that would include himself along with the disciples. Jesus spoke of his unique relationship with the Father ("no one knows the Father except the Son") and went on to add that as the unique Son he mediates that filial relationship to others ("and anyone to whom the Son chooses to reveal him" [Matt 11:27 || Luke 10:22]). God is Jesus' Father in a special way distinct from the way in which he is the disciples' Father. The Jewish leaders understood that by calling God "his own Father" (*patera idion*) in that special sense, he was making himself equal with God (John 5:18).

The Jewish Charge of Blasphemy

Jesus' claim to be the Son of God could not have been a mere messianic claim, since it was so provocative that it elicited the charge of blasphemy on the part of the Jewish leaders. This point receives particular emphasis in the Gospel of John:

- John 5:18: "This was why the Jews were seeking all the more to kill him, because not only was he breaking the Sabbath, but he was even calling God his own Father, making himself equal with God."

- John 8:58–59: "Before Abraham was, I am." So they picked up stones to throw at him.

- John 10:30–36: "I and the Father are one." The Jews picked up stones again to stone him. Verse 33: "It is not for a good work that we are going to stone you but for blasphemy, because you, being a man, make yourself God." Verse 36: "Do you say of him whom the Father

---

12. Jeremias, *Prayers of Jesus*, 11–65. Jeremias's argument has been subjected to criticism by scholars such as Geza Vermes, James Barr, and James D. G. Dunn, but others have rehabilitated it in a more nuanced form. See R. Brown, *New Testament Christology*, 86–87; Witherington, *Christology of Jesus*, 216–21; Lee, *From Messiah to Preexistent Son*, 122–36.

A TRINITARIAN VIEW

consecrated and sent into the world, 'You are blaspheming,' because I said, 'I am the Son of God'?"

- John 19:7: "We have a law, and according to that law he ought to die because he has made himself the Son of God."

Many scholars regard these statements in the Gospel of John as retrojections of the later conflict between the synagogue and the church leading to the parting of the ways. But the charge of blasphemy is not only found in the Gospel of John. It is also recorded in all three Synoptic Gospels in two separate but highly significant pericopes:

- Matt 9:3 || Mark 2:7 || Luke 5:21: "This man is blaspheming" (because he forgave the sins of the paralytic and only God can forgive sins).[13]

- Matt 26:63–66 || Mark 14:61–64 || Luke 22:67–71: "He has uttered blasphemy . . . he deserves death" (because he claimed that he was the Son of God, that he will be exalted at God's right hand in fulfillment of Ps 110:1 and Dan 7:13, and that he will come in the clouds of heaven to judge his judges).[14]

In the Jewish context of Jesus' day, claiming to be the messiah would not have provoked the charge of blasphemy worthy of death. Simon bar Kosiba was a false messianic claimant (AD 131–135), but rather than being charged with blasphemy, one rabbi accepted his claims and the other rabbis simply mocked him without calling for his death.[15] Apparently, there was something about Jesus' claim to being "the Son of God" that was regarded as much worse than being a false messiah, something blasphemous that urgently demanded his execution. As the Gospel of John explains the reaction of the Jewish leadership, they thought he deserved death "because he has made himself the Son of God" (John 19:7). It is also likely that the worship of Jesus as divine was one of the concerns that prompted Saul the Pharisee to be actively engaged in zealous and violent persecution of the first Christians.[16]

13. Johansson, "'Who Can Forgive Sins.'"

14. "To the Jewish leadership he has claimed a level of equality with God that is seen as blasphemous . . . making it apparent that more than a pure human and earthly messianic claim is present." Bock, "What Did Jesus Do," 202, 205.

15. Rabbi Yohanan ben Toreta is recorded as mocking Rabbi Akiba for being so gullible as to accept Simon's claims, saying, "Akiba! Grass will grow on your cheeks before the Messiah will come!" (*y. Ta'anit* 4.5 as quoted by Marcus, "Mark 14:61," 127–29).

16. Hurtado, *How on Earth*, 34.

THE SON OF GOD

Jesus as the Revealer or Image of the Father

Jesus as God's Son is far more than a functional agent sent by the Father. He is, in his own person, the perfect revelation of the Father. He is this because only he knows the Father perfectly, just as the Father knows him; he is therefore uniquely qualified to reveal the Father (Matt 11:27 || Luke 10:22). If Jesus is a mere creature, how could he know the Father perfectly? God himself is incomprehensible to the creature. When Philip asked him, "Lord, show us the Father," Jesus rebuked him, saying, "Have I been with you so long, and you still do not know me, Philip? Whoever has seen me has seen the Father. How can you say, 'Show us the Father'? Do you not believe that I am in the Father and the Father is in me?" (John 14:9–10). Jesus said, "I and the Father are one" (John 10:30).

The self-consciousness of Jesus as God's Son who knows and reveals the Father leads the New Testament authors to speak of Jesus in exalted terms. Paul hailed Jesus as "the image of the invisible God" (Col 1:15; cp. 2 Cor 4:4). The author of Hebrews confessed that "he is the radiance (*apaugasma*) of the glory of God and the exact imprint of his nature" (Heb 1:3). It is no wonder that the church fathers took up this theme and made it one of their key arguments for the deity of Christ. Basil the Great wrote, "The whole nature of the Father is manifest in the Son as in a seal . . . . In himself he reveals the Father in his entirety."[17] Contrast the biblical teaching with that of James D. G. Dunn, who wrote that Jesus "was as full an expression of God's creative and redemptive concern and action as was possible in flesh . . . . There was much more to God than could be seen in and through Jesus."[18] The New Testament writers would never speak that way. Paul did not say that some aspects of God could be seen in Jesus, but that "in him all the fullness of God was pleased to dwell" (Col 1:19; cp. 2:9). He is the perfect revelation of the Father. To see the Son is to see the Father.

PREEXISTENCE AND INCARNATION

We have seen that Jesus' most fundamental identity is that he is the Son of God. We have surveyed the arguments for viewing his identity as Son

---

17. St. Basil of Caesarea, *Against Eunomius* 2.16–17 (ET: DelCogliano and Radde-Gallwitz, *St. Basil of Caesarea: Against Eunomius*, 152–53). Cp. Athanasius, *Against the Arians* 1.20–21 (*NPNF2* 4.318).

18. Dunn, *Did the First Christians*, 143, 145.

A TRINITARIAN VIEW

not in a merely functional/messianic sense, but in a sense that goes much deeper, approaching something ontological in terms of his unique relationship with the Father, a relationship that was so scandalous it provoked the Jewish leadership to charge Jesus with blasphemy. In this section, I now argue that the Sonship of Christ is not something that began at some point in his earthly existence but in fact goes back to his pre-incarnate state. In other words, the New Testament teaches that before Jesus' earthly career as a man, he existed as the Son of God.[19]

Preexistence in the Johannine Literature

The majestic Prologue of John's Gospel teaches the preexistence of Christ. It begins by stating that in the beginning, the Word (the *Logos*) existed as a divine being distinct from God the Father (John 1:1–3). "He was in the beginning with God" (v. 2). In fact, he was with God prior to creation (v. 3). The Prologue then moves forward to the incarnation, stating that "the Word became flesh and dwelled among us" (John 1:14). The preexistence-incarnation motif is found throughout the Gospel of John. Jesus repeatedly speaks of his mission as one who "came or descended from heaven" (John 3:13, 31; 6:38, 42, 62). He says that the Jews do not know the Father who sent him, but "I know him, for I come from him, and he sent me" (John 7:29). "I came from God and I am here," and "before Abraham was, I am" (John 8:42, 58). Jesus even speaks of a divine action of "consecration" that took place prior to his coming to earth: he is the one "whom the Father consecrated and sent into the world" and therefore he has the right to say, "I am the Son of God" (John 10:36).

In addition, there are several passages where Jesus speaks of three phases of his existence: the time before he came into the world, his earthly ministry, and the time when he goes back to the Father. For example, he says, "I came from the Father and have come into the world, and now I am leaving the world and going to the Father" (John 16:28). Jesus expands on his three-stage career in his high priestly prayer just before he goes to the cross:

> "Father, the hour has come; glorify your Son that the Son may glorify you . . . . I glorified you on earth, having accomplished

---

19. Recent scholarly defenses of the preexistence of Christ include Lee, *From Messiah to Preexistent Son*; McCready, *He Came Down from Heaven*; and Gathercole, *Preexistent Son*.

the work that you gave me to do. And now, Father, glorify me in your own presence with the glory that I had with you before the world existed. . . . Father, I desire that they also, whom you have given me, may be with me where I am, to see my glory that you have given me because you loved me before the foundation of the world" (John 17:1, 4–5, 24).

There is only one center of consciousness, one "I" of the Son, as he speaks of his relationship with the Father as a man and as he looks back upon his preincarnate life with the Father "before the foundation of the world." It strains credulity to interpret these straightforward vignettes of the pretemporal, interpersonal relationship between the Father and the Son as mere poetic hyperbole of a personified divine attribute.

The Epistles of John also imply preexistence when they speak of Jesus' incarnation. The apostolic truth is set in contrast with error. Only prophetic spirits that confess that "Jesus Christ has come in the flesh" are to be recognized as from God (1 John 4:2; 2 John 7). The coming of Christ in the flesh, that is, his incarnation, presupposes his preexistence.

Preexistence in Paul

Some would set aside the Johannine preexistence texts as late, but there is one text in Paul that places this belief much earlier. I am referring, of course, to Phil 2:5–11. The first half of this early Christian hymn or creed speaks of Jesus' decision not to regard equality with God as something to be used for his own advantage. It goes on to say that he emptied himself and took the form of a servant, being found in the likeness of men. There are many technical exegetical questions that would need to be examined to do justice to this passage, but for my purpose, I will simply observe that New Testament scholarship has reached a firm consensus that real, personal preexistence is predicated of Jesus in this text. James D. G. Dunn has attempted to argue for ideal or metaphorical preexistence by appealing to a so-called "Adam Christology," but his exegesis is not persuasive.[20] Specific dispositions of mind and acts of will are predicated of the preexistent one,

---

20. Dunn, *Christology in the Making*, 98–128. Good critiques of Dunn's interpretation of Phil 2:5–11 may be found in Hurtado, *How on Earth*, 98–101; Lee, *From Messiah to Preexistent Son*, 305–8; McCready, *He Came Down from Heaven*, 73–80. "Dunn's conclusion that Paul did not believe in the preexistence of Christ has persuaded very few." Hagner, *New Testament*, 400 n11.

A TRINITARIAN VIEW

a self-conscious decision not to use his equality with God as something for his own advantage, and his voluntary act of humbling himself by becoming a man, viewed as the starting point of his obedience. These actions imply a real center of consciousness and will in Christ that cannot be explained away as mere poetic hyperbole or metaphor. If they were mere metaphor, how could they be used as an example for believers? "Let this mind be in you, which was also in Christ Jesus" (v. 5 KJV). The fact that this is stated so clearly in a pre-Pauline hymn pushes the origin of belief in Christ's preexistence back to the earliest period of the primitive church, within the first decade after Jesus' resurrection.[21]

There are several other important passages that some scholars accept as teaching the preexistence of Christ, such as the "I have come" texts and the "sending" texts, particularly the ones which speak of Christ's being "sent into the world," which are even more explicit.[22] Last but not least, the Epistle to the Hebrews is acknowledged by most scholars as having a very high Christology, including a preexistence-incarnation motif.[23]

TWO TESTS OF ONTOLOGICAL DEITY

There may still be some apprehension at this point. Jesus may be the Son of God in a unique sense that transcends the categories Judaism had for its messianic expectation. He may even have existed as a glorious "divine" being (in some sense) prior to his becoming a man. But does divine Sonship mean ontological deity in the sense of being eternally part of the divine being? Surely this is a "noxious exaggeration" if there ever was one! But that is precisely what I believe the New Testament teaches. I proceed now in the next stage of my argument to show that Jesus as God's eternal Son belongs within the being of the one God by showing that he passes two critical tests of ontological deity according to biblical monotheism.

---

21. Hengel, *Between Jesus and Paul*, 30–47.

22. Jesus' "I have come" pronouncements: Matt 5:17; 9:13 (= Mark 2:17; Luke 5:32); 10:34–35 (= Luke 12:51); 20:28 (= Mark 10:45); Luke 12:49; 19:10. See Gathercole, *Preexistent Son*. Coming or being sent "into the world" texts: John 1:9; 3:17, 19; 6:14; 10:36; 11:27; 12:46; 16:28; 17:18; 18:37; 1 Tim 1:15; Heb 1:6; 10:5; 1 John 4:9.

23. Heb 1:1–14; 2:5–18; 5:5–8; 7:3; 10:5–7. See Bauckham, *Jesus and the God of Israel*, 233–53.

THE SON OF GOD

Creation

The first quality that sets ontological deity apart from all else is creation, the *opus proprium Dei*.[24] Only the true God is the Creator of all things. The false gods are those who "did not make the heavens and the earth" (Jer 10:11; cp. Ps 96:5). YHWH is not like the worthless idols, precisely because he is the one who formed all things (Jer 10:16; 51:19). By definition, no creature can be the Creator of all things. With that presupposition in place, we must reckon with the astonishing implications of the New Testament's identification of the preincarnate Son as the one through whom God created all things:

> "All things (*panta*) were made *through* him (*dia* + gen.), and without him was not any thing made that was made.... He was in the world, and the world (*ho kosmos*) was made *through* him (*dia* + gen.), yet the world did not know him" (John 1:3, 10).

> "Yet for us there is one God, the Father, from whom are all things (*ta panta*) and for whom we exist, and one Lord, Jesus Christ, *through* whom (*dia* + gen.) are all things (*ta panta*) and through whom we exist" (1 Cor 8:6).

> "For *by* him (*en* + dat.) all things (*ta panta*) were created, in heaven and on earth, visible and invisible, whether thrones or dominions or rulers or authorities—all things (*ta panta*) were created *through* him (*dia* + gen.) and for him" (Col 1:16).

> "... in these last days [God] has spoken to us by his Son, whom he appointed the heir of all things, *through* whom (*dia* + gen.) also he created the world (*hoi aiōnes*)" (Heb 1:2).[25]

The phrase "all things" (*panta* or *ta panta*) is a comprehensive term that embraces all of created reality in distinction from God the Creator. Paul defines "all things" as "things in heaven and on earth, visible and invisible" (Col 1:16). The invisible things include angelic beings, as is made clear by the next phrase, "whether thrones or dominions or rulers or authorities." Other terms that comprehend all of creation are the singular *ho kosmos* (John 1:10) and the plural *hoi aiōnes* (lit. "the ages," Heb 1:2), both rendered

---

24. The exclusive/peculiar work of God. Hengel, *Son of God*, 72.

25. As many scholars recognize, these passages are undoubtedly shaped by the Jewish tradition of reflection on the mysterious figure of Wisdom in Prov 8:22–31. Wisdom, the "master workman" at God's side, the intermediary of creation, is now seen to be the eternally preexistent Son of God. Hengel, *Son of God*, 72.

A TRINITARIAN VIEW

"the world." John 1:3 is even more emphatic: "All things were made through him, and without him was not any thing (*oude hen*) made that was made." Both Paul and John go out of their way to eliminate any exceptions. All created things, without exception, received their existence and came into being through Christ. These passages do not state that "the Son created the rest of creation, but that he created *all* that was created. This excludes the Son from the created order."[26] By assigning the Son a mediatorial role in creation, the New Testament places him on the divine side of the Creator-creature distinction and makes him an eternally preexistent divine being along with God the Father and therefore part of the divine being.[27]

Aseity

Aseity is the second test of ontological deity. If the first test is a work of God, the second is an attribute of God. In fact, aseity may be the primary attribute of God's being.[28] To possess aseity means that one is *a se*, a Latin phrase which means that one has one's being "from oneself" and not from another. Only God has aseity. His name is "I am who I am" (Exod 3:14). All created reality is from God and dependent on God, but God is not dependent on anything outside of himself. The New Testament predicates aseity, and therefore ontological deity, of Jesus. The Father has granted the Son to have "life in himself" (John 5:26) and therefore he possesses the uniquely divine attribute of aseity. Jesus is unchanging, "the same yesterday and today and forever" (Heb 13:8), in contrast with the entire realm of created reality which is contingent, corruptible, and perishable: "They will perish, but you remain . . . . You are the same, and your years will have no end" (Heb 1:11–12, quoting LXX Ps 102:25–27).[29] Further demonstrating his aseity or independence from any created thing, we read that he "upholds all things by the word of his power" (Heb 1:3), and "in him all things hold together" (Col 1:17). If the entire created realm ("all things," *ta panta*) depends on him, then he cannot depend on anything in the created realm,

---

26. McCready, *He Came Down*, 82. "If He be a creature, how is He at the same time the Creator of creatures?" (Athanasius, *Circular to the Bishops of Egypt and Libya* 14 [*NPNF2* 4.230]).
27. Bauckham, *Jesus and the God of Israel*, 26–30, 238.
28. Bavinck, *Reformed Dogmatics*, 2.124.
29. Cp. Athanasius, *Against the Arians* 1.58, 36 (*NPNF2* 4.327, 340).

THE SON OF GOD

and is therefore distinct from and independent of the created realm, which necessarily determines his ontological status as divine.

The New Testament accepts the monotheistic assumptions inherited from the Old Testament and Judaism. It accepts the basic divide in reality between all that is created and God himself, who is utterly distinct from creation. And yet in the areas of creation and aseity, the New Testament places Jesus on the divine side of the Creator-creature distinction. Christ as God's Son shares ontological deity with his Father in a way that is perfectly consistent with monotheism.[30]

THE EXALTATION OF CHRIST

At this point, the ontological deity of the eternal Son has been proven. Yet the New Testament has still more to say to "seal the deal." The ontological deity of the eternal Son receives explosive confirmation from the Father's exaltation of his obedient, incarnate Son. As pointed out earlier, the New Testament envisions the Son as having a three-stage career: (1) the preincarnate state of the Son, with God the Father before and at creation, (2) the first phase of his incarnate state, that is, his earthly ministry, and (3) the second phase of his incarnate state, that is, his exaltation at God's right hand. The first and the third states are closely related. In fact, Aquila H. I. Lee has convincingly argued that the exaltation of Christ was one of the key factors that led the primitive church to the belief in his eternal preexistence.[31] Some have attempted to argue for a two-stage Christology that eliminates the preexistence phase. But this would mean that a human being has been exalted to a position of divine honor that does not properly belong to him according to his ontological nature. In other words, they argue for the deification of a mere man, a belief that would be more at home in a polytheistic context (recall the ancient Romans' belief about the apotheosis of Romulus after his death). But the exaltation of Christ, with its implication of divine status, cannot be interpreted as an apotheosis. Such a construction would be conceptually and theologically impossible within the context of an early Christian movement composed of Jewish believers raised in and committed to the strict monotheism inherited from Judaism. Therefore, the exaltation of Christ must be interpreted along different lines.

---

30. Several New Testament scholars dub this "christological monotheism," e.g., N. T. Wright, Richard Bauckham, and Larry Hurtado.

31. Lee, *From Messiah to Preexistent Son*, 280–81.

A TRINITARIAN VIEW

Rather than viewing his exaltation as an apotheosis, we must view his exaltation is the manifestation and confirmation of his identity as the divine Son of God. Paul speaks of this as his having been "marked out (*horisthentos*) Son of God *in power* . . . by his resurrection from the dead" (Rom 1:4).[32] There are several features of the exaltation of Christ which demonstrate that his divine honors in the state of exaltation are appropriate based on his ontological deity as the preexistent Son.

Sovereignty

There is only one ultimate power in the universe—only one sovereign, one king. God is "the blessed and only sovereign" (1 Tim 6:15). Thus it is remarkable that the exalted Lord Jesus shares the divine sovereignty with the Father. In fact, it was his own Father who granted him to sit at his right hand until his enemies are made the footstool of his feet in fulfillment of Ps 110:1. This crucial Old Testament verse is quoted or alluded to some twenty-two times in the New Testament with reference to Jesus. Jesus' exalted position at God's right hand and his consequent authority and sovereignty over all things are astonishing. No mere creature could be given that divine authority as Lord of all creation. The exalted Lord Jesus received the divine sovereignty from the Father (Matt 28:18), not as a temporary gift granted to a mere creature, but because he is the firstborn, that is, the rightful heir, of all creation through whom all things were created (Heb 1:2–3; Col 1:15–16).

Psalm 110:1 is not the only Old Testament prophecy fulfilled in the exaltation of Christ. Ps 8:6 is also combined with Ps 110:1 and quoted in reference to Christ's exaltation, for "God has put all things (*ta panta*) in subjection under his feet" (1 Cor 15:27; cp. Eph 1:20–22; Phil 3:21). There is also the key passage in Dan 7:13–14 that Jesus himself alluded to before

---

32. Translation mine. Although *horisthentos* can be rendered "appointed," the meaning "marked out" or "declared" (see BDAG *horizō* and most English versions) is also possible in extra-biblical Greek and is more appropriate here. Paul's framing device, "concerning his Son" ("being placed . . . outside the bracket") implies that the Son did not become the Son at his resurrection, but was the Son even before his birth: " . . . concerning his Son, who was born of the seed of David according to the flesh," i.e., "so far as his human nature is concerned" (Cranfield, *Romans*, 1.58–60). The "in power" modifier is also crucial, since it shows that the resurrection did not make him Son for the first time but powerfully exhibited what was true of him all along. Besides, as we have seen, the Gospels are explicit that he was the Son of God prior to his resurrection, going back (at least) to the Father's declaration at his baptism, "You are my Son."

the high priest at his trial. More specifically, the prophecy concerning the "Son of Man" in Daniel says that "his dominion is an everlasting dominion, which shall not pass away" (Dan 7:14), using language that is applied to YHWH's kingdom (Ps 145:13; Dan 4:34). Recall that it was precisely Jesus' claim to be that coming "Son of Man" coming in the clouds of heaven with the glory of his Father that scandalized the Jewish Sanhedrin and led to their call for his execution on the charge of blasphemy.

Worship

Worship belongs properly only to the one true God in biblical monotheism. In his indictment of the pagans for their idolatry, Paul essentially defines idolatry as an "exchange" in which they "worshiped and served the creature rather than the Creator" (Rom 1:25). Similarly, when John, the seer of the apocalypse, fell down to worship the angel, the angel rebuked him and said that worship must be given to God alone: "You must not do that! I am a fellow servant with you and your brothers who hold to the testimony of Jesus. Worship God" (Rev 19:10; cp. 22:8–9).

And yet the New Testament, which was largely composed by men brought up within and committed to strict Jewish monotheism that abhorred the worship of any creature, recorded, as if it were perfectly natural, the fact that the exalted Lord Jesus is to be worshiped as divine. By far the most important text in this regard is the second half of the pre-Pauline hymn or creed (Phil 2:9–11) that we examined earlier under preexistence. The conclusion looks ahead to the day when all sentient creatures will worship Jesus as Lord. God highly exalted him "so that at the name of Jesus every knee should bow . . . and every tongue confess that Jesus Christ is Lord to the glory of God the Father" (vv. 10–11). It is not merely that we have isolated instances here and there of people expressing their reverence for Christ by prostrating themselves before him. Rather, the Father himself has exalted him to his own right hand and calls all sentient beings to bow the knee and worship him as Lord. The striking thing is that this language is taken from LXX Isa 45:23, which is part of Isaiah's anti-idolatry polemic. This Old Testament passage, one that is "among the most fervent expressions of God's uniqueness," has been "adapted (and apparently interpreted) to affirm Jesus as supreme over all creation."[33]

---

33. Hurtado, *How on Earth*, 50.

A TRINITARIAN VIEW

The worship of Jesus in not only found in Paul. It is also found in other New Testament writers. The Gospel of John presents Jesus as claiming that the Father has given all judgment to him "that all may honor the Son, just as they honor the Father" (John 5:22–23). The author of Hebrews writes: "And again, when he brings the firstborn into the world, he says, 'Let all God's angels worship him'" (Heb 1:6, quoting LXX Deut 32:43). The book of Revelation pictures all creation worshiping Christ: "Worthy is the Lamb who was slain, to receive power and wealth and wisdom and might and honor and glory and blessing!" (Rev 5:12–14; cp. 22:3).[34]

The Divine Name

God does not share his name with creatures. "I am the LORD; that is my name; my glory I give to no other" (Isa 42:8). There is no god besides YHWH (Isa 45:21–22). And yet, according to Philippians 2:10, God has highly exalted his obedient Son Jesus at his right hand as the one who bears the divine name. In addition to Phil 2:10, there are numerous New Testament passages which demonstrate that Jesus, in his exalted state, is viewed as bearing the divine name, YHWH in Hebrew or *Kyrios* in Greek.[35] For example, Joel 2:32 ("Everyone calls upon the name of YHWH will be saved") is quoted twice in the New Testament in its Septuagint form, where YHWH has been rendered *Kyrios*, now applied to the exalted Lord Jesus Christ (Acts 2:21; Rom 10:13). The fact that the New Testament interprets Old Testament *Kyrios* texts like Isa 45:23 and Joel 2:32 as fulfilled in the exaltation of Jesus to the status of universal Lord indicates that he bears the divine name and thus participates in the identity of YHWH.[36]

Does this mean that Jesus is YHWH? I hesitate to say that Jesus *is* YHWH, which would seem to verge on modalism. Rather, I would say that, by virtue both of his ontological status and of his exaltation, Jesus bears the divine name and is thus shown to be included in the identity of YHWH.[37] If "YHWH" denotes the person who reveals himself in the Old Testament as the God of Israel, it is best to say Jesus is the Son of YHWH. Because he is his eternal Son, he shares in the identity or nature of the God of Israel.

---

34. Bauckham, "The Worship of Jesus," in *Climax of Prophecy*, 118–49.

35. See Bauckham, *Jesus and the God of Israel*, 182–232, for an examination of many other New Testament texts where the divine name (*Kyrios*/YHWH) is applied to Jesus.

36. Rowe, "Romans 10:13."

37. Bauckham's formulation in *Jesus and the God of Israel*, 24–25, 130.

THE SON OF GOD

"YHWH" is basically the name of the Father, but it is a name (unlike the name "Father") that the Father can share with his exalted Son (Phil 2:9–10). This is because the name YHWH itself does not mean "Father" but "I am who I am" (Exod 3:14). It does not differentiate his personal quality but his essential nature. The granting of the divine name, YHWH, to the Son is legitimate, appropriate, and fitting because the Son shares the Father's ontological divine nature. Thus, when the Son is exalted, he receives the divine name, YHWH, because it is fitting in terms of his ontological status. His receiving the divine name shows that he shares in the identity of YHWH.

The same situation obtains with respect to the name "God" (*ho theos*). I hesitate to say "Jesus *is* God," nor would I say "Jesus is not God." Instead, I prefer to say, as the New Testament says, that "Jesus is the Son of God." Although it is possible to construe it in a valid sense, I am cautious about the statement "Jesus is God," because the name "God" (with the definite article, *ho theos*) most frequently and properly refers to the Father. "Jesus is God" could be taken to mean "Jesus is the Father," which would be modalism. On the other hand, following John 1:1, we have strong precedent for saying that "Jesus is divine" (*theos* as anarthrous qualitative predicate nominative).[38]

Words express meaning not by reference alone, but by sense and reference.[39] A word's sense is not the same thing as the extralinguistic reality that it refers to. The words "YHWH" and *ho theos* are typically used in Scripture to refer to the Father, and very rarely if at all to refer to the Son. Yet, because their sense is such that they indicate deity as a generic concept, the terms can be applied to the Son because of his deity. Yet when the words are applied to the Son, there is usually something in the context which distinguishes him from the Father and which shows that the terms are being used qualitatively to underscore that they share the same identity or nature.

A DIVINE SAVIOR

Why is it important that Jesus be the divine Son of God? The reason, in a nutshell, is that the accomplishment of redemption depends on it. The Bible teaches that there is only one God, YHWH, the God of Israel, and that this one God has a Son through whom he created all things and through whom he redeems. Redemption is patterned on creation. Just as creation is

38. Wallace, *Greek Grammar*, 266–69.
39. Silva, *Biblical Words*, 102–7.

A TRINITARIAN VIEW

the work of God the Father through the preincarnate Son, so redemption is the work of God the Father through the incarnate Son. Earlier, I quoted 1 Cor 8:6 as one of the crucial New Testament passages which affirm that Christ is the divine intermediary of creation. But its final line affirms that Christ is also the intermediary of the new creation: "and we [believers live] through him."[40] Christ's mediatorial role in creation prepares the way for and is the basis of his mediatorial role in redemption. It is no accident that redemption is pictured as a new creation (e.g., 2 Cor 5:17; Col 3:10). Just as God created through his divine, preincarnate Son, so God saves his people and brings about the new creation through his divine, incarnate Son, and both mediatorial activities place Jesus on the divine side of the Creator-creature distinction. No wonder he is called "our (great) God and Savior Jesus Christ" (Titus 2:13; 2 Pet 1:1), that is, "our divine Savior Jesus Christ."

It is not only the objective accomplishment of redemption (new creation) that had to be by a divine person, the divine Son of God incarnate. It is also the subjective response to redemption that requires a divine person to be the object of saving faith. The fact that God has put Christ forward as the object of faith (Rom 3:25) requires that he be ontologically divine. Paul expresses the personal nature of faith in the divine Messiah in these terms: "I have been crucified with Christ. It is no longer I who live, but Christ who lives in me. And the life I now live in the flesh I live by faith in the Son of God, who loved me and gave himself for me" (Gal 2:20). We are saved by "calling on the name of the Lord" (Rom 10:13; Joel 2:32). Such absolute trust in Christ, calling upon him for salvation, is a form of worship that should only be given to a divine person, not to a creature no matter how exalted. As Charles Hodge wrote, "The man should tremble, who ventures to say: I believe in Jesus Christ our Saviour, unless he believes in his true and perfect Godhead, for only on that assumption is he a Saviour or an object of faith."[41]

In conclusion, it was not the post-apostolic church, in a desire to exalt Jesus more and more, that indulged in unwarranted "exaggeration" about the person of Jesus. It was Jesus himself who claimed to be the Son of God in an absolutely unique way. Indeed, so provocative were his claims, the Jewish leadership recoiled in horror and had him put to death on the charge of blasphemy. But God raised him from the dead and vindicated his claim to be the Son of God. Millions of ordinary Christians throughout history

40. Ciampa and Rosner, *First Corinthians*, 384.
41. Hodge, "Religious State of Germany," 520.

THE SON OF GOD

have confessed that Jesus is the Christ, the Son of God, exalted at God's right hand as sovereign Lord over all creation, and have put their faith and trust in him as their divine Savior and have worshiped him as such.

AN ARIAN RESPONSE TO A TRINITARIAN VIEW

DANNY ANDRÉ DIXON

JESUS IS THE SON OF GOD

LEE IRONS LAYS OUT a revealing summary of the number of times, and in what contexts the terms identifying Jesus as "the Son of God" in one form or another appear in five significant events detailed in the Gospel accounts of Matthew, Mark, and Luke. But none of the passages that Irons points to suggest any eternal ontological connection of Jesus to the Father.

I will stipulate the intimate language of Jesus in referring to God as "my Father" (Matt 11:27 || Luke 10:22) and similar implications in the parable of the wicked tenants where he understands himself to be the father's (God's) "beloved son" whom he calls "my son" (Mark 12:6 || Matt 21:37 || Luke 20:13); but these designations, while proving intimacy do not establish that the language exclusively proves his point.

"SON OF GOD" MUCH MORE THAN "MESSIAH"

The Holmesian game's afoot, however, when Irons introduces 2 Sam 7:14 which, in my view, sets forth the expectation that "God's Son" means functional messiah. He says there are "compelling arguments" against this view and he proposes to review the most compelling of them.

THE SON OF GOD

First, he says that there is a distinction between "Messiah" and "Son of God" in various passages, defining him as a certain *kind* of Messiah. He lists verses where the phrase "the Christ, the Son of God" appears (Matt 16:16; 26:63; Mark 1:1; 14:61; John 11:27; 20:31).

This is his argument against the admitted scholarly view of others that the two titles can be synonymous. He says, "Another way of interpreting the juxtaposition is to take the second title as adding precision and definition to the first title." He quotes a scholar, Joel Marcus, but gives little argument at this point. What we want are the *reasons for the conclusion drawn*.

He says he provides "further evidence," but it is really the same sort of argument. Irons tells us, "The baptism of Jesus is widely recognized as the moment when he was anointed by the Spirit in order to undertake his office as the Messiah," and as G. E. Ladd says, "he was already God's beloved Son and pleasing to the Father before he was chosen and appointed to be the Messiah." But isn't this begging the question? Jesus' beloved Sonship as stated by God presumes before beginning that the term does *not* mean Messiahship based upon a widely recognized understanding that he was not Messiah until he was anointed. Consider that this splitting up and sequencing of events provides *prophetic understanding* that by his very birth Jesus was Messiah. 2 Sam 7:12–16 and its parallel application to Jesus in Heb 1:5 indicate that Jesus' place in the lineage of David made him God's Son. Every king in the Davidic dynasty was "son of God." It is of Solomon that God says, "I will be his father, and he will be my son," and the writer of the letter to the Hebrews applies this verse and others to the one who would *be* the Son. For what reason, then, should the accounts of the baptism of Jesus and the descent of the Holy Spirit be seen as anything other than simultaneous, and not antecedent or synonymous? It seems that Irons is suggesting that, from a prophetic standpoint (certainly understood fully later), it was *not* God's intention that "son of God" would mean anointed king in the Davidic dynasty. Actually, it might be appropriate to ask if he thinks that *any* Son of God passage should be taken to mean "Messiah."

MATTHEW 16:13-20
(|| MARK 8:27-30; LUKE 9:18-21)[1]

In the account of Jesus' conversation with his disciples, he asks them who they think he is. "Peter answered him, 'You are the Christ'" (Mark 8:29).

---

1. For this analysis I am looking at Aland, *Synopsis*, which in the English has the RSV.

AN ARIAN RESPONSE TO A TRINITARIAN VIEW

This is the unembellished answer also found in Luke's account: "And Peter answered, 'The Christ of God.'" Neither version seeks to make any ontological conclusions about Jesus' identity. At this point, Peter simply recognizes Jesus as God's Messiah. Yet the more embellished understanding in wording is given by Matthew: "Peter replied, 'You are the Christ, the Son of the living God'" (Matt 16:16). But note that Matthew does not even care to have Jesus make a statement about any implications of Peter's observation. Does Jesus charge the disciples to tell no one that he was a certain kind of Christ, as in a Son of *God* sort of Christ? He certainly would have had a perfect opportunity to do so in the summation found in Matthew's account. But no, he simply "charged the disciples to tell no one that he was the Christ." (Matt 16:20). God's king, beginning with Solomon in the Davidic dynasty, is called his "son." Jesus, as the *last* anointed in the Davidic dynasty is called his *Son*. The anointed, the Christ, is God's Son.

Compare the preceding with Luke's account of Jesus' interview with the Jewish leaders. David Garland aptly observes that they "ask two questions of Jesus, 'If you are the Christ, tell us' (Luke 22:67), and 'Are you the son of God?'"[2] But notice carefully, however, what is *the precise wording* of the second question: "You are *then* the Son of God?" (v. 70). The second question indicates that the first question is the same as the concluding one.[3] There is nothing in the second question that sets it apart from the first.

THE MEANING OF PSALM 110:1

First, I would say that neither this passage, nor any others that Irons might have listed, is given to prove a negative, or as worded by Irons, to "exhaust" his identity. Psalm 110:1 is quoted or alluded to in the New Testament more often than any other passage from the Hebrew Scriptures. Irons crafts an answer to Jesus' question to the Pharisees posed in Matthew's version: "If then David calls him Lord, how is he his son?" Let's look at the passage:

> Jehovah saith unto my Lord, "Sit thou at my right hand,
> Until I make thine enemies thy footstool" (ASV).

2. Garland, *Luke*, 900.

3. BDAG, 736, informs us that the Greek particle *oun* is "inferential denoting that what it introduces is the result of or an inference from what precedes *so, therefore, consequently, accordingly, then*." See also Daniel Wallace who observes that the inferential conjunction *oun* "gives a deduction, conclusion, or summary to the preceding discussion." Wallace, *Greek Grammar*, 673.

THE SON OF GOD

What is David doing in writing Ps 110:1? First of all he is pointing out that Jehovah is addressing one who prophetically was the psalmist's (Jesus says David's) lord. Jesus' question is this:

> How is David's *lord* also David's *son*?

Irons does not do this, but others have tried to suggest that the first Lord, Jehovah, is speaking also to a second one who is also Jehovah designated in this second place as *Adonai*. Actually, the second referent is the Hebrew *Adoni* or "my" (Heb. *i*) "lord" (Heb. *adon*), translated "my lord." The point was that whoever the Messiah might be, he was David's superior/lord, an idea that would have stumped the Jewish leaders who would not have expected the Messiah, a descendant of David, to be greater than David. Irons's observation introduces a new figure into the equation of that particular discussion, namely, "Son of God" who must mean more than "son of David." The point actually is "son of David" is not as important as his descendant who is David's "lord."

JESUS' CALLING GOD HIS "FATHER"

We get some more statistics in a footnote as Irons advises us that Jesus refers to God as his Father about fifty times, plus nineteen direct addresses as Father. There are about seventeen references in the epistles in which God is called "our Father." Does that mathematical reality mean that our relationship with God is lacking as compared with that of Jesus? Should we negate any significance of Jesus' reference to God as "*Abba*" in Scripture only *once* (Mark 14:36) since we can claim *two* epistolary references in which *Christians* address God as "*Abba* Father" (Rom 8:15; Gal 4:6)? Why does our calling God "*Abba*" mean we do not share an intimacy with God? What is it about *Jesus* calling God "*Abba*" that means he is the only one with a "unique relationship to God"? Christians are God's sons and daughters (John 1:12), but does our ability to call God "*Abba*" mean absolutely nothing as regards a unique relationship with God as, say, those who do not share citizenship as his people? Is it not true that all believers "have access to the Father by one Spirit" (Eph 2:18)? Christ's mediating of our filial relationship as brothers and sisters to the one Father does not mean that our relationship with him is nothing. And drawing the conclusion that Jesus was "making himself equal with God" because he was "calling God his own Father" is

AN ARIAN RESPONSE TO A TRINITARIAN VIEW

clearly a specious argument created by the Jewish leaders in John 5:18. They themselves said, "The only Father we have is God himself" (John 8:41).

Jesus' claim that God was his Father was *mis*understood by the Jewish leaders, especially inasmuch as they inferred that he was claiming equality with God. Jesus went on later to finally address this misapprehension in John 10:30–33 pointing out that if they were hearing his claim to oneness with God to mean equality with God, they were sorely mistaken. He went so far as to address the misunderstanding taking it as far as it would go: He was willing to address their misconception that he was claiming to be equal to Almighty God. He argues, in fact, that were he even to claim to be *theos* ("god"), the designation would be no more inappropriate than the leaders of Israel being called *theoi* ("gods"), as in Ps 82:6 when God himself calls the judges of Israel "gods"—men who could even be called sons of God.[4] And as we will see *infra*, while the Jewish leaders did attempt to try Jesus for claiming Messianic authority once they had him in their kangaroo court, they never again brought up the claim that he was equal with God after this, Jesus' clear explanation and exegesis.

THE JEWISH CHARGE OF BLASPHEMY

Irons seems to be incredulous that Jesus' admission that he was the Son of God was an equivalent designation for Messiah for he believes claiming to be Messiah would *not* have caused the Jewish leaders to elicit the charge of blasphemy. He points out several passages of Scripture where a perceived claim to being equal with God was deemed to be a claim to equality with God deserving of death:

   a. John 5:18—Note that the verse claims that Jesus was continually "breaking the Sabbath." Jesus claimed that in healing the lame man at the Bethesda Pool, he was joining his Father in his continuing work. Some would see this as claiming a special exemption from keeping the Sabbath. But Jesus had already indicated that if it were good to act mercifully on behalf of an animal in misfortune on the Sabbath, then surely it was good to do the same for people. Thus it was "lawful to do good on the Sabbath" (Matt 12:12). The Jews had misunderstood God's will regarding the Sabbath. By implication they were also wrong in assigning to him a claim to be equal with God.

---

4. Literally, "sons of the Most high."

THE SON OF GOD

b. John 8:58—I was puzzled at Irons's mention of this verse. He lists it as evidence that Jesus was blaspheming. He does not, however, identify the blasphemy; he only quotes that Jesus claimed *to be* "[before] Abraham," and gives the report that "they picked up stones to throw at him." Perhaps Irons is leaving open the possibility of understanding *egō eimi* in the passage as meaning "I have been." The translators of the NASB (1971) list as legitimate the alternate reading, "before Abraham came into being *I have been.*" This is very much like the Greek reading from the beginning of the testament of Job, which I mention in my opening presentation. The Greek here is remarkably essentially similar to the pseudepigraphal *T. Job* 2:1: "For I have been Jobab [*Egō gar eimi Iōbab*] before the Lord named me Job [*prin ē onomasai me ho Kyrios Iōb*]." That this text would say that Jesus preexisted Abraham does not, however, suggest that Jesus was equal to God. The created angels preexisted Abraham, and are even called "sons of God" (Job 1:6; 2:1; 1 Kgs 22:19–22; Ps 148:2, 5).

c. John 10:30–36—Here, I am keying in on Irons's emphasis on verse 36 where Jesus asks his accusers if they are stoning him because he said he was God's Son. Andreas Köstenberger has suggested that Jesus is using a *qal wahomer* rabbinic argument made from the lesser to the greater. Köstenberger writes: "Jesus' point is that if Israel can in some sense be called 'god' in the Scriptures, how much more appropriate this designation is for him, 'whom the Father consecrated and sent into the world' and who truly is the Son of God."[5] Perhaps that is Irons's point. But it isn't a definite point. He is not arguing what the Son of God *is*.

d. John 19:7—The Jewish leaders argue that Jesus ought to die because he claimed to be the Son of God. Were they offended because it was *Jesus* who was making this claim? Was it because the claim was made *at all*? Or was it that the claim was that the association was being made with being *God's* Son? And why was one of these (or something else) a problem? Irons doesn't tell us.

e. Matt 9:3—Irons points out that blasphemy was assigned to Jesus because he claimed to do something that only God could do—forgive sins. But he fails to point out in the argument here that Matt 9:8 demonstrates, first, that the people marveled because such authority

---

5. Köstenberger, "John," in Beale and Carson, eds., *Commentary*, 465.

AN ARIAN RESPONSE TO A TRINITARIAN VIEW

had been *given*. Irons has already admitted that Jesus was both human and divine while on the earth. While his alleged divine identity would have been masked from the people, the Father would not have been confused that the one who shared in his nature and identity—his co-God if you will—was in fact embodied as Jesus. As God there was nothing that the God part of Jesus lacked, so authority to forgive sins would have been something that Jesus already possessed. It also shows, second, that the power to forgive sins had been given *to men*—and here the man under consideration was Jesus. Is Matthew writing of the people's perception or his own spiritually informed perspective about Jesus as a man and only as a man?

JESUS AS THE REVEALER OR IMAGE OF THE FATHER

At this point I feel compelled to say that none of the observations that Irons makes negates an understanding of Jesus' status as Son of God as Messiah. If Jesus had a heavenly preexistence, he would have knowledge of the Father that he could indeed uniquely communicate to others. Revelation is indeterminate regarding the period of time or the nature of the Son's existence with the Father in heaven before his advent. So I am not one who thinks of Jesus as a "mere creature." Certainly I share with Irons an understanding that there are humanly unknowable details about the relationship of the Father and the Son before he became the man Jesus. I implied as much in my first paragraph of this presentation. Yet Irons quotes John 14:9–10 without comment on what Jesus means when he tells Philip that to see him is to see the Father. We cannot even get an idea of what he means when, in the next sentence, he quotes Jesus who says, "I and the Father are one" (John 10:30). Jesus says in the same book that his disciples are to be "one" as he and the Father are one; and he adds that they in him and he in them share the same oneness (John 17:21–23).

The best picture of being "one" that is understandable (since Irons offers no commentary) is that Jesus is talking about unity of the believing community as they seek to have a better understanding of God's nature and heart. Certainly Jesus is spoken of in exalted terms. In saying Jesus is "the image of the invisible God" (Col 1:15), however, is to admit that he is not the same as God. Jesus in an *eikōn*, a "*likeness, image,* or *portrait,*" of another. It is decidedly *not the real thing*. Even to describe Jesus as the

THE SON OF GOD

charaktēr of God (Heb 1:3) is to present Jesus not as the real God, but as a *stamp* or an *engraved likeness* impressed into a piece of metal like Washington on a quarter or Jefferson on a nickel.

This is not to detract from what Jesus *is,* but it is to guard against saying what he is *not*—God himself. Jesus can communicate God, represent God, reveal God, imitate God, provide the highest pixel resolution of God possible on one's computer or mobile device, but he is not God himself. Irons will, as we shall see, join Bauckham and use other terminology, but it means the same thing (or something polytheistically worse for Trinitarians if God and one who shares in his identity is another entity!). Irons cites Col 2:9 which states that the fullness of deity lives in Jesus in bodily form. Could anything be greater? Yet is it not true that Paul prays that each believer in Ephesus be filled to the measure of all the fullness of God also (Eph 3:19)? Does not Peter assure his readers that it is possible for them to participate in the divine nature (share in God's identity?) and escape the world's corruption caused by evil desires (2 Pet 1:4)?

Irons believes that all of this inheres in Jesus' identity as God's Son, but not because the Son is the Messiah, but rather because the Son comes from God. This is because he does not see that the penultimate revelation of God announced on the day of Pentecost is very great indeed: Jesus was formally proclaimed Lord and Messiah at that time. The Dan 7:13–14 prophecy that the Messiah (a Son of Man) would enter into God's presence and receive authority, glory, and sovereign power, and that he would be worthy of universal worship, reigning over an eternal kingdom, was fulfilled. Irons indicates further in his essay an appreciation for certain aspects of this paragraph, particularly regarding Ps 110:1 and Dan 7:13–14. Darrell L. Bock makes clear that Jesus' castigation of the Jewish leaders in the context of claiming for himself a place at the right hand of God coming against them in judgment is what pushed the Jewish leaders to the edge in condemning Jesus. Jesus also claimed to be the Christ, which, although it may not be the main reason for his condemnation, could not have been welcome, a claim coming from one whom they saw as being unworthy for a number of reasons.[6]

PREEXISTENCE AND INCARNATION

I have very little disagreement with this section of Irons's essay I wonder, though, why Irons can speak of Jesus as preexistent *Logos* who "existed as a

---

6. Bock, *Blasphemy and Exaltation,* 202ff.

AN ARIAN RESPONSE TO A TRINITARIAN VIEW

divine being distinct from God." Although he seems to embrace the historic view of the Trinity as set forth in *The Westminster Confession of Faith*, he uses the word Trinity only twice and within only an inch or two of space of each reference to it, and has a very unconventional but apparently scholar-welcome (e.g., Richard Bauckham) conception of it. The references he gives from John's Gospel and the Johannine epistles seem on-target (at least, I agree with his brief listing of them), and I can even agree that Phil 2:5–11 may very well be a very early statement of Christian understanding predating liberal scholarship's erroneous view that the high Christology found in the Gospel of John is something developed and finalized well into the second century.

TWO TESTS OF ONTOLOGICAL DEITY

Creation

Without question Jesus is set forth in Scripture as being creator (John 1:3, 10; Col 1:16; 1 Cor 8:6).[7] Irons examines the wording of all the passages emphasizing the all-inclusive language in which both "Paul and John go out of their way to eliminate any exceptions." But note that, for example, Hebrews 2:8 says that "God has put *all things* in subjection under [Christ's] feet. For in that he [God] put *all* in subjection under him, he left *nothing* that is not put under him." Someone might read Heb 2:8 without acknowledging Scripture as a whole and argue against the existence of any exception to those things that are put under Christ.

However, 1 Cor 15:27 shows that there *is* an exception to "all things" under Christ, saying: "When he saith *all* things are put under him [Jesus], it is manifest that he [God] is *excepted*, which did put all things under him."[8] The idea that is presented is that given certain things one would understand from prior knowledge based on other Scripture, some things are *manifestly* excepted. Leaving theological presuppositions aside before making lexico-graphical decisions permits taking the Greek word *prōtotokos* to pertain literally to birth order (as applied to Jesus in Col 1:15).[9] Consider also Jesus'

---

7. But the affirmation of Heb 1:2 that the Son created "the world" is a bit more specious since *aiōn* in Heb 1:2 is more properly translated "age," and many of the ancient sources for the rendering "the world" as a spatial concept may be more appropriately listed as "a segment of time as a particular unit of history." See BDAG 32.

8. Kerrigan, *Biblical Christ*, 57.

9. BDAG 894. Also see Thayer who, although not without providing discussion to

THE SON OF GOD

affirmation that the Father granted that the Son would have life in himself (John 5:26). He also says in connection with his sending commission by God, "I live because of the Father" (John 6:57). Jesus came into being as first-born *from* (Gk. *ek*) God, and the rest of creation came into existence *through the agency of* (Gk. *dia*) Christ.

Aseity

Irons presents several examples of attributes of God which he says are tests of his ontological deity. Indeed, he joins Herman Bavinck in affirming aseity as what may be the primary attribute of God's being. These are characteristics that only God has from himself. Then regarding John 5:26 he observes that God who has life in himself *grants that status to Christ*. One cannot have that which he has not obtained, so there is a logical problem with Irons's understanding of the biblical phrase "has life in himself" as applied to Christ. John's wording does indeed start from the perspective that life was something that the Father already had without consideration in the text of the origin of that life. So it is self-existent. But Jesus' status as a living entity has a beginning. Christ's nonexistence—when he did not have life in himself—changes from the point that the Father gave him life and certainly continues from that point forward. Irons lists Heb 13:8, which says "Jesus is unchanging, 'the same yesterday and today and forever,'" and argues that the statement implies eternity.

Certainly "forever" can extend unendingly into the future. But it is an absurd idea that just because a status begun at a point in time yesterday continues to every yesterday past. Finally along this line Irons cites Heb 1:11–12, pulled from the Septuagint reading of Ps 102:25–27, where the Lord's created heaven and earth are contrasted with his continuity into future eternity. The passage does not speak of this Lord's eternal existence into *both* past and future. It identifies this Lord as having been the cause of the created order (discussion *supra* [v. 10] notwithstanding), predicts creation's end (vv. 11–12a), and declares the Lord's steady status from that point forward (v. 12b). The *Logos*, whose beginning was when he was given life by God (and as a consequence now has life in himself, John 5:26; 6:57),

---

the contrary, specifically lists Col 1:15 as an instance of *prōtotokos* as appropriately applied to Christ as one "who came into being through God prior to the entire universe of created things." See Thayer, *Greek-English Lexicon*, 555.

AN ARIAN RESPONSE TO A TRINITARIAN VIEW

was God's agent of creation, which has a fiery future (2 Pet 3:10–13). He is presently remaining and Scripture says he will remain into eternity future.

THE EXALTATION OF CHRIST

Despite a number of problems considered above, Irons believes the Son's ontological deity has been proven. He begins at Rom 1:4 where Jesus is "Son of God in power" modified by the Greek word *horisthentos*, which he translates as "marked out" or "declared" in keeping with standard lexicons and, he says, most English versions. The controversy is as simple as identifying whether Jesus as Son always had authority or was granted it. It has been my position that Jesus' ability as a man to do miracles was authority given by God (Matt 9:8), subject to limitation (e.g., in Nazareth "he *could not* do any miracles," Mark 6:5). *All* authority in heaven and on earth was given to him after his resurrection (Matt 28:18). And as Peter announces to Israel, God "*has made* him both Lord and Messiah this Jesus whom you crucified" (Acts 2:36). These are not statements "sealing the deal" of Christ's aseity. They are statements acknowledging that he was a being limited in his abilities by God who is ontologically superior to and apart from him.

Sovereign

Irons's understanding of God is puzzling. Since reading his discussion I am amazed that he calls himself a Trinitarian. He holds that God the Father alone is the ultimate power in the universe (1 Tim 6:15). Yet he says God exalts Jesus to share that divine sovereignty with him. I note in an elementary way that one cannot exalt someone who already and always held the position to which he was raised. Irons is admitting there was a time when Jesus did not have the status he has now. Yet he says Jesus' Sonship is eternal. This is a philosophical contradiction. While Irons does not see that a mere creature could be given that divine authority, I demonstrate in my opening essay that the idea was not foreign to the Jewish mind at the time Jesus lived. That the Jewish leaders had a particular problem with Jesus specifically seems to go without saying. But they seem to arbitrarily regard pretenders to the office of Messiah. And Jesus said enough at his trial to cause them to reject him.

THE SON OF GOD

Worship

Irons affirms that worship belongs properly only to the one true God. But worship is also reserved for anyone whom God has granted the authority. The angel Irons mentions in Rev 19:10 did *not* have that authority. Yet 1 Chron 29:20 tells us that David told the people, "'Now bless Jehovah your God.' And all the assembly blessed Jehovah, the God of their fathers, and bowed down their heads, and worshiped Jehovah, and the king." That I agree with the various passages Irons lists indicating that Jesus was worshiped does not mean one should therefore conclude that only God can be worshiped. God has exalted Jesus to be worshiped. That is within his prerogative to do so.

The Divine Name

While God does not give his glory to others, he does tell the Israelites to listen to the angel that he had sent ahead of them: "Do not rebel against him; he will not forgive your rebellion, since my Name is in him" (Exod 23:20–21). I agree with other verses Irons lists indicating that "in his exalted state" Jesus bears God's name Jehovah (which he writes as "YHWH"). My argument has been that one who is exalted did not hold the position or bear the name earlier.

It is this phrase "participates in the identity of YHWH" that is so interesting. Irons has a chronological problem. I am compelled to call him out and have him clearly explain what he means by it. An angel bears God's name in Exodus. Perhaps Irons believes it also shares in Jehovah's identity. Is there a distinction to be made between angels and Christ? If Christ was exalted, what was he before that happened? Irons "hesitates to say Jesus *is* YHWH," and he rejects modalism. It seems to me that Irons cannot escape some form of binitarian divine reality. Jesus is a second individual sharing in God's identity. That makes Irons's position polytheistic. Nor can he escape it by saying, even with me, that "Jesus is divine" based on the Greek in John 1:1. Angels are divine. Jesus, though not an angel, is divine. God is the ultimate and supremely divine One. Jesus is a divine *other* one.

AN ARIAN RESPONSE TO A TRINITARIAN VIEW
A DIVINE SAVIOR

I have little disagreement with Irons's understanding that Jesus the Messiah is "our divine Savior." The language is appropriate for the references he gives (Titus 2:13; 2 Pet 1:1). It is through him—Jesus as God's agent—that he accomplishes our salvation. It is because God decided that Jesus was the one to accomplish this that makes it necessary, not that Christ had to be divine (although he was!).

A SOCINIAN RESPONSE TO A TRINITARIAN VIEW

DUSTIN R. SMITH

I WISH TO APPLAUD LEE Irons for his stimulating presentation of Jesus as the divine Son of God. His engagement with both ancient and modern sources is both noteworthy and commendable. I particularly value his eager honesty which comes out when he openly wrestles with how some of the more difficult evidence should be understood. His arguments demonstrate that he has pondered these issues over an extended period of time while at the same time assessing their implications. His case aims to illustrate that Jesus is the divine Son of God, one who eternally preexisted with the Father. At the incarnation, the Son of God took up man's nature, becoming both divine and human. After his earthly ministry, God exalted him to his right hand and bestowed upon him divine honor. Irons additionally intends to demonstrate that this very position is taught within the New Testament.

Irons's presentation, in my opinion, suffers from a variety of flaws. Unfortunately, the space allotted to me will only allow me to respond to a selection of my concerns. Nevertheless, I intend to raise objections regarding what seems to me to be some of the most pressing areas of contention. My hope is that through gentle dialogue and questioning, Irons and I can find some common ground in our attempts to engage the biblical data seriously as believing Christians.

My initial concern is the language which Irons regularly employs regarding the "divinity" and "deity" of Jesus. He begins his presentation in an attempt to define these terms, citing an example from the Latin historian Livy as evidence of what he does not intend. Irons fails to clearly articulate

A SOCINIAN RESPONSE TO A TRINITARIAN VIEW

what these terms *do in fact mean*, leaving me somewhat bewildered. He states that Jesus is "eternally divine" and that he "belongs on the divine side of the Creator-creature distinction." It is difficult to define a term when you use the word within its definition. I am unable to agree or disagree with whether Jesus is "divine" or "deity" if there is no consensus on what these terms, slippery as they can be, clearly mean or entail. I suggest that we jettison these two words, both because of the obscurity that comes from defining them and because they are absent from modern English translations of the Bible.[1]

This leads to my next point of apprehension. By arguing that Jesus Christ is "eternal" and that he belongs on the Creator side of the spectrum, Irons is essentially saying that Jesus has always existed. A significant corollary to his point would be an insistence that Jesus was *never* brought into existence, since he does not belong to the category of "created creatures." I find these claims to be significantly at odds with the biblical data. For one, Jesus is certainly not alive and active anywhere within the pages of the Hebrew Bible.[2] In fact, there is a scholarly consensus that the title "Son of God" is used in three different ways within the Hebrew Bible (referring to the Davidic king, the people of God, and the heavenly hosts), but never in a manner which refers to a preexisting personal being alongside the Father.[3] Furthermore, Yahweh is routinely described as the one who has no equal (2 Sam 7:22; 1 Chr 17:20; Jer 10:6, 7), with no other besides him (Deut 4:35, 39; Isa 45:5, 6, 21, 22; 46:9; Joel 2:27). I am curious how it could be that the Son of God literally preexisted alongside God the Father when the biblical authors repeatedly acknowledge God by saying, "You *alone* are Yahweh" (2 Kgs 19:19; Neh 9:6; Pss 83:18; 86:10; Isa 37:20), "there is no one like you" (Exod 8:10; 9:14; 1 Sam 2:2; Ps 86:8). This unique God, Yahweh, is one and the same as the Father, whom Jesus identifies as *the only true God* (John 17:3). What about Isa 44:24, which plainly indicates that Yahweh, the sole creator, was *all alone* at creation, by Himself?

I additionally wish to question why Irons ignored the massive birth narratives and genealogies in Matthew and Luke, both of which, it seems

---

1. An exception could be made for how *theos* is to be understood in John 1:1c, where I feel an adjectival sense is expressed.

2. In fact, the author of Hebrews argues that God used to speak through prophets, but *in these last days* He has spoken to us through a Son (Heb 1:1–2) indicating that God didn't speak through a Son in the Hebrew Bible.

3. Fossum, "Son of God"; Caragounis, "*bēn*"; Michel, "Son"; Donaldson, "Son of God"; Haag, "*bēn*."

THE SON OF GOD

to me, clearly indicate that Jesus was brought into existence in the womb of Mary (Matt 1:18, 20; Luke 1:35). If the Bible's two birth narratives feature the miraculous birth of Jesus by highlighting his coming into existence, in what sense can we rationally speak of Jesus as "eternal?" If Jesus is indeed brought into existence, this actually puts him on the creature side of the Creator-creature distinction. I look forward to Irons's interaction on these important points.

Irons's presentation raises another issue concerning monotheism. If Jesus is on the divine side of the Creator-creature distinction, then how many persons are in that group? In other words, how many are on the divine side of this split? Isn't the Son of God numerically distinct from the Father, whom Irons (correctly) identifies as Yahweh? Does this not make two, one who is Yahweh and one who is the son of Yahweh? This certainly calls monotheism into question. If there are only two on this side, is this even Trinitarianism anymore? It sounds more like binitarianism. Perhaps some clarification will shed some light on my puzzlement.

Another concern I wish to raise regards his argument that the title Son of God applied to Jesus means something "far more" than an indicator of messianism. In fact, Irons is convinced that this title is indicative of Jesus' "divine Sonship" (I confess that I am still unsure what "divine" means). I respectfully suggest that these conclusions go beyond the available evidence. The authors of the New Testament (and the historical Jesus himself) were influenced by Jewish literature and traditions wherein "Son of God" was used in a variety of ways. Within the Hebrew Bible, Pss 2:7, 89:26-27, and 2 Sam 7:14 lay the foundation for messianic interpretations regarding God's Son.[4] In fact, the context of 2 Sam 7:14 equates the Son of David with the Son of God, leading to subsequent Jewish readings which do the same (4QFlor). Luke 1:32 calls Jesus the Son of the Most High while at the same time calling David his father (i.e., Son of David). Even Paul argues in his description of the gospel that Jesus is both a descendant of David and God's Son (Rom 1:1-4). Irons argues that the "Messiah Son of God" is not the same as the "Messiah Son of David." Ps 2:7 and 2 Sam 7:14 can be detected as influential within the New Testament (Matt 3:17; Mark 1:11; Luke 3:22; Acts 13:33; Heb 1:5), suggesting that these understandings of messianism are the most appropriate contexts for interpreting Jesus' sonship. N. T. Wright's admission is most helpful at this point: "We must stress that in the first century the regular Jewish meaning of this title ['son

---

4. Hurtado, *Lord Jesus Christ*, 103.

A SOCINIAN RESPONSE TO A TRINITARIAN VIEW

of God'] had nothing to do with an incipient trinitarianism; it referred to the king as *Israel's representative*."[5]

Irons asserts that Jesus never spoke of God as "our Father" in a way which might include him with his disciples. This is a debatable conclusion, particularly in light of the Lord's Prayer ("Our Father," Matt. 6:9). Additionally, John 20:17 recalls Jesus saying, "I have not yet ascended to the Father; but go to my brethren and say to them, 'I ascend to *my Father* and *your Father*, and my God and your God.'" It seems that Jesus is not only including himself with the disciples in defining the Father, but also mentioning that they all share the same God! These texts further weaken Irons's case for defining "Son of God" as he does.

I disagree with Irons's assertion that Jesus' claim to be Son of God "could not have been a mere messianic claim" since it brought forth the claim of blasphemy. This seems to me to be a failure to understand how the Jews interpreted Jesus and his claims, particularly within the Gospel of John, where Jesus could have been understood as a *rebellious son* taking prerogatives which are not rightfully his. One example Irons supplies is John 5:18 where Jesus calls God his own Father, making himself equal to God. It needs to be stated that within first century Judaism, a claim to sonship implied obedience and dependence, not equality (Deut 21:18; Sir 3.6–16; Philo, *Conf.* 63; *Dec.* 118). In other words, for a son to claim equality with one's father in a manner which laid claim to the father's unique prerogatives (thus dishonoring the father) would make the son into a rebellious son.[6] If the Johannine 'Jews' understood Jesus as a rebellious son, who illegitimately claimed the right to break the Sabbath and give life, then they would have interpreted Jesus' claim to messianship as a false claim. In their eyes, Jesus was a *false Messiah*. In order to counter this claim, Jesus stated, "the son can do nothing of himself, unless it is something he sees the Father doing" (John 5:19, 30). In other words, Jesus responded to this misunderstanding (a prevalent motif in the Fourth Gospel) by claiming to be an *obedient son rather than a rebellious son*.[7] Along similar lines, Irons notes the episode where Jesus forgave sins as one which elicited the charge of blasphemy. The story continues to note that "God has given such authority to men" (Matt 9:8), a statement with which Jesus agrees (Matt 9:6). God has authorized Jesus to forgive sins (see John 20:23, where

---

5. Wright, *Jesus and the Victory of God*, 485–86, emphasis his.
6. McGrath, *John's Apologetic Christology*, 87.
7. Borgen, "God's Agent," 69.

THE SON OF GOD

the disciples are similarly authorized). My question to Irons would be, how is Jesus authorized (by God) to forgive sins if he already possessed that right as the divine Creator?

I also object to Irons's argument that, "If Jesus is a *mere creature*, how could he know the Father perfectly?" First of all, this is setting up a straw man and knocking it down. I do not think that the Bible described Jesus as a mere creature. He is the sinless, miraculously begotten, messianic king of the coming kingdom of God, who died for the sins of humanity. Secondly, the Bible *never* claims that a creature is unable to fully understand God. His argument seems confused as he admits that Jesus is ignorant of the eschatological day and hour (Matt 24:36; Mark 13:32). How can Jesus know the Father perfectly and at the same time be unaware of certain facts?[8] Are these texts really teaching that Jesus is ontologically divine, coequal with the Father? I suggest that they are not. In order for coequality with the Father to logically stand, the Son must likewise be omniscient, which he clearly isn't.

Another problem appears when Irons writes that "the Sonship of Christ is not something that began at some point in his earthly existence but in fact goes back to his preincarnate state." I desire that Luke 1:35 get a fresh look, a text which highlights the spirit's miracle *as the precise reason* for the begotten child being called the Son of God. Irons continues by citing John 1:1–3 as proof that the Word was a "divine being distinct from God." In addition to again raising the question of monotheism, this definition of the Word goes beyond anything taught within the Hebrew Bible, where God's *davar* is never described as a separate divine being.[9] Irons brings a straightforward reading to the "came or descended from heaven" references, a reading which ignores the Jewish idiom (Jas 1:17; 3:15, 17), misses that Jesus' "flesh" is what descended (John 6:51), and fails to grasp the *figurative* nature of the dialogue which is pervasive. Jesus unquestionably was sent from God (John 7:29), but so was John the Baptist (John 1:6). I invite Irons to interact with the argument which I detailed regarding John 8:58 and 17:5 in my response to Dixon, particularly where I demonstrated that Jews often spoke of preexistence within God's plan. It is certainly true that Jesus was consecrated before his birth (John 10:36), but is this really so different than the beginning of Jeremiah's commissioning (Jer 1:5)?

---

8. Note the examples I provided in my initial essay where Jesus is not omniscient.
9. See my reading of the Johannine Prologue which I noted in my response to Dixon.

A SOCINIAN RESPONSE TO A TRINITARIAN VIEW

Irons further argues that John 16:28 is indicative of three phases of Jesus' existence. However, this suggestion fails to take seriously the chiastic structure of the verse:

I came forth from the Father (A)
  and have come into the world (B)
  I am leaving the world again (B1)
and going to the Father (A1)

This seems, rather than teaching three phases, to indicate two phases. At the end of this section, he suggests that these disputed passages in John's Gospel need to be interpreted as "straightforward vignettes." Yet I feel the need to ask, "straightforward to whom?" To us as twenty-first century Westerners, who are nearly two millennia detached from the culture, context, idioms, and customs of the first-century-Jewish world? Does not Jesus characteristically speak in metaphor, parable, and typology within the Fourth Gospel? I respectfully suggest that the Judaism out of which the Fourth Gospel was composed needs to be accounted for before we assume that such statements need to be read with such wooden literalism.

Irons objects to a theology of two stages of Christology which eliminates preexistence. He argues this reconstruction would result in a human being exalted to a position of honor which is inconsistent with his "ontological nature." In other words, Irons assumes that Jesus *has to be ontologically divine* in order to make sense of his exaltation. In response, I wish to bring to the discussion texts within Judaism where human figures are described as greatly exalted (without any reservation given by the authors). The *Testament of Abraham* depicts a glorified human figure (revealed to be Adam) seated upon a golden throne overseeing the judgment of souls (*T. Abr.* 11.4–12). The same document depicts Abel, a human judge, exalted to a position of enthronement after his death (*T. Ab.* 12.4–11; 13.1–4). *Fourth Ezra* has Ezra receiving the promise of exaltation to live with God's son (*4 Ezra* 14.9). The second-century-BCE document, the *Exagōgē* of Ezekiel the Tragedian, drawing on the vision of the throne chariot in Ezek 1, portrays Moses as a man seated upon a heavenly throne ruling and governing humanity (*Ezek. Trag.* 68–86). Some of the speculation about the location of the elusive Elijah crystallized in Sirach, who describes him as exalted ("taken up") without dying (Sir 48:9–10). Similarly, the book of *1 Enoch* testifies about the speculation of the figure by the same name who was promoted to heaven apart from death

THE SON OF GOD

(*1 Enoch* 12.4). Are Adam, Abel, Ezra, Moses, and Enoch being given divine honors representing their ontological nature? I would be eager to hear how Irons feels about these passages, about which James Dunn summarizes, "this raises the possibility that even within the monotheistic Judaism of the first century that thought of a great human figure being exalted to heavenly status, and thus receiving honor due to such a one, was not so far from being admissible."[10] Irons is making a rather bold claim to assert that the (omnipotent) Father is unable to exalt a human being.

The next objection I wish to raise with Irons's presentation runs along similar lines, as he assumes, "No mere creature could be given that divine authority as Lord of all creation." His statement is problematic for a number of reasons. First, as I have already mentioned, a sinless, miraculously begotten Son of God who will one day rule as the king of the kingdom could never be called a "mere creature." This again sets up the straw man. Secondly, I am surprised that Irons finds no parallel to human figures being given universal dominion. Was not Adam told, "rule over the fish of the sea and over the birds of the heavens and over the cattle and *over all the earth and over every creeping thing that creeps on the earth*" (Gen 1:26–27)? What about the anointed king in Ps 2 (God's son) who is guaranteed the nations as his inheritance along with the very ends of the earth as his possession (Ps 2:7–8)? Was not the Son of Man promised to receive "dominion, glory, and a kingdom, that all the peoples and nations might serve him" (Dan 7:13–14)? It is not surprising that Jesus is called the "second Adam" by Paul (1 Cor 15:45), not only because of his implicit "Adam Christology" but also because Jesus was to receive the dominion originally marked out for Adam (1 Cor 15:23–28). If God *rewarded Jesus* for his life of faithfulness with power and authority on heaven and earth, then *Jesus did not previously possess it!* Jesus is the heir of all creation, indeed, but Paul says that Christians are coheirs with Christ (Rom 8:17). If Jesus had to be given this authority and power from God, in what sense can we say that they are sharing some ontological nature? Irons correctly points out that the exaltation of Jesus was in fulfillment of Psalm 110:1. However, upon a closer examination of this passage in Hebrew, we find that Yahweh exalts *adoni* ("my lord"), a term in each of its 195 occurrences never refers to God or deity.[11] It always denotes a human superior, sometimes even an angel. Therefore, if Ps 110:1 is the passage which the New Testament authors cited to explain the

---

10. Dunn, *Did the First Christians*, 89.
11. The LXX confirms the vowel placement of *adoni* by translating it as *kyriō mou*.

A SOCINIAN RESPONSE TO A TRINITARIAN VIEW

exaltation of Jesus, and this passage illustrates Yahweh exalting a created human (or angel) superior, then why is it so difficult to conceive that God can exalt the human Messiah Jesus to a mediator's position (1 Tim 2:5)?

Another issue which needs to be raised is Irons's understanding of the act of worship. He assumes that only the Creator is worthy of worship, and since Jesus is worshiped this must mean that the early Christians understood Jesus as the Creator. However, this argument possesses many flaws. For one, Jews had no problem ascribing worship to human beings, apparently without any hesitation that there is any compromise to the worship due to the one true God. One example is located in 1 Chr 29:20 where the assembly of Israelites "worshiped" both Yahweh and King David. The Greek verb *proskyneō*, which the New Testament authors used to describe the act of homage toward Jesus, is also used of Joseph (Gen 33:7 LXX), Boaz (Ruth 2:10 LXX), Daniel (Dan 2:46 LXX), Peter (Acts 10:25), and even Christians (Rev 3:9). Irons cites the example in Rev 5 where the Lamb is declared worthy of awesome worship. However, the Apocalypse of John argues that the Lamb is to be worshiped *for a different reason* than the one seated upon the throne (God). Rev 4:11 details why God is worthy of worship, "You created all things, and because of Your will they already existed, and were created." On the other hand, the Lamb receives worship because, "you were slaughtered, and purchased for God with your blood those from every tribe and tongue and people and nation" (Rev 5:9). Therefore, God is worthy to receive worship because he is *the* Creator, while Jesus is worthy to receive worship because he died and redeemed humanity in his blood. Rev 5 continues by recording the song, "To Him who sits on the throne and to the Lamb, be blessing and honor and glory and dominion forever and ever (Rev 5:13). Both the Creator and the slaughtered Lamb are given prostration, while at the same time *remaining distinct from each other*. Furthermore, if the Lamb is distinct from the person who created all things (Rev 4:11), doesn't this specify Jesus as being one who was created? In short, Irons's assessment of how the New Testament uses the act of worship toward Jesus fails to take account of all the available data.

Irons tries to make the case that "God does not share his name with creatures." His argument continues by demonstrating that God has indeed shared his name with Jesus, which allows him to participate in the "identity of YHWH." Certainly Irons is not unaware that within Judaism God has bestowed his name onto various agents. The Israelites were guided by God's angel, of whom God commanded the people, "Be on your guard before him

THE SON OF GOD

and obey his voice . . . since My name is in him" (Exod 23:21). The prophet like Moses, according to Deuteronomy, would be given God's words and would speak "in My name" (Deut 18:18–19). Similarly, the angel Yahoel in the *Apocalypse of Abraham* is commanded by God, "Go . . . through the mediation of my ineffable name, consecrate this man for me" (*Apoc. Abr.* 10.3). Yahoel later speaks of the authority granted to him by the creator God, "I am Yahoel, and I was called so by him . . . to shake, a power through the medium of his ineffable name in me" (*Apoc. Ab.* 10.8). It seems that, on occasion, God certainly did share his name with creatures, all of whom acted as his authorized agent. I would like to request Irons to flesh out what exactly he means by "participating in the identity of Yahweh." This language is very slippery and unhelpfully vague. It is a phrase wholly absent from both the biblical authors and the church fathers. By identity, does he mean coequality? I wonder if Solomon, who is mentioned as sitting upon Yahweh's throne (1 Chr 28:5; 29:23), even being placed upon it by Yahweh himself (2 Chr 9:8), fits into this definition of participating in the identity of Yahweh. The use of the title *kyrios* for the exalted Jesus in Acts 2:21 and Rom 10:13 makes sense in light of the principle of agency, where the agent bears the name and authority of the one who sent him (cp. Yahoel again). Irons downplays agency as an inadequate way of understanding the relationship between Yahweh and Jesus. I suggest that the Jewish definition of agency, where "a person's agent is equivalent to the person himself" (*b. Qidd.* 42b, 43a), best accounts for the relationship between God and Jesus.

I found Irons's wrestling with the question "Is Jesus Yahweh?" to be quite admirable and honest. Irons seems to conclude that Jesus is not the same person as Yahweh, feeling more comfortable with saying that "Jesus is the Son of Yahweh." Along similar lines, Irons rightly hesitates to say "Jesus *is* God." He feels more relaxed (rightly) with the phrase "Jesus is the Son of God." The logic here, of which I desire to be corrected if I am mistaken, is that Jesus is not God precisely because God cannot be his own Son. In other words, if Jesus is the Son of God then he is *numerically distinct from the one whose Son he is*. Irons and I are in agreement with his admission that Yahweh and *ho theos* are typically used in Scripture to refer to the Father. And this Father, Jesus teaches, is his God and our God (John 20:17).

This brings me to a few lingering misgivings regarding Irons's presentation as a whole about which I would value his input. There seems to be some hesitation on his part to state plainly that Jesus, the Son of God, died completely in every respect. The New Testament has no problem admitting

A SOCINIAN RESPONSE TO A TRINITARIAN VIEW

that Jesus was asleep in the grave (Matt 12:40; Acts 2:27; 1 Cor 15:4, 20) until he was raised up (literally: "woken up") on Easter Sunday (Acts 3:15; 1 Cor 6:14; 2 Cor 4:14). Isa 53, upon which both Jesus and the New Testament authors drew to understand the death of the Messiah, speaks of the suffering servant who "poured out his soul to death" (Isa 53:12; Phil 2:9). I would like to understand further how Irons fits in the death of Jesus, about which the New Testament authors speak without any reservation, with Jesus' "divinity." If Jesus is the [immortal] Creator, how can he truly die? Gal 2:20 indicates that the "Son of God" died on behalf of the Apostle Paul. Can an "eternal" Son die, thus requiring another to raise him from the dead? No doubt Irons is aware of how central the claim of Jesus' death and resurrection are to the Christian gospel message. It seems that if God is immortal (Rom 1:23; 1 Tim 1:17) and if Jesus died, then Jesus is not the immortal God (and did not possess the quality of immortality). I suggest identifying Jesus as the human Messiah, who died and was raised to eternal life, makes better sense of these problems. Nevertheless, I eagerly look forward to hearing how Irons sees these pieces fitting together.

Finally, I want to interact with Irons's closing remarks that "it was not the post-apostolic church, in a desire to exalt Jesus more and more, that indulged in unwarranted 'exaggeration' about the person of Jesus." I agree that Jesus is the unique Son of God, and that this confession was central to the early Christian proclamations. Amen! However, a Son of God defined by texts like 2 Sam 7:14 and Ps 2:7 is something quite different from the extra-biblical phrase "God the Son." Therefore, I am not entirely sure where Irons is going with the word "exaggeration." It would certainly be an exaggeration to assert that the doctrine of the eternal generation of the Son is taught, hinted at, or alluded to in Scripture. Jesus, who called the Father "the only true God" (John 17:3), is not using the post-apostolic teaching found in the confession of Chalcedon. Irenaeus seems to be exaggerating when he writes, "This Christ passed through Mary just as water flows through a tube," something radically different from Matthew's and Luke's insistence that Jesus was brought into being inside his mother Mary.[12] I wonder if Irons agrees with Tertullian's understanding of God when he says, "[God] could not have been a Father previous to the Son, nor a judge previous to sin. There was, however, a time when neither sin existed with him, nor the Son."[13] What about Gregory of Nyssa, who argues that "[The

---

12. Irenaeus, *Against Heresies* 1.7.2.
13. Tertullian, *Against Hermogenes* 3.

THE SON OF GOD

Trinity represents] the middle between the two opinions [of polytheism and Jewish monotheism]."[14] I echo the observation of many church historians who contend that the church's view of Christology certainly did develop over the course of the next few centuries.[15] In addition, the fact that some of the textual scribes altered the texts of Scripture in order to elevate the Christology in various passages has been well documented.[16] Perhaps I should reemphasize that I believe everything that both the Old and New Testaments teach about Jesus Christ. My contention is that the Messiah can uniquely represent God as a miraculously begotten, sinless, and completely obedient human being.

I wish to thank Lee Irons for his time and energy spent composing his lengthy presentation concerning how he understands Jesus Christ, the Son of God. I value and appreciate his honesty, scholarship, and reverent approach. He should be congratulated for his research efforts, which have apparently taken place over an extended period of time. Irons's tone has been nothing short of what is to be expected of a Christian gentleman. I remain unpersuaded of his overall thesis, though I agree with a variety of his points. My hope and desire is that through vigorous and fruitful dialogue we can continue to grow in our understanding of humanity's Savior, Jesus Christ.

---

14. Gregory of Nyssa, *Oratio Catechetica Magna* 3.2.

15. E.g., Hanson, *Image*, 87; Armstrong, *History of God*, 81. James McGrath correctly admits that "the earliest Christians were not trinitarians in the modern sense." See his *Only True God*, 100, 114–5 n15.

16. See Ehrman, *Orthodox Corruption*.

A TRINITARIAN REPLY

CHARLES LEE IRONS

I APPRECIATE THE SPIRIT IN which both Danny Dixon and Dustin Smith have written in response to my positive statement. Both have raised some important challenges and questions that I need to respond to. A good number of the challenges I attempt to answer in my responses to their positive statements, especially their argument about exalted beings in Jewish literature. Thus I will use this rebuttal section to respond to the issues that I do not address there. Hopefully this dialogue will at least clarify our fundamental differences.

THE TERMS "DIVINE" AND "DEITY"

Smith raises an objection to my use of the terms "divine" and "deity," and suggests that we stop using these terms because, in his opinion, they are vague and hard to define. However, I addressed this at the outset of my positive statement, and I thought I had made two key points to address Smith's concerns. First, I added the adjectival qualifier "ontological" to make clear that I am using the term in a way that ascribes deity to someone as a matter of ontology or essence. This added adjective could never be applied to angels, for example; although in a sense they are "divine beings," they are not ontologically divine. Second, I defined deity with reference to the Creator-creature distinction. Among things that exist, there is a fundamental divide. So fundamental is the divide that all existent beings fall into one of two categories: either they are on the Creator side or the creature side of the ontological divide. Any existent being that had a beginning,

THE SON OF GOD

and a time when it did not exist, is a creature and hence not ontologically divine. Any existent being that is referred to in Scripture as Creator is ontologically divine. This definition is not circular, as Smith claims. I do not use the term I am trying to define in the definition. The definition uses terms like "Creator" and "creature," and hence it is a logically sound definition. It is not surprising that Smith wants to discard the terms "divine" and "deity" and would prefer to speak only of "God." He has an a priori commitment to the belief that there is only one person in the universe who is God. But I fail to see how Smith can have a legitimate objection to my use of this terminology, as I have defined it, unless he simply wants to win the debate by definition.

IS MY VERSION OF THE TRINITY IDIOSYNCRATIC?

Both Dixon and Smith wonder if my version of the Trinity is idiosyncratic. They express amazement or puzzlement with some of the language I use to formulate the relationship between the Father and the Son. I will try to provide clarification. One thing that may help is to understand that within Trinitarianism there exist two main streams of thought—both regarded as orthodox. One tradition, which is typically associated with the Latin-speaking Western church and which has Augustine as its main theologian, begins with the oneness of God and then proceeds to try to understand how there can be three persons in the one God. The other tradition, which is typically associated with the Greek-speaking Eastern church, begins with the three persons (or hypostases) and then proceeds to try to understand how the three are one. Most of us are more familiar with the Western approach to the Trinity, but my thinking has been greatly influenced by the Eastern tradition, primarily through the writings of Athanasius and the Cappadocian fathers.[1] Hence my starting point is with the three distinct persons, particularly the distinction between the Father and the Son. The reason my language has been a source of puzzlement to Dixon and Smith is likely because they were expecting me to begin with the oneness of God and then to explain how that one being of God can be understood as personalized in a threefold manner.

If I had the opportunity, I would defend the doctrine of the Trinity on the basis of Scripture incrementally. *First*, I would begin (as I did in my

1. Basil of Caesarea, his brother Gregory of Nyssa, and Gregory Nazianzen.

A TRINITARIAN REPLY

positive statement) with the fact that the Father has an eternal Son, and that the Son falls on the Creator side of the Creator-creature distinction. Now we have two ontologically divine persons. *Second*, I would attempt to prove the personality and deity of the Holy Spirit, showing that the Spirit is a distinct person (more than God's power) and that he too falls on the Creator side of the Creator-creature distinction. (A discussion of the Holy Spirit would perhaps require another book in itself.) *Third*, having established a triad of divine persons, I would then move to the doctrine of the twofold eternal procession of the Son and the Spirit from the Father. The eternal generation of the Son, when properly understood, enables us to understand how the essence of God can be one and yet the persons within that essence can be multiplied in a manner consistent with the singular essence of God. I would attempt to demonstrate the generation of the Son and the procession of the Spirit exegetically from the New Testament, especially from the Gospel of John. Then, *fourth*, I would attempt exegetically to show that the doctrine of the simplicity of God is a theoretical linchpin of the triune nature of the one God who is not divided into three parts. *Finally*, I would attempt exegetically to demonstrate how the simplicity of God leads to the inseparable operation of each of the three persons of the Trinity. The last three steps are sub-parts of an exegetical, biblical-theological argument showing how the three persons can be distinct in their personal operations and yet be one in essence. That is merely a sketch of how I would go about attempting to demonstrate the doctrine of the Trinity from Scripture. I would begin, in Eastern style, with the individual hypostatic entities of the Father, Son, and Holy Spirit, and then progressively move from that starting point to the unity of the Godhead.

DOES THE TRINITY VIOLATE MONOTHEISM?

Both Dixon and Smith charge the doctrine of the Trinity with violating monotheism. They both understand monotheism to require that God be one individual or one person. Therefore, to speak of three persons within the Godhead is to violate monotheism in their view. It is beyond the scope of this book to engage the doctrine of the Trinity in depth, but it is clear that we disagree that monotheism entails that God is one person. The fact that God has sent his Son and that the Son sent the Spirit clearly reveals God to be three persons. It is revealed by anticipation in the Old Testament (esp. Ps 2:7; 110:1) and it is revealed definitively in the history of redemption in

THE SON OF GOD

the incarnation, life, ministry, and exaltation of Jesus—both in his claim to be the unique, divine Son of God and in the Father's vindication of that claim by exalting him to the highest place at his right hand. To me, this is sufficient proof that monotheism does not mean that God is numerically one person. The New Testament's focus on Jesus' Sonship explains how Jesus is eternally divine and distinct from God the Father, and yet there is only one God. Sonship is the key that unlocks the door to the doctrine of the Trinity, because it captures both the Son's equality as one who is of the same substance with the Father (*homoousios*) and the Son's subordination as one who is divine in a way that is distinct from the Father as the Father's offspring. He is not a second God competing with the Father. He is the Father's Son, fully dependent on the Father. He has his full divine nature from the Father in such a way that there are not two gods but one God.

PARTICIPATING IN THE IDENTITY OF YHWH

Both Dixon and Smith also wonder what I mean when I use Bauckham's language that Jesus "participates in the identity of YHWH." I can understand how this might be confusing. It seems to suggest that there are at least two separate individuals who are both God, leading to the charge of "binitarianism." I should mention that I view the term "identity" and the more traditional term "essence" as near synonyms. The only difference is that "identity" focuses on our knowledge of the divine essence, rather than God's essence in and of itself. When I say that Jesus "participates in, or is included in, the identity of YHWH," I mean that, by his exaltation, God the Father has made it clear that his Son belongs within the one essence of God, that is, he belongs to the Creator side of the Creator-creature distinction. The key point is that the exaltation of Christ manifests, reveals, and makes clear his identity. It does not create it. The Son always was included within the divine identity or essence, eternally, by the Father's eternal generation of the Son. The exaltation of Christ does not change, create, or add to it. It merely makes it evident to us so that we can now see what was true of him all along. The reason the exaltation of Christ is needed is because the Son emptied himself by becoming man, thus temporarily and partially hiding aspects of his divine identity. He appeared "in fashion as a man" (Phil 2:7). Thus, the exaltation of Christ was necessary in order to bring to light and publicly manifest his true divine identity that had been temporarily concealed to a degree, although it did shine through at various points in

A TRINITARIAN REPLY

his earthly ministry prior to his exaltation, particularly in his miracles of power over nature and the voice from heaven declaring "This is my beloved Son" at his baptism and his transfiguration.

"SON OF GOD" AND THE BLASPHEMY CHARGE

Both Dixon and Smith dispute my interpretation of the title "Son of God." Here we have a fundamental difference of interpretation. I think that I made some strong arguments for taking the "Son of God" title in a sense that means ontological deity and equality with God, and not just as a synonym for "Messiah," but Dixon and Smith did not address many of my arguments: the voice from heaven at the baptism of Jesus; Jesus' dialogue with the Pharisees concerning Ps 110:1; Jesus' use of the *Abba* title to address the Father; and Joel Marcus's argument that the Jews did not regard false messiahs as blasphemers worthy of death. Dixon and Smith think that the Jews rejected Jesus merely as a false messiah. But if Jesus only claimed to be the Davidic Messiah and did not claim to be the unique, divine Son of God, they cannot explain the precise nature of the Jewish reaction. The Jewish reaction fits the mold of the standard "zeal" response to blasphemy and idolatry.[2] Many Jews felt that anyone who engaged in such extreme violations of the first commandment must be immediately put to death in order to uphold the exclusive claims of YHWH as the only true God.

I recognize that Dixon and Smith did not ignore the blasphemy argument, but they went down different paths to try to explain it. Dixon appeals to Darrell Bock's book on Mark 14:53–66.[3] Dixon represents Bock as claiming that what pushed the Jews to condemn Jesus to death was "Jesus' castigation of the Jewish leaders in the context of claiming for himself a place at the right hand of God coming against them in judgment." In other words, the thing that incensed the Jews was that Jesus claimed to have authority over them and that he would one day judge them as the exalted Son of Man. This interpretation enables Dixon to get around the notion that the Jews condemned Jesus for claiming to be the divine Son of God.

---

2. Jewish zeal was based on the model of Phinehas (Num 25:1–13; Ps 106:28–31) and was essentially vigilante justice in response to extreme violations of the Torah, like blasphemy or idolatry (*Jub.* 30:18; Philo, *Special Laws* 1.54–55, 2.253; Gal 1:13–14; Phil 3:6; *m. Sanh.* 9.6).

3. Bock, *Blasphemy and Exaltation*.

THE SON OF GOD

However, there are two problems with Dixon's argument. First, Dixon misrepresents Bock. Bock is too careful a scholar to argue that Jesus' claim to have authority as judge was the *only* reason the Jews charged Jesus with blasphemy. In a more recent article published in 2012, Bock makes clear that Jesus' claim to equality with God was also part of the reason they charged him with blasphemy.[4] After all, Bock is a Trinitarian, so we should not be surprised that Bock's scholarship does not support Dixon's Arian position.

Second, the thing that is missing in Dixon's argument is a connection with blasphemy in particular. It is one thing to say that the Jews condemned Jesus to death because he claimed the authority to act as eschatological judge. But Dixon has not shown how this claim could be construed as "blasphemy" by the Jews. "It is not for a good work that we are going to stone you but *for blasphemy*, because you, being a man, make yourself God" (John 10:33).

Smith takes a different approach, relying on the contention of James McGrath that the Jews regarded Jesus as behaving in a manner unworthy of a son by claiming equality with God, which made him a rebellious son worthy of death in their eyes per the Mosaic law (Deut 21:18–21).[5] Smith argues that a good (non-rebellious) son would only claim to be subordinate to his father, never to be equal with his father. The moment he started to claim to be equal with his father, he would become a bad (rebellious) son. Thus, the Jews wanted Jesus to be put to death, not because he claimed to be divine, but because he was acting as a rebellious son.

In response to Smith's argument, I would like to make two points. First, in John 5:18 the thinking of the Jews is represented in these words: Jesus, they reasoned, "was even calling God his own Father, [thereby] making himself equal with God." In other words, the Jews interpreted Jesus' assertion that God was "his own Father" (that is, in a special and distinctive manner) as "making himself equal with God." The Jews seemed to think that a claim to sonship does in fact imply a claim to equality. Thus John 5:18 seems to contradict Smith's contention that "within first-century Judaism, a claim to sonship implied obedience and dependence, not equality."

Second, Smith's reasoning is flawed because it contains an admission that gives away his whole case. Smith writes: "For a son to claim equality

---

4. See my opening statement, note 14.
5. McGrath, *John's Apologetic Christology*, 87. The argument is also found in an older article by McGrath, "Rebellious Son," and in his more recent book, *Only True God*, 58–61.

A TRINITARIAN REPLY

with one's father in a manner which laid claim to the father's unique prerogatives (thus dishonoring the father) would make the son into a rebellious son." So Smith admits that Jesus claimed (or at least that the Jews took Jesus to be claiming) equality with God in a manner which laid claim to the Father's unique prerogatives![6]

In sum, Dixon and Smith seem unable or unwilling to heed the clear statements in the Gospels and instead go off on a speculative search, fabricating other Jewish charges against Jesus than the ones stated in the Gospels. The Gospels fail to mention the specific crimes speculated by Dixon (claiming authority as eschatological judge) and Smith (being a rebellious son). Instead, the Gospels explicitly inform us that it was Jesus' claim to be the Son of God that was precisely the problem. Recall, again, how explicit the Fourth Gospel is. John tells us: "This was why the Jews were seeking all the more to kill him, because not only was he breaking the Sabbath, but he was even calling God his own Father, making himself equal with God" (John 5:18). When Jesus asked them for which good work they were going to stone him, they replied: "It is not for a good work that we are going to stone you but for blasphemy, because you, being a man, make yourself God" (John 10:33). And later, the Jews explained to Pilate: "We have a law, and according to that law he ought to die because he has made himself the Son of God" (John 19:7). In all three texts, the verb *poieō* is used in a sense that means "to make oneself out to be someone."[7] The issue is Jesus' claim concerning his ontological identity. The debate is over who Jesus is. Is he the divine Son of God as he claims? The Jews think that Jesus, being a mere man, has infringed upon monotheism and deserves to be put to death for blasphemy. This is a strong argument, and neither Dixon nor Smith has provided a convincing rebuttal.

THE CHRONOLOGICAL OR LOGICAL PROBLEM

Let us move to another key issue that both Dixon and Smith raise in objection to my interpretation of the exaltation of Jesus. Dixon refers to it sometimes as a "chronological problem," and sometimes as a "logical problem," but I take him to be making the same point. Both Dixon and Smith use

---

6. "Saying that he has made himself 'equal to God' (*ison theōi*) sounds much more as if Jesus is accused of assuming the same status as God, *i.e.*, of infringing monotheism." Van der Horst, "Review," 414.

7. BDAG *poieō* 2hβ.

the argument that "what is granted, could not have been his beforehand." Their point is a seemingly rational one, at least if we are talking about the way things work with ordinary people who are merely human. When an employee is granted a promotion at work, logically they could not have had the new position before receiving the promotion, otherwise it would not be called a promotion. That is how things work with ordinary persons. But Jesus is no ordinary person. He is the eternal Son of God who became man. Thus, when he is exalted to God's right hand, he is receiving honor, glory, authority, and worship that he already possessed, but he is now receiving it in a new mode, *as the incarnate Son*. He possessed all authority in heaven and earth even before his incarnation, as the preexistent Logos, but now the Father has granted him all authority as man (Matt 28:18; Acts 2:36).

As I explained in my positive statement, I believe the Bible teaches a three-phase Christology: preexistence, incarnation, and exaltation. Furthermore, the middle phase, incarnation, is a phase of humility in which the Son "emptied" himself and took on the form of a bondservant (Phil 2:5–8)—that is, he voluntary chose not to exercise all of his divine attributes and prerogatives, making himself appear as a mere human, although his divine glory did shine through at times even during his humiliation and prior to his exaltation. Therefore, the exaltation of Christ not only gives him these divine prerogatives in a new mode (as man) but it also provides a public manifestation and vindication of his true identity as the divine Son of God in the face of the evidence that seemed to contradicted it—his sufferings and crucifixion by those who rejected his claims. Thus, there are two things that he receives at his exaltation that he did not receive before: (a) receiving authority, honor, and glory as the incarnate Son, and (b) receiving public vindication by God. It is not that he received authority, honor, and glory that he did not possess before, for certainly he had all of these things from eternity past. Rather, it is that he now exercises these divine prerogatives in his incarnate human state and as his vindication by God in light of his being rejected by the Jewish nation.

John 17:5 supports what I am saying. Jesus prays, "And now, Father, glorify me in your own presence with the glory that I had with you before the world existed." Jesus is asking that he might receive the same glory that he had before he became a man in his preexistence phase, but that he might now receive it as a man. It may sound rational to say, "If he was granted glory and authority, then he did not possess it before." But Jesus himself explicitly and clearly asks to be granted the glory that he possessed before!

A TRINITARIAN REPLY

There is no logical contradiction, as long as one understands the New Testament's three-phase Christology.

Phil 2:5–11 supports this understanding as well. Many scholars have noticed the "parabola" of Jesus' career, which begins with the preincarnate Christ existing "in the form of God" and "being equal with God," then moves to his descent as he humbles himself by becoming a man. But after his humiliation and obedience to the point of death, he is exalted to a position that in some sense he had before, being given the divine name and receiving universal worship. So he receives again what he possessed all along, but he receives it in a new mode (as a man) and with a new scope (the recognition by all the universe of sentient beings, that is, all men and angelic/demonic beings).

UNANSWERED ARGUMENTS

At this point, I would like to express my disappointment that Dixon and Smith did not really answer what I consider to be my strongest arguments: Jesus as the revealer of the Father and the two qualities of Jesus that demonstrate his deity (creation and aseity). To me these are absolutely crucial arguments. As I wrote in my positive statement, the granting of divine prerogatives to Christ in his exaltation (sovereignty, worship, and the divine name) are only confirmatory evidences of his deity. The real proof of his deity lies here.

Revealer of the Father

Smith simply ignores this argument. Dixon does not ignore it, but he fails to really grapple with it. Perhaps I was not clear enough. I do not mean that Jesus reveals the Father the way any prophet might, by means of propositional statements about God, informing us that God is a heavenly Father. I mean that Jesus, because of his ontological identity as the Son of God, reveals that God is the Father, for if God has a Son, then he must be the Father's Son (John 8:19; 14:7, 9; 2 John 3). Furthermore, Jesus' Sonship reveals that God's Fatherhood is not a voluntary relationship that began at a certain point in time, but something profound about who God is, eternally and necessarily. If Jesus were not the eternal Son of God, then the Father would not be eternally Father. But he is eternally Father. That is who he is. God's identity as Father is part of his essential eternal identity, not something he became at a point in time. "For us there is one God, the Father" (1 Cor 8:6).

Creation

Again, Smith ignored this argument. Dixon did not ignore it but his response was feeble in my opinion. First, Dixon admits that the preexistent Logos created. Well, then, if he created he must be the Creator and must fall on the Creator side of the Creator-creature distinction, meaning that he must be eternal and could not have had a beginning of existence. For any existent being that had a beginning, a time when it did not exist, is a created being, a creature, and therefore not the Creator. There is no such thing as a creature who is also the Creator. It is an ontological and metaphysical impossibility according to the biblical world view.

Second, Dixon tries to get around the meaning of "all things" by appealing to 1 Cor 15:27, pointing out that there can be unstated exceptions to "all things," for example, God the Father himself, as Paul says. But this point, while true, completely misses the mark. I did not argue that "all things" must include all things that exist, but that it must include all created things. If it included all things that exist, then it would include God the Father himself, which would mean that God created himself—an obvious absurdity. Rather, I argued that "all things" in biblical terminology means "all created things," as John 1:3 takes pains to spell out: "All things were made through him, and without him was not anything made that was made." Thus, when we are told that God created "all things" through the Logos or the Son or Christ (John 1:3, 10; 1 Cor 8:6; Col 1:16; Heb 1:2), it follows that the Logos cannot himself be a created thing. This is an exceedingly powerful argument that Dixon and Smith have yet to really reckon with. My prayer is that the profound weight of these New Testament passages that speak of God creating "all things" through the intermediation of the Logos or the Son will begin to weigh upon their minds until they come around to seeing that it proves that the second person of the Godhead is eternal (in the sense of having no beginning) and ontologically divine.

Aseity

Yet again, Smith ignored this argument; Dixon did not, but his response was not well thought out. I had quoted John 5:26, "As the Father as life in

A TRINITARIAN REPLY

himself, so he has granted the Son to have life in himself." My argument was that this verse ascribes to the Son the divine property of having "life in oneself" or aseity (from the Latin terms *a* + *se*, that is, "from oneself"). This is not a property that can be ascribed to any creature, for a creature, by definition, has life or existence from the Creator, not from himself or itself. Therefore, if the Son has "life in himself," and if he has it in the very same way that the Father has it, then he must be ontologically divine and not a created being.

Dixon's response is not well thought out insofar as he makes an argument that clearly does not work; in fact, it dissolves the verse into a self-contradiction. He points to the fact that the same verse states that the Father "granted" this property of aseity to the Son. Dixon argues that if he was "granted" or "given" this property, then he did not have it before being granted it. Therefore, Dixon, argues, this verse can be used to support his view that the Son is not eternal and that there was a time when he did not have life or existence. However, I do not think he has thought this through. If it is true that the verb "granted" means that there was a time when he did not have it, then it would contradict the other element of the verse, which states that he has life "in himself." If there was a time when the Son did not have life or existence, and then at a certain point he received it from the Father, thus causing the Son to be brought out of nonexistence into existence, then he does not have life "in himself," but rather has it from God *in the same way that all other created beings do*. On this interpretation, John 5:26 becomes self-refuting.

There must be a better solution. I would argue that we should interpret the verb "granted" as an analogical term in which something from the realm of the temporal and mutable creation is used to describe something about the eternal and unchangeable Creator. The verb "grant" (*didōmi*), when used in its ordinary meaning, that is, when it is predicated of creatures, normally implies a temporal sequence in which a creature comes into possession of something it did not previously possess. But that ordinary meaning does not fit here, otherwise the verse would be self-contradictory. Therefore, it is best to see the Father's "grant" of life to the Son as an eternal or timeless grant—admittedly not an ordinary use of the verb "grant," but then again this is no ordinary context. It seems likely that the term is being used in John 5:26 without its inherently temporal limitations because it is predicated of a "granting" that transcends the creaturely limitations of time and space. In other words, the Son eternally owes his life to the Father,

THE SON OF GOD

because the Father is the source and cause of his being, in a manner that transcends time, and therefore in a manner utterly distinct from creatures.[8]

JOHN 10:34-36

At this point, I want to address this passage in the tenth chapter of John's Gospel. It is admittedly a difficult one for my case for the ontological deity of Christ. In the context, John tells us that Jesus has just made the astounding claim, "I and the Father are one" (v. 30), prompting the Jews immediately to pick stones to stone him (v. 31). Jesus reminds them that he did many good works (miracles) and asks them, "For which of them are you going to stone me?" (v. 32). The Jews reply that they are going to stone him, not for doing a good work "but for blasphemy, because you, being a man, make yourself God" (v. 33). So far, the passage seems to support the ontological deity of Christ.

But then in vv. 34–36, Jesus' argument in reply to their charge of blasphemy seemingly plays into the hands of the deniers of the ontological deity of Christ. Jesus responds by asking a question that forms an argument of some sort, although it is not immediately clear what the argument is. He asks:

> "Is it not written in your Law, 'I said, you are gods' [Ps 82:6]? If he called them gods to whom the word of God came—and Scripture cannot be broken—do you say of him whom the Father consecrated and sent into the world, 'You are blaspheming,' because I said, 'I am the Son of God'?" (John 10:34–36 ESV).

Dixon argues that the Jews misunderstood Jesus' claim to be the Son of God. Jesus (on Dixon's view) did not mean that he was equal with God or ontologically divine but that he was divine in the same sense that Ps 82 applies the term *elohim* (= "gods") to the human judges of Israel. Once Jesus clarified what he meant, Dixon tells us, "they never again brought up the claim that he was equal with God after this, Jesus' clear explanation and exegesis."

---

8. The begetting of the Son is "beyond the sphere of time, and above the grasp of reason" (Gregory Nazianzen, "Third Theological Oration," §3; *NPNF2* 7.302). "Whereas it is proper to men to beget in time, from the imperfection of their nature, God's offspring is eternal, for His nature is ever perfect" (Athanasius, *Against the Arians* 1.14; *NPNF2* 4.315).

A TRINITARIAN REPLY

But it is not true that "they never again brought up" this claim. According to John's Gospel, they brought up this charge to Pilate: "We have a law, and according to that law he ought to die because he has made himself the Son of God" (John 19:7). This caused Pilate to become very afraid; so he went back to Jesus and asked, "Where are you from?" (v. 9). Pilate knew that they weren't just accusing Jesus of being a rebellious son or of not being appointed by God to be God's agent. He knew they were accusing him of something far more troubling. We see this right here in our context in John 10. A few verses after his quotation of Psalm 82:6, John has Jesus repeating his claim that "I and the Father are one" (the claim that caused this argument with the Jews in the first place) but in different words: "Even though you do not believe me, believe the works, that you may know and understand that *the Father is in me and I am in the Father*" (John 10:38). When he reiterates the claim of union and equality with the Father, they again seek to arrest him (v. 39). The "misunderstanding" is definitely not cleared up!

Most commentators agree that Jesus is employing an *a fortiori* argument. This type of argument usually takes the form, "if x, then how much more y," although it can be implicit as here. Dixon claims to agree with this, citing Andreas Köstenberger in support.⁹ But I do not see how Jesus, on Dixon's interpretation, could be seen as making an *a fortiori* argument. To paraphrase, Dixon thinks Jesus is arguing, "If the Scripture calls mere men, the judges of Israel, *theoi* [= 'gods'], then it cannot be blasphemous for me to claim to be *theos* [= 'a god'] as well, even though I am a mere creature, like them." In other words, on Dixon's view, if it is not blasphemy to call x "god," then it is not blasphemy to call y "god," since both x and y belong to the same class, namely, created beings. This is not an *a fortiori* argument, since it compares two entities that belong to the same class. To have a genuine *a fortiori* argument, Jesus must put himself on a different ontological level than the "gods" of Ps 82. I think the following paraphrase by W. Gary Phillips more helpfully brings out what Jesus is saying:

> Let Me remind you that, incredible though it may seem, Scripture says that wicked human beings were called by divine title, simply because they were commissioned by God. It was not blasphemous for them to bear the divine label (and you cannot escape the truth of this, for Scripture asserts it). Therefore how much more may I,

---

9. Köstenberger, "John," in Beale and Carson, *Commentary*, 465. It is inappropriate for Dixon to call Köstenberger to his support, since Köstenberger is a Trinitarian who believes that Jesus' divine Sonship is "infinitely greater" than that of the beings (human or angelic) in Ps 82:6. Ibid., 466.

THE SON OF GOD

the eternal Son of God, go by My divine title. I have received (a far greater) divine commission, and I bear the divine title not by grace (as they did) but by nature. To accuse Me of blasphemy is ludicrous.[10]

That is a clear and helpful paraphrase, but there is another detail in the text that makes Jesus' argument even clearer. In Greek the phrase "to whom the word of God (*ho logos tou theou*) came" (v. 35) could be taken as an allusion to the preexistent divine Logos of John 1:1, a view held by some church fathers and some modern commentators.[11] If this is correct, Jesus would then be arguing that when the Scriptures refer to creatures, whether humans or angels,[12] as "gods" and "sons of the Most High" (Ps 82:6), they do so because these creatures are such through their participation in the eternal Logos, who is the Son by nature. The others are "gods" and "sons of the Most High" in a creaturely and derivative manner through him who is the ontological Son of God.[13]

SMITH'S ARGUMENTS AGAINST THE DEITY OF CHRIST

Smith argues that there are two factors which prove that Jesus is not divine: first, his ignorance of the day of his second coming (Matt 24:36 || Mark 13:32); and second, his death. Since God is omniscient and immortal, Jesus' lack of omniscience and his death prove that he cannot be divine. I am a little surprised that Smith would use such arguments. It suggests that he has a rather superficial understanding of what Trinitarians believe about Christology. Trinitarians hold to the historic doctrine of the two natures of Christ, that is, the doctrine that Jesus is both God and man in two natures and one person, a doctrine that was defined at the Council of Chalcedon in the fifth century (AD 451), but which was held by the church fathers long before then. For example, in the previous century, Gregory Nazianzen laid down this rule, that "what is lofty you are to apply to the Godhead"

---

10. Phillips, "John 10:34–36," 414.
11. E.g., R. Brown, *John*, 410.
12. Commentators take the *elohim* of Ps 82 in two main ways, as angels or as humans (in which case they are either Israelite judges or Israel at Sinai). As I noted in my response to Dixon, 11Q13 assumes the angelic interpretation. It is not necessary to decide that question here.
13. This was Athanasius's argument in *Against the Arians* 1.39 (NPNF2 4.329).

A TRINITARIAN REPLY

and "all that is lowly"—all that implies limitation or that might seem to be inconsistent with deity—you are to apply to his human nature.[14] When Jesus said that he does not know the day or the hour of his parousia, he is speaking of himself in terms of his self-imposed limitations as one who took on a true human nature.[15] When the Gospels tell us that Jesus died by crucifixion, they are not saying that the divine nature of Jesus died—which is impossible—but that his human nature died, or, more accurately that Jesus the Son of God died according to his human nature.

The Council of Chalcedon, based on the teaching of Scripture, helped define for the church the language and the theological grammar that ought to be used in speaking of the two natures of Jesus. Jesus is one person, a person who has both a divine and a human nature, and the human nature receives personhood in union with the person of the Son or eternal Logos. Although the Bible sometimes uses paradoxical language, e.g., the blood of God (Acts 20:28), or the Son's ignorance (Matt 24:36 || Mark 13:32), these statements are not to be taken in a way that confuses the two natures of Christ, but as involving a semantic communication of attributes in which something that is proper to the human nature is ascribed to the divine nature because of the unity of the two natures in one person. "The Son does not know the day or the hour of his coming" means "The Son, according to his human nature, does not know the day or the hour of his coming." "The Son died" means "The Son died according to his human nature." The divine nature of the Son is omniscient and immortal. But because of the incarnation, the Son has taken a true human nature into personal union with himself, so that the Son can experience human things like not knowing everything, being tested and tempted, hungering and thirsting, dying, being raised from the dead, and so on. As Leo (d. 461) so clearly taught in his famous *Tome*, each nature in Christ retains its proper character without diminution. The divine nature is not diminished by the human nature, and the human nature is not diminished by the divine nature. Furthermore, the Son performs the acts or experiences the experiences in that particular nature to which those actions or experiences pertain. It was in his divine nature that the Son raised the dead, stilled the sea, and turned water into wine. But it was in his human nature that the Son was tempted, was hungry

---

14. Gregory Nazianzen, "Third Theological Oration," §§17–20 (*NPNF2* 7.307–9).

15. "We are to understand the ignorance [of the Son] in the most reverent sense, by attributing it to the Manhood, and not to the Godhead." Gregory Nazianzen, "Fourth Theological Oration," §15 (*NPNF2* 7.315).

THE SON OF GOD

and thirsty, and experienced human emotions like sorrow. As applied to the death of Christ, "the Son of God is said to have been crucified and buried, inasmuch as he underwent this, not in his actual Godhead . . . but in the weakness of human nature."[16]

CONCLUSION

There is much more that could be said as we follow up the threads of the various arguments, but this must suffice for now. Dixon and Smith have raised some good questions and challenges for my view. I recognize that there are thorny exegetical and theological issues that need to be wrestled with on all sides. I hope I have also given Dixon and Smith some things to think about as they search the Scriptures. May we all come to understand more deeply the true significance of Jesus' identity as the Son of God.

---

16. The *Tome* of Leo (*NPNF2* 14.254–58, see 256). Although it is called a *Tome*, it was actually a relatively brief letter to Flavian, bishop of Constantinople, concerning the error of one Eutyches. Eutyches taught that there is only one nature in Christ after the union. But this implies that Christ's human nature is not consubstantial with ours, which imperils his ability to die for our sins and represent us as the Second Adam. When Leo's letter was read at the Council of Chalcedon, the gathered bishops cried out, "This is the faith of the fathers, this is the faith of the Apostles. So we all believe, thus the orthodox believe." *NPNF2* 14.259.

Part Two

AN ARIAN VIEW
Jesus, the Life-Given Son of God

DANNY ANDRÉ DIXON

INTRODUCTION AND OUTLINE

I HAVE TRIED TO DETERMINE my burden in this debate. Although I have not read their initial presentations, I anticipate I will share similarities with Smith or Irons on various points. I sense that Irons will demonstrate some sense of Jesus' identity with God. I can agree with that. If Jesus received life (John 5:26; 6:57) from his Father Jehovah or Yahweh,[1] there is, in that unqualified statement, the implication that Jesus shares in God's nature; he is a divine being. I must also maintain that, divine as he may have been (John 1:1), he is *not* eternal in the sense of having had no beginning, nor is he Almighty God—mighty and exalted as Jesus the Christ may be, any more so than God's other children will eventually be (John 1:12; 1 John 3:1–2). I depart from Smith in my understanding of the literal origin of Christ. I believe the one who became Jesus came to have existence with God as a sentient individual at some unrevealed time before becoming a human individual, born as miraculously as was Adam the *original* human son of God (Luke 3:38) or his helper who corresponded to him (Gen 1:26–27; 2:18–25).[2] Furthermore, I believe that before the miraculously born Jesus

---

1. "YHWH," "Yahweh," and "Jehovah" are all attempts to render in English the Hebrew proper name of the God of Israel and have been used in Bible translations and, more commonly, in biblical scholarship.

2. I say Jesus, Adam, and Eve were all "miraculously" born, because humans since

THE SON OF GOD

became flesh, he was God's agent-architect commissioned by God to bring about "all things"—especially this world as we know it (John 1:3; 1 Cor 8:6; Col 1:15–16). Having said all this, I hope to develop the following observations in the following pages:

1. The one and only "God" ought to be understood as Jews of Second Temple monotheism understood him to be.
2. The exclusiveness of Father-God Yahweh/Jehovah is not compromised by exalted, worshiped, and Yahweh-functioning human or angelic figures who are also presented in the Second Temple-period writings as gods.[3]
3. Jesus' position and treatment is a result of his exaltation, which parallels secondary figures in Judaism.
4. Jesus' life is derived from the Father.

To understand how members of early Jewish and Christian communities understood God requires examining their Scriptures and noncanonical writings. Jack Lewis has correctly observed:

> With the recovery of the Dead Sea Scrolls, the already-keen interest in the Jewish background of the N. T. has experienced a rebirth. Jesus and his disciples were Jews who spoke in the vocabulary and thought forms of first century Judaism. Even though their teaching has been preserved for us in *Koine* Greek, it is really to first century Judaism that one must first turn if he is to understand them. The Gospels assume this background without describing it.[4]

The Bible affirms that there is only one true God (Deut 6:4; John 17:3; 1 Tim 2:5), and while it would be easy for a believer to say that because there is only one God all other gods are false, this would be an oversimplification

---

Adam and Eve are neither created from dirt or ribs, nor are they begotten with only twenty-three chromosomes from virgin mothers.

3. I want to thank David Barron for his encouragement, instruction, and assistance in this debate. Without his selfless insight and generous help, my approach would have been overly simplistic, especially as it regards exalted figures in Second Temple Judaism. I would not have known many areas in which to read current thinking on these matters, and I would have missed addressing important areas of thought in preparation and discussion particularly in this first presentation. I do shudder, however, as I think about the amount of money expended to bring my personal library up to par in just this area! Thank God, Yahweh, Jesus, Yahoel, Melchizedek, Enoch's Son of Man figure, or someone else for used books on Amazon.com!

4. Lewis, "Jewish Background," 209.

AN ARIAN VIEW

from the standpoint of the biblical data. As Carl Mosser has observed, "Moderns are often unaware that *theos* had a much broader semantic range than is allowed for G/god in contemporary Western European languages."[5] And Larry Hurtado correctly notes the same thing in his comment:

> If we are to avoid a priori definitions and the imposition of our own theological judgments, we have no choice but to accept as monotheism the religion of those who profess to be monotheists, however much their religion varies and may seem "complicated" with other beings in addition to the one God.[6]

Even so, while extra-biblical texts *inform* understanding of the Jewish culture and thought, which in turn often clarify biblical investigations, this is not to say they *determine* theology. However, to use good methodology in Christology and theology, we must let early Jewish writers tell us what *they* considered appropriate for one exalted by God.

GOD EXALTS DIVINE AGENTS

Upon examination of the evidence, it is undeniable that these writings describe individuals (exalted figures) who came to be granted divine attributes, prerogatives, and designations, and even the name of God himself. Yet the writings revealing this are not perceived as being blasphemous, since these figures are not seen as displacing God's individuality. The Bible points this out, various early Jewish texts reveal it, and contemporary scholars recognize it. Consider James McGrath:

> Agency was an important part of everyday life in the ancient world. Individuals such as prophets and angels mentioned in the Jewish Scriptures were thought of as "agents" of God. And the key idea regarding agency in the ancient world appears to be summarized in the phrase from rabbinic literature so often quoted in these contexts: "The one sent is like the one who sent him." The result is that the agent can not only carry out divine functions but also be depicted in divine language, sit on God's throne or alongside God, and even bear the divine name.[7]

---

5. Mosser, "Earliest Patristic Interpretations," 22.
6. Hurtado, *How on Earth*, 113–14.
7. McGrath, *Only True God*, 14.

THE SON OF GOD

An important Gospel pericope provides a biblical example of how this concept of agency played out and was demonstrated in inspired text. Matt 8:5–13 presents a centurion as having personally come to Jesus, asking him to heal his servant. Jesus assents to come. The centurion responds by admitting that he is not worthy for Jesus to go to his home, and that if Jesus would merely speak, then the healing would be certain. Jesus sends the centurion back and the servant is healed. As Luke relates the incident (Luke 7:1–10), however, the centurion never personally comes to speak with Jesus. Rather, he sends certain "Jewish elders" (Luke 7:3) to represent him, encouraging Jesus personally to perform the requested healing. Jesus agrees to heal the servant and while approaching to perform the miraculous healing the centurion sends friends to explain to Jesus that the centurion sees himself as not even worthy for Jesus to enter his home (Luke 7:2–10). Rather than taking this as a contradiction between synoptic accounts, I believe we have here an example of agency as understood in the ancient world. For all practical purposes, an agent was considered to be the sender himself holding the sender's complete authority.

The Jewish historian Josephus provides another example of the same principle in his retelling of the events found in 1 Sam 21–22. His account demonstrates how those having the authority of a sender were considered. Josephus has the high priest Ahimelech say that since he had thought that David was sent to accomplish Saul's purpose, to not assist David would be to act in contradiction to Saul rather than to David (*Ant.* 6:257).

GOD EXALTS MOSES "AS GOD" OR "AS A GOD"

God tells Moses he would be as "a god to Pharaoh" (Exod 7:1).[8] While God has not, in his exalting Moses, made him something beyond human, God did give him authority to act on his behalf, allowing Moses to speak for him and carry out his works.

Characters other than Moses are exalted and called gods, as in Psalm 82 and its introductory statement by Asaph revealing that "God . . . gives judgment among the 'gods'" (Ps 82:1).[9] Ash and Miller reject two interpretations: (1) that the *elohim* represent "God's judgment against heathen

---

8. The NET Bible textual note here admits that "'like' is added for clarity," appealing to Exod 4:16. Note the translation there: "He will speak for you to the people, and it will be as if he were your mouth and as if you were his God" (Exod 4:16 NET Bible).

9. Unless otherwise noted, quotations of Scripture are from the NIV (1984 edition).

AN ARIAN VIEW

deities, placing them in a subordinate role to that of God and threatening them with death," and (2) that "disorders [are] caused in the world by 'the spiritual hosts of wickedness in the heavenly places'" (per Eph 6:12). Instead, Ash and Miller take Psalm 82 as a "polemic against human judges and rulers in Israel."[10] However, they admit:

> One major objection to this interpretation has been that the word 'elohim would not be applied to human beings. However, the word is definitely used of a Davidic king in Ps 45:6–7, which we give here with the word 'elohim transliterated.
>
> [6] Your throne, O 'elohim, is for ever and ever;
> A scepter of equity is the scepter of your kingdom.
> [7] You have loved righteousness and hated wickedness;
> Therefore, 'elohim your 'elohim, has anointed you
>   With the oil of gladness above your fellows.
>
> Since both verses are addressed to the same person, the pronouns *your* preceding 'elohim of verse 6 refers to the king (cf. 45:1). Since human judges in Israel stood in the place of God in their role as judges (cf. Deut 1:17; 2 Chr 19:6–7; Exod 22:8–9), the judge, as God's deputy, may be called 'elohim.[11]

GOD EXALTS THE "SON OF MAN" FIGURE IN 1 ENOCH

The Son of Man/Elect One within the *Similitudes* (or *Parables*) *of Enoch* (*1 Enoch* 37–71) is arguably the most exalted of mankind within known Second Temple-Jewish writings. Although there is "no consensus, however, on whether this identification is implied throughout the Parables, or indeed on how it should be understood,"[12] some think that the figure is probably Enoch himself (*1 En.* 71:14). Enoch sees the Elect One/Son of Man and "his dwelling-place under the wings of the Lord of the Spirits" (*1 En.* 39:6). He is "named in the presence of the Lord of the Spirits" and this was done even previously, "before the stars of the heaven were made" (*1 En.* 48:2–3). Noting *1 Enoch* 48:6, where "he has been chosen and hidden before Him, before the creation of the world and for evermore," Nickelsburg and VanderKam comment "that it is the Son of Man himself and not just his name that

10. Ash and Miller, *Psalms*, 285.
11. Ibid., 286.
12. Collins, "Enoch and the Son of Man," 221.

THE SON OF GOD

preexists his eschatological functions."[13] Such literal preexistence is evident in 62:7 as he was hidden "from the beginning" and "preserved . . . in the presence of [God's] might."

The Son of Man is depicted as eschatological judge (*1 En.* 45:3; 49:4; 61:9; 69:27) and guide to the righteous (*1 En.* 48:4). Those who "have denied the Lord of Spirits and His Anointed" shall receive judgment (*1 En.* 48:10). This pairing of the Son of Man with God exemplifies the importance and exalted nature of his position. He further comes to sit upon God's throne, "the throne of glory" (*1 En.* 51:3; 45:3; 55:4: 61:8; 69:27).

THE SON OF MAN IS WORSHIPED OR GIVEN HOMAGE

- "All who dwell on earth shall fall down and worship before him [the Son of Man], And will praise and bless and celebrate with song the Lord of Spirits" (*1 En.* 48:5).
- "And the kings and the mighty and all who possess the earth shall bless and glorify and extol him who rules over all, who was hidden" (*1 En.* 62:6).
- "And all the kings and the mighty and the exalted and those who rule the earth shall fall down before him on their faces, and worship and set their hope upon the Son of Man, and petition him and supplicate for mercy at his hands" (*1 En.* 62:9).

In *1 En.* 48:5 the worship of the Son of Man is performed along with the worship of God.[14] While full worship of the Son of Man might be rejected within a proper monotheistic devotion, with his enthronement and exaltation before all by God, it may be understood that it is God's desire for the Son of Man to receive this worship. Here, the Son of Man becomes an exception defined by God himself to the strict monotheistic standard of worshiping none but God *only* because God chooses to exalt him and place him upon his own throne to be worshiped. This dual worship had been seen before:

---

13. Nickelsburg and VanderKam, *1 Enoch 2*, 173.
14. "All those who dwell upon the earth shall fall and worship before him; they shall glorify, bless, and sing the name of the Lord of the Spirits." *OTP* 1.35.

AN ARIAN VIEW

> And David said to all the assembly, "Now bless Jehovah your God." And all the assembly blessed Jehovah, the God of their fathers, and bowed down their heads, and worshiped Jehovah, and the king (1 Chr 29:20 ASV).

Significantly, the language in *1 En.* 62:6 where all on earth will "bless and glorify" the Son of Man is the same language used to describe the worship of God at 63:2. While this language and that of 48:5 will permit such an understanding of the Son of Man figure, Bauckham mitigates the force of this perceived status:

> The Son of Man is here described in terms used elsewhere of the worship of God (cf. 39:12; 48:5; 61:9, 11, 12; 69:24). In 48:5 and 62:9, the language could be used of submission to a ruler without necessarily connoting divine worship, but, as in so many cases, it is not the gesture or the terms used but the context which must determine whether the Son of Man is receiving the worship due only to God.[15]

Yet, since Bauckham's particular theological position regarding Christ is that this kind of worship and sitting upon God's throne includes one within his "divine identity,"[16] he is left with no other choice but to say that the Son of Man figure "is the exception that proves the rule."[17]

In addition to depicting the Son of Man as exalted and worshiped alongside of God, Tilling says, "The author(s) of the Similitudes could also apply OT God and YHWH texts to this figure, as in 52:6, but also, for example, in 62:6."[18] At the very least this demonstrates the author's comfort in reapplying such passages to a secondary, exalted figure, though perhaps these passages find their ultimate fulfillment in him as God's agent.

Here, the Son of Man participates in worshiping God (61:3), so throughout he is independent of God. Bauckham could join McGrath in his view of divine identity and admit that his is a "highly problematic interpretation."[19] Suppose we would agree with Bauckham and see the Son of Man as a recipient of full worship within a monotheistic context; it is the justification for doing so that is significant: *it is God's exaltation of the figure coupled with God's desire for him to receive such worship that makes it*

15. Bauckham, *Jesus and the God of Israel*, 170–71.
16. Ibid., 172.
17. Ibid., 171.
18. Tilling, *Paul's Divine Christology*, 210.
19. McGrath, *Only True God*, 122n10.

THE SON OF GOD

allowable. The worship would stem from how the people "see and recognize how he sits on the throne of glory" (62:3). Scholarly honesty demands that a concept of an exalted Son of Man is an exception in how one defines monotheistic worship. But it would also demand that even in exaltation the Son of Man figure *would not be included, nor would any other figure (like Jesus of Nazareth) need to be included in a similar scenario within the divine identity!*

GOD EXALTS ANGELS; ANGELS ARE SPOKEN OF AS BEING GOD[20]

Besides exalted men, angels are called gods, exalted and portrayed at times as divine agents, but also as beings of a higher nature. The appropriateness of designating angels as gods because they are higher beings is evident with a careful analysis of Ps 8:5. Verse 4 asks, "What is man that You are mindful of him, and the son of man, that You visit him?" implying amazement that God even takes notice of men who are so far beneath him. Yet what follows is a statement of man being just "a little lower than *'elohim*" (god/God *or* gods).[21] Neil R. Lightfoot rightly concludes that the Septuagint "has preserved the correct sense of the passage, interpreting the Hebrew *'elohim* to stand for 'divine beings' or 'angels.'"[22] Ps 138 begins with praises

---

20. Presently, I only mention the appearance of angels to Abraham, Jacob, Moses, Joshua, and others, spoken of either in their immediate contexts or in other places as being God himself. While I doubt that Smith or Irons will question the presence of these figures, I will revisit them in more detail as necessary later. I only want to say that they demonstrate the almost universally understood principle of agency in which an authorized personage is frequently called God himself in Scripture. What confuses me is how this point, although parallel to Christ in many ways, is rejected as carrying much weight to see him as God's agent as opposed to being one who, in that role, shares God's identity (Bauckham) or receives worship because he *is* God (Hurtado and others).

21. Hebrew "nouns that are plural in form but singular in meaning usually take the singular verb." Seow, *Grammar*, 151. E.g. *'elohim.*

22. See Lightfoot, *Jesus Christ Today*, 72 n8. Interestingly, B. F. Westcott says, "The original meaning is probably less definite than either 'a little less than angels' or 'a little less than God.' It would more nearly correspond to 'a little less than one who has a divine nature.' 'Thou hast made him to fall little short of being a God' (compare 1 Sam 28:13). To our ears 'than God' would be equivalent to 'than the Eternal,' which would have been wholly out of place in the Psalm. And on the other hand 'than angels' obscures the notion of the 'divine nature' which lies in the phrase." *Hebrews*, 44. Regarding Heb 2:9 Westcott concludes, keeping entirely in the original context of the psalm: "The words of the Psalm have an unexpected accomplishment. The man spoken of as little less than angels (so

AN ARIAN VIEW

sung to Jehovah "before the gods" (v. 1), understood by the Septuagint to be "angels," while the Targum renders this "judges," a possible meaning, though seemingly unlikely given that there is no indication David would go specifically before judges in his worship. Anywhere he might be could be construed as before angels, so the Septuagint here makes good sense. This corresponds to what is found within the Dead Sea Scrolls, where exalted beings are frequently portrayed as gods.[23]

YAHOEL/IAOEL–THE EXALTED ANGEL BEARING GOD'S NAME

The *Apocalypse of Abraham* is a Jewish work, perhaps from the late first century or second century AD, constituting a story of Abraham's youth and his perception of idolatry. Abraham loses faith in idols prone to physical destruction and asks God to reveal himself. He reports that God commands the angel: "Go, Iaoel of the same name, through the mediation of my ineffable name, consecrate this man for me and strengthen him against his trembling. The angel he sent to me in the likeness of a man came, and he took me by my right hand and stood me on my feet" (*Apoc. Abr.* 10:3–4). Iaoel speaks to Abraham: "I am Iaoel and I was called so by him who causes those with me on the seventh expanse, on the firmament, to shake, a power through the medium of his ineffable name in me" (*Apoc. Abr.* 10:8). Eventually, the angel Iaoel and Abraham both bow down in worship to God and begin to praise him. They sing to the one who is "eternal" (*Apoc. Abr.* 17:8, 13, 15), God is said to be "eternal, mighty . . . holy, Saboath, most glorious El, El, El, El, Iaoel" (*Apoc. Abr.* 17:13). So Abraham and the angel Iaoel address God with the same name Iaoel.[24]

"Iaoel" combines "Ia" (Yah) and "El" or "Yahoweh" and "El." Amazingly, Iaoel and God share the same name in this text, although it is difficult to imagine the angel possessing God's name of himself, as his own personal name. Furthermore, the author gives a mere angel God's own, personal

---

great is he) is represented by Jesus, the Son of God become flesh, and so made little less than angels (so full of condescension was He) and in that humanity which He has taken to Himself crowned with glory." Ibid., 45.

23. I have examined numerous references to these gods, who are angels, as may be seen in "The Songs of the Sabbath Sacrifice" (4Q400–407). García Martínez and Tigchelaar, *Dead Sea Scrolls*, 807–37.

24. R. Rubinkiewicz translates *The Apocalypse of Abraham*. H. G. Lunt revises and annotates it in *OTP* 1.693, 697. I do not modify the "Iaoel" spelling in this edition.

name. Amazing as it is, the angel is given this name by God because His name dwells in the angel who is also given the authority to do his work.[25]

Of course Bauckham won't let this go unchallenged:

> It is identical to a form of the divine name as used of God, but used as an angel's name it need not be understood as actually naming the angel by God's name. Rather it can be taken as an affirmation that "YHWH is God." It does not identify Yahoel with God (any more than the equivalent name Elijah identifies that prophet with God), but it designates him the angelic high priest who bears the divine name and employs its authority in priestly blessing.[26]

That the angel is granted divine authority and called by the name of God himself, strongly suggests that the angel, God's agent, bears God's very name, and not the same name with an entirely different meaning. It seems unlikely that since Yahoel is "of the same name" as God, they would share form but not meaning. Yet Bauckham maintains that bearing God's name constitutes inclusion "in the unique identity of YHWH."[27] Is this to say, by Bauckham's reasoning, that Iaoel, *bearing* God's name, also should *be* Almighty God?

Bauckham appeals to *Sefer ha-Razim* to establish that Yahoel holds an "unimportant position among the hundreds of named angels in *Sefer ha-Razim*,"[28] contradicting his own argument that Yahoel "exercises a delegated authority on God's behalf as the angelic high priest, the heavenly and cosmic equivalent of the Aaronide high priest in Jerusalem."[29] Such would have necessarily indicated that Yahoel's holds a highly exalted place. Further arguing against Bauckham's interpretation is the significant time between this work and the text to which he appeals. As previously mentioned, the *Apocalypse of Abraham* dates from the late first century to early second century, while *Sefer ha-Razim* is dated two hundred years or more later. The two authors worked from very different opinions, with one of significantly later dating.

---

25. McGrath says, "The name Yahoel is clearly made up of the two divine names, Yah(weh) and El. Yet the reason the angel bears his name is not because he has been confused with or absorbed into God but because the angel has been given the divine name by God." *Only True God*, 49.

26. Bauckham, *Jesus and the God of Israel*, 226–27.

27. Ibid.

28. Ibid., 226 n105.

29. Ibid., 227.

AN ARIAN VIEW
"DIVINE BEING" MELCHIZEDEK ACTS AS GOD

Among the Dead Sea Scrolls, 11Q13 presents an eschatological view of a heavenly Melchizedek. Although the document is fragmentary, what remains today is significant, not only because of the appellations and exalted language the author felt at liberty to grant Melchizedek, but even more so due to the application of Old Testament Yahweh passages to Melchizedek.

A significant modification of Isa 61:2 occurs early on in what remains of this scroll. Where the divine name had appeared in Isaiah, it is replaced with Melchizedek. So rather than "the year of Yahweh's favor," we read, "For this is the time decreed for the year of Melchizedek's favor." What had been Jehovah's year is interpreted to be Melchizedek's. Whether Melchizedek is here understood to be God's agent and therefore bearer of His name is unclear. Perhaps the author intended only to suggest that "the year of Yahweh's favor" was the same as "the year of Melchizedek's favor," without having Melchizedek bear God's name. On the other hand, the author may have provided an interpretation of Isaiah, revealing his view that here Yahweh was Melchizedek, and he himself bore God's name. Either way, this exemplifies the application of one Old Testament Yahweh passage to an exalted figure.

Psalm 82 is cited from verse one, wherein the first instance of *elohim* is interpreted to be Melchizedek. Bauckham suggests

> that, in the first statement ('*elōhîm* will stand up in the assembly of *ēl*'), '*elōhîm* must be a different person from *ēl*. Since the assembly—the heavenly council of judgment—is said to be that of *ēl*, he naturally supposed that *ēl* is YHWH, while '*elōhîm* is the angel Melchizedek, who stands up in the divine council to condemn Belial and his evil angels (Ps 82:2, as interpreted in 11QMelch 2:11–12).[30]

It is not expressly clear that two distinct individuals are in view as *el* was a common rendering for the YHWH within the Dead Sea Scrolls. But a possible distinction is carried over from the preceding, where Melchizedek "will, by his strength, judge the holy ones of God (*el*)." So Melchizedek would be distinguished as judge from the one to whom the holy ones belong.

---

30. Ibid., 222.

THE SON OF GOD

MELCHIZEDEK JUDGES THE PEOPLES

The citation from Ps 7:7b–8a is of greater significance, since the source passage contains the divine name (as in Isa 61:2). Instead of substituting Melchizedek in its place, the author provides ʾēl, following common practice. Again Bauckham makes a suspect distinction between ʾēl and Melchizedek, following 82:1:

> ʾēl is here the scribal substitution for the Tetragrammaton, a standard practice in the Qumran texts, and (especially in view of the fact that our exegete has taken ʾēl in Ps 82:1 to be YHWH) it must be understood to refer here not to Melchizedek but to YHWH. However, since the first line quoted (Ps. 7:8b [Hebrew; v. 7b in the English Bible]) is an imperative, whereas the second line (7:9a [Hebrew; v. 8a in the English Bible]) speaks of YHWH in the third person, our exegete has supposed that the person addressed in the first line must be someone other than YHWH, and takes him to be Melchizedek.[31]

The scroll's author relates what is said to be what is said about Melchizedek. If the author did not intend for the reference to be understood as about Melchizedek there is little reason for the portion of text to have been included at all. Citing Ps 82 wherein Melchizedek had "taken his place," this scroll's author turns to Ps 7 with him having ascended to "the height." As Melchizedek was the one in Ps 82 who "holds judgment," it only follows that he does the same in Ps 7, as the one who "will judge the peoples." Thus Wise, Abegg, and Cook translate, "A divine being will judge the peoples."[32]

The use of *el* for Ps 7 may be due to the author's view of interchangeability with *elohim*, for there is no particular limiting factor in applying one term or the other to Melchizedek. Yet, it may well be that the author intentionally used this term to connect Jehovah with Melchizedek, serving to identify him as one bearing Jehovah's name. In fact, whether this is explicit or not, it is certainly implicit, for the one spoken of in Ps 7:7 can be interpreted to be none other than Jehovah (Ps 7:6–7). If *el* in Ps 7:7 is identified with Melchizedek, it is likely that *el* is also identified with Melchizedek in the citation of Ps 82.

---

31. Ibid., 223.

32. Wise, Abegg, and Cook, *Dead Sea Scrolls*, 592. García Martínez and Tigchelaar translate, "God will judge the peoples" (*Dead Sea Scrolls*, 2.1207).

AN ARIAN VIEW

The final significant citation stems from Isa 52:7: "Your God reigns." Restoring what was here fragmented text, Wise, Abegg, and Cook articulate this view by rendering the last of the three quotes, "'Your divine being' is [Melchizedek, who will del]iv[er them from the po]wer of Belial."[33] The ability of a Jewish author to speak of one who is an exalted divine agent as "your God" demonstrates just how far agency was understood to go—even to the point of permitting the transfer of God's titles to God's specially appointed agents.

MELCHIZEDEK FORGIVES SINS AND IS "SAVIOR"

Beyond appellations and OT citations the scroll's author presents two other significant statements concerning Melchizedek. He was granted the authority to grant forgiveness of sins, for he would be "forgiving them of all their sins," an ability mistakenly limited by at least some Jewish leaders to God alone (Matt 9:2–3, esp. v. 8; Mark 2:7.), though Melchizedek is likely only working in providing their forgiveness, not actually granting it, like the seraphim in Isa 6:6–7. After restoration of the text, it is "Melchizedek who will deliver them from the hand of Belial," thus serving as a savior to the people. These statements demonstrate that in addition to God's name and titles, his functions can also be transferred to certain agents.

Manzi has suggested that Melchizedek is Jehovah himself,[34] but unless we are to believe this Jewish author viewed God as in some way binitarian, this is exceedingly unlikely.[35] Not only have we already noted a distinction between Melchizedek and the One to whom the holy ones belong, another clear distinction exists: "The statement that Melchizedek is to 'exact the vengeance of God's (*'el*) judgement' seems to presuppose that Melchizedek and God are two different beings."[36] Further, at places such

---

33. Ibid., 593.

34. Manzi, *Melchisedek*.

35. Van de Water has attempted a middle ground, suggesting 11Q13 portrays "Melchizedek as Yhwh and at the same time as God's intermediary." "Michael or Yhwh?," 85. Acknowledging the distinction between the two, Van de Water follows Manzi in simultaneously identifying Melchizedek with Jehovah. With the acknowledgement of Melchizedek as an intermediary, not established is why the move beyond viewing Melchizedek as an exalted divine agent should be made. Melchizedek is Jehovah, but in what sense?

36. Aschim, "Melchizdek and Jesus," 135.

THE SON OF GOD

as 4Q401 a likely reconstruction has Melchizedek as a heavenly priest of God.[37] Though it is possible that the different authors had various ideas concerning Melchizedek, it seems unlikely that a figure elsewhere recognized as one other than God would be so altered to become God himself.

Many similar examples could be given, but the preceding is sufficiently strong evidence that Second Temple Judaism observed a great deal of flexibility in the use of the term "God." Various exalted figures could bear God's very name, carry out his will, and even appear on his behalf. This is especially so with the Son of Man figure in *The Similitudes of Enoch*. Other exalted figures could even be exalted alongside of God and rightfully worshiped, though such occurrences were the exception rather than the rule, since God required strict devotion only to himself. At any rate that this exists in the literature of this period speaks to the acceptability of the concept; it was not blasphemous in the minds of Second Temple Jews.

JOHN 5:23—THE SON IS HONORED IN THE SAME MANNER AS THE FATHER BECAUSE JUDGMENT WAS GIVEN TO HIM

Bowman and Komoszewski emphatically conclude about John 5:23:

> "Anyone who does not honor the Son does not honor the Father who sent him" (John 5:23). . . . That Jesus is here claiming divine honor is evident from the immediate context. Jesus has just claimed that he does whatever the Father does (v. 19) and that he "gives life to whomever he wishes" (v. 21). The Father even has entrusted to the Son (v. 22) the responsibility of rendering eternal judgment over all people. According to Jesus, the Father did so precisely so that everyone would honor him, the Son, as they honor the Father (v. 23). In short, we are to honor Jesus as the one who holds our eternal future in his hands—as the one who has the power of life and death. We can assign no higher honor or status to someone than that of our ultimate, final Judge.[38]

John's own commentary on this particular pericope is very telling. "The Jews" had formed a perspective about Jesus—not that they were correct in it, but they were in their own minds very certain of it. At this stage of his ministry, they saw that he was overturning traditions of their oral law

---

37. Collins and Collins, *King and Messiah*, 82.
38. Bowman and Komoszewski, *Putting Jesus in His Place*, 31.

AN ARIAN VIEW

right and left, while he was referring to God in ways that they were not used to doing themselves. Jesus had said, "My Father is working until now, and I am working" (John 5:17), and their conclusion about that was that he was even "calling God his own Father, making himself equal with God."

In his response, Jesus makes several things clear. First, he was not a rogue figure, for he acted in accord with the will of his Father (John 5:19). Second, he was acting as one in appropriate intimacy with God in saying "the Father loves the Son and shows him all that he himself is doing" (John 5:20).

As God is a life-giver, so also is the Son, which certainly was beginning to hit close to home as to the depth of relationship he was claiming existed between him and God, particularly as God declared himself the giver of life (John 5:21; cp. Deut 32:39). When he claims that he as the Son has "all judgment," however, he does not claim it as an inherent and eternal quality. Rather he says that the Father "*has given him authority* to execute judgment" (John 5:27, emphasis mine). Like a number of persons seen earlier in this presentation similarly Jesus is an exalted figure, especially here in his prerogative to dispense judgment on men.

Recall an earlier occasion in Jesus' ministry where he is perceived as blaspheming because he claims a prerogative reserved for God when he healed a paralytic and declared that the man's sins had been forgiven (Matt 9:2), which, on the basis of Isa 43:25 would probably have been considered something that only God could do ("I, even I, am he who blots out your transgressions, for my own sake, and remembers your sins no more," God says). Based on other information that we have seen regarding Melchizedek, the seraphim (Isa 6:6–7, declaring Isaiah's forgiveness and atonement), the Son of Man figure, and Enoch (notwithstanding the perspective of the Jews disputing with Jesus in John 5), Second Temple-Jewish thought allowed that an exalted figure could judge others. And here, those with better insight are astonished, as Matthew comments: "and they glorified God, who had given such authority to men" (Matt 9:8).

JOHN 8:58; 17:3-5—JESUS PREEXISTED ABRAHAM: ANAMNESIS VS. PROLEPSIS

John 8:58 legitimately reads, "Before Abraham came into being, I have been."[39] The Greek here is remarkably essentially similar to the

---

39. Margin readings are, among other things, "alternate translations" or "explanatory equivalents," NASB Preface (1971 edition), viii.

THE SON OF GOD

pseudepigraphal *Testament of Job* 2:1: "For I have been Jobab [*Egō gar eimi Iōbab*] before the Lord named me Job [*prin ē onomasai me ho Kyrios Iōb*]." Here Jesus reflects on his conscious existence, remembering his "glory" shared with the Father before the world came into existence and recalling his being sent as God's Messiah. These are perfect examples of the Greek figure of speech "anamnesis" or "recalling"—as in John 17:3–5—recollecting the past. Here anamnesis stands directly opposite of "prolepsis" at John 17:3–5, which anticipates and speaks of "future things as present."[40]

PHILIPPIANS 2:9-11–ALL WILL BOW AND CONFESS CHRIST AS LORD BECAUSE GOD EXALTED HIM

Gathercole rightly says, "For many scholars, Philippians 2 constitutes the highest point of Christological reflection in the NT. Certainly for a number the so-called 'Philippians hymn' is the clearest statement of preexistence."[41] He points out that Murphy-O'Connor and James Dunn have raised the most well-known objections to seeing preexistence in Philippians 2. His first difference with Murphy-O'Connor's "cavalier dismissal" formulated in "questioning the standard view of the 'form of God' (*morphē theou*), which he [Murphy-O'Connor] thinks is the sole ground for preexistence."[42] His main argument, however, is with Dunn, who he says "refuses to see any preexistence of Christ independent of Adamic imagery," and he quotes Dunn: "It is the prehistorical existence of Adam as a template on which a vivid Adam Christology begins to be drawn,"[43] concluding that Dunn does not give much weight to the statement that Jesus "emptied himself" (*heauton ekenōsen*). Of course, even Gathercole does not present an argument for preexistence from this passage but simply says that not only in this passage, but in others, "What is most striking is that [Paul] very often *assumes* it, rather than arguing for it."[44]

I think Phil 2:9–11 plays to the present balcony in that the reason anyone will bow before Christ is not because the passage or the context presumes his preexistence as God or as a divine being, but because "God

40. See Bullinger, *Figures of Speech*, 918, 914.
41. Gathercole, *Preexistent Son*, 25.
42. Ibid.
43. Ibid.
44. Ibid., 31.

AN ARIAN VIEW

highly exalted him" (v. 9). That the Scriptures value what Jesus accomplished through his service, humility, and obedience to the point of death must not be considered lightly. Nor may we devalue the significance of that emptying and humility, for it is precisely because of this (Gk. *dio*[45]) that Christ is exalted to the glory of God the Father.

Mat 28:18—Jesus bears his authority not because it was his by nature, but *because it was given to him*. I agree with Davies and Allison's comment and exegesis here, which remind us of much of what has gone before in this presentation. They quote Hare and make some additional observations about the sentence, "All authority in heaven and on the earth has been given to me":

> "Jesus is not waiting passively in heaven for his glorious arrival as judge and king but is already exercising his Lordship as God's plenipotentiary Son . . . ." Compare 4.8–9 (where Jesus refuses Satan's offer of world rule); 9.8; 11.27 [noting appropriately that "The parallelism between 11.27 and 28.18 is imperfect: the former has to do with revelation, which is not exactly the same as authority . . .]; 13.37–43 (where the Son of man rules over the cosmos); 21.23; also Ezekiel the Tragedian in Alexander Polyhistor *apud* Eusebius, *Praep. ev.* 9.29.4–6 (where Moses is given God's crown and scepter); Dan 7.13–14 (where dominion is given by God to the one like a son of man); 4Q521 frag. 2 ('heaven and earth will obey his messiah'); Philo, *Vit. Mos.* 1.155–6 (on the universal authority given to Moses); *T. Job* 3.5 (*dos moi exousian*); Jn 3.35; *Sib. Or.* 5.414–16; Hermas, *Sim.* 5.6.4; *3 En.* 10. (God makes Metatron ruler over all heavenly kingdoms). The Son of man, who was once handed over to the power of others, now has authority over them [citing Jeremias who sees the Greek *edothē* as an "ingressive aorist": "has just been given"]. The sense corresponds not to the Latin *omnipotens* (the ability to do all things) but the Greek *pantokratōr*: Jesus is the ruler of all.[46]

The point I am making is that Jesus says he has what he has—his authority—because it was *given to him*, not returned to him, or always was his.

---

45. Not only is *dio* "an inferential conjunction" (BDAG 250), Dana and Mantey observe that this "is the strongest inferential conjunction," meaning "on which account, wherefore." *Manual Grammar*, 245.

46. Davies and Allison, *Matthew 19–28*, 682 and n31.

THE SON OF GOD
JESUS' DERIVED LIFE

Jesus had a beginning in Bethlehem. (I am sure we will be told that by Smith if we didn't already know it!) The Christ or the Word of God whose existence "was"[47] back into time indefinitely stated and who was with God was, at some point, also given life (John 1:1). Luke has Gabriel use the strongest inferential conjunction in Greek, *dio*,[48] to affirm the reason for Mary's pregnancy. It was precisely because of the conception caused by the overshadowing of holy spirit—God's power he says in parallel rendition—that Jesus would be called God's Son. We have already seen that Adam was God's Son (Luke 3:38), precisely because of no less an impressive miraculous making out of dirt. If God could make a man out of clay (or make Eve from a man's bone), he could weave together twenty-three Y chromosomes, join them with those of Mary, and give Jesus human life. Yes, this is pedantic, but only because if ever there was a secret thing that belonged to God and not to man (Deut 29:29) this is it! Jesus affirms, without explanation, that he was given life: "For as the Father hath life in himself, even so gave he to the Son also to have life in himself" (John 5:26; cp. 6:57).[49] The commentaries lack logic and coherency on these verses, except to say Jesus has eternally been given life by the Father.[50]

---

47. "In the beginning *was* The Word" (John 1:1). The use of the Greek imperfect indicative active *ēn*, "was," ought not to be taken lightly. Nor should any other aspects of syntax or lexicography for the first fourteen verses of John 1. Leon Morris, not frustrating the expectation, is informative on the point. He writes in a note on John 1:1: "'Was' is *ēn* not *egeneto*, which is used in vv. 3,6, 14 . . . . It is relevant to notice that exactly the same verb, *ēn*, occurs in the next clause, where Knox brings out the continuous force by rendering, 'God had the Word abiding with him'. Westcott draws attention to the fact that, whereas the opening of Genesis takes us back to the beginning and that which starts from that point, 'St. John lifts our thoughts *beyond* the beginning and dwells on that which "was" when time, and with time finite being, began its course.' Calvin thinks little of any argument derived from the tense of the verb and looks for 'weightier reasons', *viz.*, 'that the Evangelist sends us to the eternal sanctuary of God and teaches us that the Word was, as it were, hidden there before He revealed Himself in the outward workmanship of the world.'" Morris, *John*, 73–74 n9.

48. See note 45 supra.

49. Acknowledging the interpretative force of a constative or culminative use of the aorist here might help understanding, although it would offend an ear presuming a more gnomic perspective to save a doctrine. On the uses of the aorist tense, see Dana and Mantey, *Manual Grammar*, 195–97.

50. E.g., on John 6:57, George R. Beasley-Murray comments: "As the Son lives 'through the Father,' i.e., has life from and is sustained by the Father" (Beasley-Murray, *John*, 95). At least F. F. Bruce presumes Trinitarian eternal begetting when he says of John

AN ARIAN VIEW
THE VALUE OF SUCH A DISCUSSION

While I do not believe that one's Unitarian or Trinitarian bent will matter one whit in determining one's salvation on judgment day, I believe that anything that God has revealed is fair game for his servants to explore (Deut 29:29). I have a few thoughts about the implications of Jesus' preexistence, which may impact this point if the debate wends toward a consideration of supposed advantages Jesus may have had that none of "his brothers"—a class, his fellow humans, to which he belongs—would have had in living a faithful life. Who wins a debate like this? I would not agree that discussions like this are pointless. I changed my position on this topic at the age of forty-three and modified it again after considering finer points three years later. I eagerly await Smith's and Irons's responses.

5:26–27: "It is an eternal act, part and parcel of the unique Father-Son relationship which existed already 'in the beginning.' In the eternal order the Father, as Father, imparts to the Son, as Son, that life-in-himself which it is the Father's to possess and impart." Bruce, *John*, 132.

A TRINITARIAN RESPONSE TO AN ARIAN VIEW

CHARLES LEE IRONS

Danny Dixon has given us an opening statement in which he defends the position that Jesus is "a divine being" distinct from God Almighty. Unlike Dustin Smith, Dixon affirms the preexistence of Christ: Jesus had "existence with God as a sentient individual at some unrevealed time before becoming a human individual." This preexistent divine being was also God's agent in creating all things. However, Dixon does not believe in the eternal preexistence of Christ, which sets his view apart from mine. This preexistent divine person "became flesh" by being miraculously born of the Virgin Mary. Dixon's Christology seems to be similar to that of Arianism in the fourth century and of the modern-day Jehovah's Witnesses.

What is Arianism? Historically, it is the belief that the Son was created out of nothing; hence, he is different in essence from the Father. He may be called "God" or "divine," but only in a lesser sense than God the Father. As the first, greatest, and highest creature, he possesses a lesser form of deity that makes him like God but not ontologically on par with God. Because he is created, there was a time when he did not exist. Although he is called the Son of God, he is not eternally God's Son. The Son was created before any other creature, and through him God created the rest of creation.[1]

---

1. Athanasius reports the teaching of Arius in these quotes: "'The Son was not always;' for, whereas all things were made out of nothing, and all existing creatures and works were made, so the Word of God Himself was 'made out of nothing,' and 'once He was not,' and 'He was not before His origination.'" *Against the Arians* 1.5 (*NPNF*2 4.308–9).

A TRINITARIAN RESPONSE TO AN ARIAN VIEW

Historically the Christian church has rejected Arianism because of its fundamental failure to reckon with the Creator-creature distinction. The Bible makes two things unequivocally clear. First, it makes clear that there is an absolute distinction between the Creator and the creation. Biblical revelation about God is uncompromising in setting God apart from all created reality as ontologically distinct and transcendent. Whereas the creation had a beginning, God has no beginning, no end, and exists eternally. Whereas the creation is dependent on God, contingent and inherently subject to corruption, God is totally self-sufficient and independent of creation. Based on the teaching of Scripture, Basil of Caesarea stated it this way: "There are two realities, creation and divinity."[2] In this biblical view of reality, there is no room for hybrids, that is, beings that are in some sense both created and divine.

Second, with that ontological divide in view, the Scripture tells us that the Son falls on the Creator side of the Creator-creature divide. This can be seen in the passages which tell us that God created all created things through the Son (John 1:3, 10; 1 Cor 8:6; Col 1:16; Heb 1:2, 10). Commenting on John 1:3, Athanasius's predecessor as Bishop of Alexandria, said:

> The same John affirms that the Word of God is not classed among things created out of the non-existent, for, he says that "all things were made by Him".... In their ignorance and want of practice in theology [the Arians] do not realize how vast must be the distance between the Father who is uncreated, and the creatures, whether rational or irrational, which He created out of the non-existent.[3]

The fact that the Son is not created is also implied when we are told that the Son has "life in himself" in the same way that God has "life in himself" (John 5:26) (something that could never be said of a creature). Additionally, the same point is made when the Scriptures inform us that "all things" (*ta panta*) are dependent on and sustained by the Son (Heb 1:3; Col 1:16), which could not be the case if Christ were part of the "all things," that is, part of creation. In another passage, the perishable creation is contrasted with the changeless Creator:

> Of old you laid the foundation of the earth,
> and the heavens are the work of your hands.

---

2. Basil of Caesarea, *Against Eunomius*, 2.31 (ET: DelCogliano and Radde-Gallwitz, *St. Basil of Caesarea*, 178).

3. "Epistle of Alexander, Bishop of Alexandria" (*NPNF2* 3.36, 39).

THE SON OF GOD

26 They will perish, but you will remain;
   they will all wear out like a garment.
You will change them like a robe, and they will pass away,
27 but you are the same, and your years have no end (Ps 102:25–27).

Athanasius pointed out long ago that this passage is quoted by the author of Hebrews in such a way that "they will perish" is applied to the creatures, and "you will remain" is understood as referring to Christ in distinction from the creatures (Heb 1:10–11).[4] Here, Christ is said to have an eternal divine nature that puts him squarely on the Creator side of the Creator-creature distinction. Therefore, he cannot be classed among the creatures.

In addition to the argument from the Creator-creature distinction, another biblical argument against Arianism is that it envisions a Son who is not truly revelatory of God the Father. Arianism fails to grasp that the concept of sonship means that a son possesses the same nature as his father. That is what the metaphor of sonship requires. As applied to Christ, if he is the Father's Son, then he possess the Father's divine nature and is therefore, in his being, able to reveal the Father. This is what the New Testament claims. "No one has ever seen God; but the only begotten God, who is in the bosom of the Father, he has made him known" (John 1:18 translation mine). Jesus said, "Whoever has seen me, has seen the Father" (John 14:9). The Son is "the radiance of the glory of God and the exact imprint of his nature" (Heb 1:3). If the Son is merely a creature, then his nature is not the same as the Father's nature. Arianism's Jesus is a creature, not the Son; therefore, Arianism's Jesus is not capable of revealing the Father.

Considerations such as these were decisive in the fourth century debate that led the church ultimately to reject Arianism as unfaithful to the biblical witness concerning the Son's fundamental identity as one who is the eternal, ontologically divine Son of God.

At this point, I turn now to respond more directly to Dixon's essay point by point. I will take Dixon's four points in his first paragraph as the structuring device for my response.

SECOND TEMPLE-JEWISH MONOTHEISM

Dixon asserts that "the one and only 'God' ought to be understood as Jews of Second Temple monotheism understood him to be." But why should our

---

4. Athanasius, *Against the Arians* 1.36, 58 (*NPNF2* 4.327, 340).

A TRINITARIAN RESPONSE TO AN ARIAN VIEW

understanding of God be restricted to what Second Temple Jews thought? Jesus has come and has revealed the Father, thereby also revealing that he is the Father's Son! The redemptive revelation that blazed out from the lightning strike of the incarnation, life, death, resurrection, and exaltation of the Son of God compelled a major reconceptualization of the very nature of God himself. God's revelation of himself as the Father through the sending of the Son is a profound event in the history of redemption, one that non-Messianic Jews reject. For this reason, I as a Christian cannot accept Dixon's premise that "God" ought to be understood as Jews of Second Temple monotheism understood him to be.

YAHWEH-FUNCTIONING HUMAN OR ANGELIC FIGURES

Dixon writes: "The exclusiveness of Father-God Yahweh / Jehovah is not compromised by exalted, worshiped, and Yahweh-functioning human or angelic figures who are also presented in the second temple period writings as gods." This is the heart of Dixon's argument. I will now deal with the three "Yahweh-functioning" figures to which Dixon appeals.

The Enochic Son of Man

"The Son of Man" in *1 Enoch*—also called "the Chosen One," God's "Anointed One," and "the Righteous One"—is a mysterious figure that has long puzzled scholars and provoked a voluminous secondary literature. Aside from Jesus' own self-designation as the Son of Man in the Gospels, there is hardly anything like it in the literature of early Judaism. What is more, and potentially damaging for proponents of the ontological deity of Christ, there are three verses that seem to say that this figure is worshiped as he sits upon the throne of God while executing the final judgment as God's vice-regent (*1 En.* 48:5; 62:6, 9). Seizing on these three verses, Dixon argues that "the Son of Man becomes an exception defined by God himself to the strict monotheistic standard of worshiping none but God only." The implication is that Jesus may be another one of these exceptions defined by God. Even Richard Bauckham, a staunch advocate for the inclusion of Christ within the divine identity, is prepared to concede that the Son of

THE SON OF GOD

Man as depicted in *1 En.* is "the exception that proves the rule" that God alone may be worshiped.[5]

But I am not ready to raise the white flag of surrender. A closer examination of the three verses cited by Dixon reveals that the "worship" of the exalted Son of Man in *1 En.* is not in fact an exception to strict monotheism's prohibition against worshiping creatures. I would argue that the Enochic Son of Man does not violate the Creator-creature distinction. This is not a case of a creature receiving divine worship, but of a transcendent angelic figure who represents God and receives prostration (not divine worship) as the representative of God.[6]

In *1 En.* 48:5 we read these words: "All those who dwell upon the earth shall fall and worship before him [= the Son of Man]."[7] This same scene is reprised later in *1 En.* 62:6–9, where the kings try to appease the Son of Man by falling down and worshiping him in an unsuccessful bid to avoid punishment for oppressing and persecuting the righteous:

> (These) kings, governors, and all the landlords shall (try to) bless, glorify, extol him who rules over everything, him who has been concealed . . . . On that day, all the kings, the governors, the high officials, and those who rule the earth shall fall down before him on their faces, and worship and raise their hopes in that Son of Man; they shall beg and plead for mercy at his feet. But the Lord of the Spirits himself will cause them to be frantic, so that they shall rush and depart from his presence. Their faces shall be filled with shame, and their countenances shall be crowned with darkness. So he will deliver them to the angels for punishments in order that vengeance shall be executed on them (*1 En.* 62:6, 9–11).[8]

There is no hint in the text that God ("the Lord of Spirits") has commanded the kings and those who dwell on the earth to worship the Son of Man; it is their own idea. It is akin to a deathbed conversion intended to curry God's favor in order to escape judgment at the last moment.

---

5. Bauckham, *Jesus and the God of Israel*, 171.

6. What sets divine worship apart from lesser forms of honor that might legitimately be offered to a creature (human or angelic) is that divine worship (a) is authorized and commanded by God and (b) is offered with the intention of offering worship to the only being that is properly the object of divine worship, namely, the one true God.

7. ET: E. Isaac, "1 (Ethiopic Apocalypse of) Enoch," in *OTP* 1.35.

8. ET: Ibid., 1.43.

A TRINITARIAN RESPONSE TO AN ARIAN VIEW

Most importantly, the word "worship" should be translated "prostrate themselves."[9] In keeping with the general dependence of *1 En.* upon Isaiah's picture of the Servant of YHWH, the reference to kings "prostrating themselves" before the Son of Man is probably derived from Isa 49:7: "Thus says the LORD, the Redeemer of Israel and his Holy One, to one deeply despised, abhorred by the nation, the servant of rulers: 'Kings shall see and arise; princes, and they shall *prostrate themselves*'" (ESV). The Hebrew word *ḥāwâ* (in the Hishtaphel) is frequently used in the OT in both senses: (1) obeisance or prostration before a king or noble, and (2) worship of YHWH. It is usually rendered *proskyneō* in the LXX, a Greek word having the same double usage as the Hebrew word it renders. For example, on one occasion, "David bowed with his face to the earth and *paid homage*" to King Saul (1 Sam 24:8; cp. 2 Sam 9:6). In *1 En.* 48:5, the added prepositional phrase "before him" supports the translation, "they shall fall on their faces and prostrate themselves *before him*." The text of *1 En.* does not say that they offer divine worship directly to the Son of Man, but that they physically bow before him, acknowledging his authority as the one appointed by God to execute final judgment.

Yahoel

The second exalted being that Dixon appeals to is the figure of Yahoel in the *Apocalypse of Abraham*. The book is about the youthful Abraham, brought up in a pagan, idolatrous environment, searching for the true God. God appointed Yahoel to go to Abraham in order to strengthen and instruct him. When Yahoel meets Abraham, he identifies himself as follows: "I am sent to you to strengthen you and to bless you in the name of God, the creator of heavenly and earthly things" (*Apoc. Ab.* 10:6).[10] Yahoel is clearly an angel, but not just any angel. He is special because he bears God's name(s): God "put together his names in me." A few verses earlier, God refers to him as "Iaoel [= Yahoel] of the same name, through the mediation of my ineffable name" (*Apoc. Ab.* 10:3).[11] His bearing the divine name(s) is consistent with his role as the angel sent to Abraham to reveal the name of God to Abraham. The idea that an angel can bear the divine name in a limited sense is not in itself startling. After all, YHWH said of the angel that he sent

---

9. Nickelsburg and VanderKam, *1 Enoch 2*, 172.
10. ET: R. Rubinkiewicz, "The Apocalypse of Abraham," in *OTP* 1.694.
11. Ibid., 1.693

THE SON OF GOD

before the Israelites, "Do not rebel against him, for he will not pardon your transgressions, for *my name is in him*" (Exod 23:21). The question is, "In what sense is this figure bearing the divine name?" In the present case, we can see that the name of YHWH was "in" an angel as a theophany, as part of temporary agency, but not for the purpose of being included in the divine identity in order to receive divine worship. Yahoel is a creature temporarily commissioned to act as God's agent.

The Creator-creature distinction is not compromised by the *Apocalypse of Abraham*'s depiction of Yahoel. Indeed, maintaining that clear distinction is one of the themes of this Jewish pseudepigraphal work, since it begins with Abraham destroying the idols of his father Terah and searching for "which god is in truth the strongest" (*Apoc. Ab.* 1:1).[12] Finally, Abraham tells his father, "Let me proclaim to you the God who created all things" (*Apoc. Ab.* 7:10 alternate reading[13]), "the God of gods, the Creator" (*Apoc. Ab.* 8:3). When God appears to Abraham, he identifies himself as "the God who created previously, before the light of the age" (*Apoc. Ab.* 9:3). Yahoel himself recognizes that he is distinct from and sent by "the creator of heavenly and earthly things." Later, when the angel Yahoel instructs Abraham how to worship the one true God, he does not receive worship from Abraham but rather stands at his side and shows him how to worship God. Abraham and the angel both bow down and worship God (*Apoc. Ab.* 17). One scholar rightly concludes: "This angelic being [Yahoel] is thus God's vicegerent, second only to God Himself. Yet he may not be worshiped, but rather himself sets Abraham the example of worshiping God."[14]

Qumran's Melchizedek

The third exalted being that Dixon makes much of is the exalted figure of Melchizedek as presented in a fragment found in Cave 11 of the Dead Sea Scrolls (11QMelch = 11Q13). This fragmentary text belongs to a genre of writing called *pesher*, a type of biblical commentary characterized by quotations of verses from the Hebrew Bible, followed by statements usually introduced with the words, "its interpretation is . . . ." There is no doubt that, in the eyes of the Qumran sect, the biblical figure of Melchizedek (mentioned only twice in the Hebrew Scriptures—Gen 14; Ps 110) is not

---

12. Ibid., 1.689.
13. Ibid., 1.692.
14. Box, with Landsman, *Apocalypse of Abraham*, xxv.

A TRINITARIAN RESPONSE TO AN ARIAN VIEW

a historical, ordinary human being but "an enormously exalted divine being."[15] As Dixon points out, the high estimate of this exalted being is seen in the fact that 11Q13 rewrites Isa 61:2, substituting "Melchizedek" for "YHWH," resulting in the phrase, "the year of Melchizedek's favor" or "the acceptable year of Melchizedek" (line 9). Three additional scriptural passages (Ps 82:1; 7:7–8; and Isa 52:7) containing the words *el* or *elohim* are interpreted as references to Melchizedek. When those terms appear in the Hebrew Bible in reference to YHWH, they are usually rendered "God," but in these three instances in 11Q13, they are more appropriately rendered "godlike or divine being." Additionally, this exalted being is granted the power to exercise divine prerogatives, specifically executing eschatological judgment on the enemies of God.

The use of the word *elohim* to refer to an angel, understood as a godlike being, is not surprising. On several occasions, the *elohim* (or the sons of *elohim*) are interpreted as "angels" in the Septuagint (Gen 6:2; Deut 32:8; Job 1:6; 2:1; 38:7; Ps 8:6; 97:7; 138:1). Another illustration is Ps 82:1, quoted by 11Q13: "God has taken his place in the divine council; in the midst of the *elohim* he holds judgment." This verse seems to have been interpreted by the Qumran sect as a reference to the heavenly council of the angels. My point is that it even in the Old Testament itself, we have cases of angels being called *elohim*.[16] 11Q13 is not going beyond anything found in the OT.

Dixon also claims that Melchizedek is said to have the power to judge and to forgive sins. But it is not clear that this is what 11Q13 says. Dixon relies on one particular English translation of the Dead Sea Scrolls to make this point. The translation quoted by Dixon puts both sentences relating to forgiveness and atonement in the active: "*He* [Melchizedek] will proclaim to them the Jubilee, thereby releasing them from the debt of all their sins . . . . *He* shall atone for all the Sons of Light."[17] But another translation uses the passive, thereby making it ambiguous whether it is Melchizedek or God who is doing the forgiving and atoning: "And liberty shall be proclaimed to them, to free them from the debt of all their iniquities . . . atonement shall

---

15. Wise, Abegg, and Cook, *Dead Sea Scrolls*, 455.

16. See also Ps 29:1; 89:6–7. For more on *elohim* as divine (angelic) beings, see Heiser, "Deuteronomy 32:8."

17. Wise, Abegg, and Cook, *Dead Sea Scrolls*, 456.

THE SON OF GOD

be made for all the sons of light."[18] The ambiguity of the latter translation accurately captures the ambiguity of the Hebrew.[19]

But even if 11Q13 should be interpreted as explicitly as the translation Dixon uses does, we have seen the notion that the angel of the Lord seemingly has the power to pardon the Israelites' transgressions (Exod 23:21). We should not take this to mean that the angel literally forgives sins—for "who can forgive sins but God alone?" (Mark 2:7)—but that as the destroying angel his passing over the Israelites and not executing God's judgment on them is tantamount to "pardoning" them. To say that the angel "pardons" them is another way of saying that by not punishing them the angel is bringing to bear the legal consequences of God's prior act of forgiveness.

In sum, the author of 11Q13 "clearly thought of [Melchizedek] as an angelic *creature* who would participate in the last judgment."[20] Qumran's Melchizedek figure does not violate the Creator-creature distinction, since he is regarded as a mere angel who remains very much a created being under God and subordinate to God's authority.

Assessing Dixon's Argument

What is the point of Dixon's appeal to the Enochic Son of Man, the angel Yahoel in the *Apocalypse of Abraham*, and Melchizedek as understood by the Qumran sect? He seems to be making the argument that, according to early Jewish conceptions of God, God can exalt secondary, created agents and grant them various divine prerogatives. And God can do that, just because he is God. If God wills that a creature be exalted as his agent to represent him, be seated on the throne of judgment, receive the divine name, be called "God," and be the object of worship—that is God's right. Such exalted figures are beings distinct from YHWH functioning as agents of YHWH. In that role as agents of YHWH, they are granted a godlike role, filling in as it were for YHWH and are even called "God," even though they are not YHWH himself. These early Jewish texts, Dixon writes, "demonstrate that in addition to God's names and titles, his functions can also be transferred to certain agents." All of this "speaks to the acceptability of the concept

---

18. *DSSR* 2.25.

19. "Melchizedek may have been regarded as the subject of the atonement, but this is by no means certain, because it is always possible that the author thought of God . . . as subject." De Jonge and van der Woude, "11Q Melchizedek," 306.

20. VanderKam, *Dead Sea Scrolls*, 53 (emphasis added).

A TRINITARIAN RESPONSE TO AN ARIAN VIEW

[of agency] without it being blasphemous in the minds of Second Temple Jews." Dixon's implicit point seems to be: the New Testament's application of the title "God" or the divine name "YHWH/*Kyrios*" to Jesus need not be interpreted as indicating that Jesus is YHWH, but may be interpreted (using these Jewish figures as an analogy) as an instance of agency. To be consistent, if the New Testament writers say that Jesus is exalted, called "God," given the name YHWH, and is worshiped, we should not view these things as proof that Jesus is ontologically equal with God or that he is part of the divine identity. Rather, we should see him as still a creature who has been exalted by God just as the Enochic Son of Man, the angel Yahoel, or Melchizedek were in these Jewish texts. Ultimately, such exaltation of a creature rests on God's desire or will, and none of this violates strict monotheism.

But in my opening essay, I did not make the simplistic arguments that Dixon seems to be attempting to answer with his appeal to three "Yahweh-functioning" figures in Jewish literature. I did not argue, "Jesus is worshiped as divine or is given the name YHWH in the New Testament; therefore, Jesus is YHWH." My argument for the ontological deity of Christ rested primarily on the self-consciousness of Jesus as the Son of God and the fact that he is the creator and has aseity. I stated that the case for the ontological deity has already been made before I discussed the exaltation of Christ. I did discuss his exaltation and the results that flow from it—exercising divine sovereignty at God's right, being worshiped, and receiving the divine name. But I argued that these are confirmatory of his deity (which has been established on other grounds), and that this treatment of the exalted Christ is appropriate because of his prior status as ontologically divine.

Even more importantly, none of the exalted secondary figures to which Dixon appeals ever claimed to be the Son of God in a way that made them equal with God. But Jesus did make that claim, and he was subsequently raised from the dead and exalted at God's right hand and given the divine name. This approving action of God is tantamount to God's vindication of Jesus' claim to be the ontological Son of God—precisely as Jesus said when he was being interrogated by the high priest. God's exaltation of Jesus is God's approval and vindication of the claims of Jesus to be the divine Son of God, thereby cosmically confirming the absolute, full deity of Christ.

The first chapter of the Epistle to the Hebrews seems to have been written precisely to counter the kind of thinking that Dixon advocates, namely, viewing Jesus as merely another exalted angel. I suspect that Dixon would

THE SON OF GOD

not say that Jesus "is" an angel, but he has appealed to three Jewish texts, all of which are about exalted angels, to make his case for seeing Jesus in similar terms as a divine being who is nevertheless a creature and distinct from YHWH. So even if he holds back from calling Jesus an angel, in terms of the structure of his argument, that is essentially what his Christology amounts to. But the author of Hebrews points out how far superior Jesus is to an angel, no matter how exalted, godlike, or God-functioning (Heb 1:1–14).

THE EXALTATION OF JESUS

Dixon writes: "Jesus' position and treatment is a result of his exaltation, which parallels secondary figures in Judaism." I do not agree that there are genuine parallels between the exaltation of Jesus and the exaltation of secondary figures in Judaism. To be sure, there are similarities, but the secondary figures of Judaism (at least the ones cited by Dixon) fall short of what we see in the case of the New Testament's three-stage Christology: (1) eternally preexistent Son of God who was the instrument of God in creation, (2) incarnation, i.e., becoming man, and (3) the exaltation of the incarnate Son returning to the glory he had before becoming man but now receiving that glory as a man. There is nothing in Judaism that approaches this. The closest we get is the Son of Man in *1 Enoch*, who does exist prior to creation and who is exalted to a very high position as executor of final judgment. But the Enochic Son of Man is not eternally preexistent, is not the intermediary of creation, never has an incarnation phase, and when he is exalted is not granted *divine* worship. The kings of the earth prostrate themselves before him in a vain attempt to curry favor at the last minute to avoid judgment, but the Enochic Son of Man is not exalted by God in order to receive worship from all creation, as Jesus is. As to the other secondary agents of Judaism cited by Dixon (Yahoel and Melchizedek), neither of them is eternally preexistent, and neither of them became incarnate. True, we see a few examples of exaltation—an angel bearing God's name, seated on God's throne, exercising delegated authority to judge, and being the object of prostration and obeisance in recognition of that delegated authority. But such exaltation is not the same as the exaltation of God's Son, eternally divine and then incarnate. They are mere angels or angel-like beings, created beings given delegated temporary authority to represent God in some way.

A TRINITARIAN RESPONSE TO AN ARIAN VIEW

None of the exalted secondary figures appealed to by Dixon violates the Creator-creature distinction. All three exalted beings fall on the creature side of the Creator-creature distinction. All three are angels or angel-like beings. Jesus, by contrast, is clearly not an angel or an angel-like being according to the New Testament. He is far superior to the angels. As the author of Hebrews asked, "To which of the angels did God ever say, 'You are my Son, today I have begotten you?'" (Heb 1:5). Jesus the Son of God possesses qualities that set him apart from even the most exalted of Jewish secondary figures: eternal preexistence, intermediary of creation, and ontological Sonship.

JESUS' LIFE DERIVED FROM THE FATHER

In the last portion of Dixon's essay he says Jesus was a "divine being" whose life was derived from the Father. But what kind of "divine being"? An angel? If not, how is he different from an angel? Would Dixon say God created the preexistent Son "out of nothing" as Arius taught? If he is a mere creature, what was the preexistent Son's role in the act of creation? How can a creature create or be an agent of creation? What happened to the preexistent Son when he was born of Mary as a human? Did he cease being a "divine being" in order to become exclusively human? Or did he retain his "divine being" while also taking on human nature? This final section begs many questions.

CONCLUSION

In conclusion, Dixon's Arian Christology is not convincing. It leaves us with a Son who is a creature, who is not eternally the Son, and who cannot reveal the Father. Arianism is contradicted by the teaching of the New Testament that the Son falls on the Creator side of the Creator-creature distinction, and that Jesus as God's Son is the perfect revelation of the Father.

A SOCINIAN RESPONSE TO AN ARIAN VIEW

DUSTIN R. SMITH

DANNY DIXON SHOULD BE congratulated for his tightly argued proposal regarding how he understands the identity of Jesus Christ. His knowledge of the ancient sources demonstrates his desire to properly situate the passages of the Bible within their proper context. Dixon writes with honesty, genuineness, and a desire to let the evidence speak for itself. I appreciate his openness regarding how he has shifted positions based upon his prolonged study of such a tremendous topic, since I also admitted making changes in my Christology. For these and many other reasons, he should be commended. Dixon's case is, stated positively, that Jesus existed prior to the incarnation as a created being distinct from Yahweh.

Before I raise a few objections, I feel the need to admit that it was an utter delight to read Dixon's presentation, primarily because so much of his position is broadly the same as my own. In particular, we agree that God exalts his agents within Second Temple Judaism, and that this fact needs to illumine responsible readings of the New Testament texts. We likewise acknowledge that the title "God" was legitimately given to such figures as Moses, the Davidic king, human judges, etc. Furthermore, we recognize that within Second Temple Judaism various exalted figures are worshiped in manners and circumstances which are tolerated and not accused of idolatry. Dixon and I share the desire to let the angel Yahoel, the messenger who bears the name of God in the *Apocalypse of Abraham*, "join us at the table" as we discuss Christology. Together we insist that Jesus possesses his authority precisely because God has bestowed it upon him (not because

A SOCINIAN RESPONSE TO AN ARIAN VIEW

it originally belonged to him). I appreciate that these points are honestly communicated in Dixon's presentation.

I have already corresponded with Dixon regarding my various concerns of his thesis. One of my primary objections involves his inability to precisely define who (or what) Jesus was as a divine being before the incarnation. In other words, Dixon argues that Jesus existed prior to his birth as an undefined "divine being" who is neither Yahweh nor an angel.[1] One has to wonder *what else Jesus could be* in this preincarnate form.[2] Dixon calls Jesus a "sentient individual," but he fails to provide any scriptural evidence to supplement this claim. He also surprisingly states that "Jesus became flesh," but "Jesus" is the human name, not a designation of some preexistent being.[3] It seems that certain passages, which Dixon interprets as teaching that Jesus was God's architect of this world, have forced Jesus backwards into some unknown preincarnate form. I am confused how it is that someone as important as the architect of all things (as Dixon asserts) is never described or identified in any meaningful detail within the Bible. What sort of divine being, other than Yahweh (or an angel), has the power to create all things? I respectfully suggest that the most appropriate inference to draw on the Bible's silence regarding Jesus' preexistent identity is that *there is no biblical teaching on the matter*. Dixon presents a Jesus having a preincarnate identity about which the Bible says absolutely nothing. I find such an argument to be unpersuasive.

One of the corollaries of Christologies which posit a preexisting divine being who literally becomes incarnate in the womb of Mary is that the legitimacy of Jesus' humanity is called into question. If the core of who Jesus really is, in his identity, is something other than a full-fledged human being, then the incarnation fails to produce a true member of humanity. Dixon insists that Jesus belongs to the class of his fellow human beings, but this seems inconsistent with his argument that Jesus was created as a nonhuman divine being prior to creation. One of the qualifications for the office of Messiah was that the candidate had to be a human descendant of King David. Dixon's Jesus does not fit this requirement. My original essay demonstrated the extent which both testaments insisted that the promised

---

1. Dixon privately acknowledged that Jesus it not an angel (Heb 1:5).

2. The only things which conceivably come to mind (all of which are not even serious considerations) are an animal, bird, fish, a second god, or a demon.

3. A scholarly consensus exists on this point, e.g., Davies and Allison, *Matthew 1–7*, 155.

THE SON OF GOD

messiah would be a human descendant from the lines of such figures as Abraham, Jacob, Judah, and David. Dixon does not deal with these texts. Perhaps greater clarity on his understanding of the humanity of the Messiah would be achieved if he engaged with Gen 3:15; 49:8–10; Num 24:17; Deut 18:18; 2 Sam 7:12; Ps 132:11; Isa 11:1; Jer 30:9; 33:17; Ezek 34:23; or Zech 6:12. Why does Matthew's Gospel commence by devoting over 340 Greek words in detailing the origin of Jesus as descending from the family lines of Abraham and David? I would like to ask Dixon if Matthew's genealogy teaches that Jesus literally preexists his birth. Even John's Gospel stresses the humanity of Jesus (eighteen times) with *Jesus himself* stating that he is a human (John 8:40). It is my contention that a messiah who is not 100 percent human down to the very core of his identity fails to qualify for the messianic vocation described in the Bible.

Dixon's presentation similarly fails to admit that Jesus was *begotten* in time, a statement about which a variety of New Testament authors regularly speak as the starting point of his existence (and implicitly objecting to literal preexistence). Matthew describes the genesis of Jesus Christ (1:18) and details how Jesus was begotten in Mary (1:20). Dixon alludes to Luke 1:35, which clearly links the miraculous begetting of Jesus with his sonship. Are we to understand this text as referring to a preincarnate divine being who travelled *through* Mary? Even Paul makes mention of Jesus' birth in Romans 1:3 and Galatians 4:4. What does he mean when Jesus was "born out of (*ek*) the seed of David" and "born out of (*ek*) a woman?" What is the significance of the *monogenēs* language used of Jesus (John 1:14, 18; 3:16, 18; 1 John 4:9)? Jesus told Pilate that he *was born* for the purpose of kingship (18:37). Dixon's particular position is indicative of a lack of consideration of the Bible's "begetting" language used of Jesus.

Another significant concern I wish to raise regards his reading of the Prologue of John. Dixon cites John 1:1 as evidence for literal preexistence. However, his argument is open to rebuttal. Firstly, Dixon uses "Christ" and "Word" interchangeably, a link never mentioned in John 1:1–18. Secondly, he regards the *Logos* of John 1:1 as an actual being, living and distinct from God. I am confident that Dixon is aware of the debate over whether John understood the *Logos* as a personification of God's creative speech or as a literal "self" existing alongside God. Dixon has not given his reasons for interpreting the *Logos* as a personal being. I am curious how he would interact with Dunn's insistence that "nowhere either in the Bible or in extra-canonical literature of the Jews is the word of God a personal agent or on

A SOCINIAN RESPONSE TO AN ARIAN VIEW

the way to become such."[4] Isa 44:24 declares that Yahweh was unaccompanied during the act of creation: "I, Yahweh, am the maker of all things, stretching out the heavens *by Myself* and spreading out the earth *all alone*." How could it be that the *Logos* is an *actual personal being* alongside Yahweh when this passage uses singular verbs to described the creative acts, says "by myself", and additionally insists that God was all alone?" I find it hard to be convinced that "by myself" and "all alone" language means that there was more than one person or being involved.

It is more likely that the Prologue is poetically personifying God's creative utterance. The following parallels account for the context in which John thinks and writes:

> "By the *word* of Yahweh the heavens were made, and by the *breath of His mouth* all their host" (Ps 33:6).
>
> "To Him who made the heavens with *understanding*" (Ps 136:5).
>
> "Yahweh by *wisdom* founded the earth, by *understanding* He established the heavens. By His *knowledge* the deeps were broken up" (Prov 3:19–20).
>
> "By his *knowledge* everything shall come into existence, and all that does not exist he establishes with his *calculations* and nothing is done outside of him" (1QS 11:11).
>
> "By the *knowledge* of the Lord they were distinguished" (Sir 33:8).
>
> "O God of my ancestors and Lord of mercy, who have made all things by your *word*" (Wis 9:1).
>
> "Worship the God of heaven, who causes the rain and the dew to descend on the earth and does everything upon the earth, and has created everything by his *word*" (Jub. 12:4).
>
> "*Wisdom* being his mother, through whom the universe arrived at creation" (Philo, *Fug.* 109).
>
> "*Wisdom*, by means of whom the universe was brought to completion" (Philo, *Det. Pot.* 54).

These examples do not indicate that there was an actual personal being alongside God (Word or Wisdom).[5] Rather, these texts character-

---

4. Dunn, *Christology in the Making*, 219.

5. Wisdom in Prov 8 and Wis 6, although significantly personified, was not intended to be understood as a distinct person from Yahweh.

THE SON OF GOD

istically insist that God's creation came about because of his powerful speech, or through God's Wisdom. The creation is indicative of a wise and knowledgeable ordering.[6] This data persuades me to read John 1:3 ("All things were made through Him") as a metaphorical portrayal of God speaking creation into existence reminiscent of Gen 1. Rather than saying that all things were made through a personal being, the *Logos*, it is more likely that John intended his readers to pick up on the personification of God's Word (or Wisdom) so pervasive in the examples above. Similarly, the statement of John 1:1b ("the *Logos* was with God") draws from such poetic passages as the following:

> "Yet these things You have concealed in Your heart; I know that this is *within* You" (Job 10:13).
>
> "For He performs what is appointed for me, and many such decrees are *with* Him" (Job 23:14).
>
> "What is *with* the Almighty I will not conceal" (Job 27:11).
>
> "My son, if you will receive my words and treasure my commandments *within* you" (Prov 2:1).
>
> "Wisdom is *with* you" (Wis 9:9).
>
> "All wisdom is from the Lord and is *with* Him forever" (Sir 1:1).

To summarize, in the beginning was God's creative and personal utterance, who (personified as a male figure within the bounds of the Prologue's poetry) was with God, i.e., in his mind and plan, and who was *Theos* (without the article), "fully expressive of God."[7] This creates a context wherein John 1:14 can say that this self-expressive *Logos* of God became embodied in the human Jesus. I am curious how Dixon feels about this interpretation, especially in light of such noteworthy parallels as: Philo's description of Moses as the *embodiment* of Torah (*Moses* 1.162; 2.4), Philo's close *identification* of Sarah with Wisdom (*Leg.* 2.82; *Det.* 124; *Congr.* 1.12–13), Simon ben Onias's being depicted as the *embodiment* of Wisdom (Sir 50), and the

---

6. Carter, *John*, 199.

7. Cf. the distinction Philo makes with using *theos* with the article and without it (*Somn.* 1.229). William Barclay similarly reads John 1:1c by ascribing a qualitative characteristic to the anarthrous *theos*: "When in Greek two nouns are joined by the verb to be and when both have the definite article, then the one is fully identified with the other; but when one of them is without the article, it becomes more an adjective than a noun, and describes rather the class or sphere to which the other belongs." *Jesus as They Saw Him*, 21.

A SOCINIAN RESPONSE TO AN ARIAN VIEW

Torah's characterization as the *quintessence* of Wisdom (Bar 3:23–4:1; Sir 24:23). Is the Fourth Gospel really doing something so different than his Jewish contemporaries? It seems to me that John 1:14 is effectively declaring that Jesus is God's authoritative spokesman *par excellence.* This sets up a significant motif within the Gospel narrative wherein Jesus is depicted as speaking the very words of God the Father (John 3:34; 7:16–17; 12:47–50; 14:10, 24; 17:6, 14). I offer this reading of the Prologue as a plausible and persuasive alternative to popular interpretations which often read to the Prologue as saying what their cherished traditions teach.

I think some dialogue would yield fruitful results regarding how Dixon understands Luke 1:35. He rightly notes that this passage indicates the causal link between the miracle in Mary's womb and the identification that Jesus will be called God's Son. I wish to kindly remind him that this passage additionally speaks of the Son of God as "the holy child begotten," that is, the one who was brought into existence. This establishes on a timeline the *terminus a quo* of Jesus' existence.[8] Since Dixon argues for Jesus' literal preexistence, I would be curious to hear how he sees Luke 1:35 fitting into this scheme. I offer up a few questions as I seek clarity on this point. Does Luke 1:35 only begin the human part of Jesus' life, essentially adding humanity onto a preexisting person? It would be helpful if Dixon were to flesh out (no pun intended) how he understands the specifics of incarnation. Does Jesus possess two distinct natures, a preexisting divine nature in addition to a human nature? If so, is Jesus Christ really two persons? If not, which of the two natures is the core consciousness? Perhaps Dixon feels that the preexisting divine person ceased to exist once the human Jesus was born. If so, in what sense is there any continuity with the preexisting person with the subsequent human counterpart which bears any meaningful relevance? Many scholars have admitted that no text shows Jesus displaying any consciousness that he had two natures, as it would create a significant theological problem.[9] I suggest that it would be helpful if Dixon could explain further how he resolves these noteworthy difficulties. Such a response would hopefully bring clarity to what seems to me more than a few marked contradictions.

---

8. James D. G. Dunn rightly echoes my concern: "To be sure, the imagery of birth (the coming into existence of a new human being) *does not immediately mesh* with the idea of incarnation (the enfleshment of one already preexistent)." "Incarnation," in *ABD* 3:403, emphasis mine.

9. See esp. Haight, *Jesus*, 39; Robinson, *Human Face*, 103–5; Ohlig, *One or Three?*, 108–9.

THE SON OF GOD

Another misgiving I have with Dixon's presentation concerns two passages in John (8:58; 17:5) which are interpreted with a rather wooden literalism suggesting that Jesus reminisced about his preexistent life and glory. I contend that interpreting these texts in this manner raises *more problems* than it solves. For one, it creates the conundrum over whether or not Jesus has two natures. If so, does the human Jesus share the mind of his divine nature? If yes, doesn't this mean that Jesus, possessing two consciences, is actually two persons? If however the divine nature ceased to exist when the human Jesus was born, how could the memories be passed onto the mind of an unborn fetus? John's Gospel doesn't seem to engage in such theological gymnastics in an attempt to convey that the human Jesus understood the memories of a second nature or a preexisting divine being.

I suggest that modern readers of the Gospel of John who come to the text uninformed about how Jews regularly spoke about preexisting things in God's mind and plan will fail to grasp what exactly is conveyed in these two passages. In other words, I deem it of no small importance that John 8:58 and 17:5 be properly situated in the context of Jewish preexistence discourse,[10] which characteristically spoke of noteworthy concepts as predetermined by God to fulfill their purpose and function, particularly as they affected God's creation and people.[11] I offer the following passages in dialogue about the nature of preexistence:

> "Seven things were created before the world was made, and these are they: Torah, repentance, the Garden of Eden, Gehenna, the throne of glory, and house of the sanctuary, and the name of the Messiah" (*b. Pes.* 54a; cf. *b. Ned.* 39b).

> "[God] will reveal His Messiah whose name is spoken from the beginning" (*Tg. Zech.* 4:7).

> "Abraham and Isaac were created before any work" (*Pr. Jos.* 1:2).

> "But He did design and devise me, and He prepared me from the beginning of the world to be mediator of His covenant" (*T. Mos.* 1:14).

> "The architect moreover does not build it out of his head, but employs plans and diagrams to know how to arrange the chambers and the wicket doors. Thus God consulted the Torah and created

---

10. Cf. McGrath, who remarks that John is "firmly rooted in Jewish thought." *John's Apologetic Christology*, 20.

11. Harnack, *History of Dogma*, 1.102–3.

A SOCINIAN RESPONSE TO AN ARIAN VIEW

the world, while Torah declares, 'In the beginning God created,' 'beginning' referring to the Torah, as in the verse, 'The Lord made me as the beginning of His way'" (*Gen. Rab.* 1.1).

"Six things preceded the creation of the world; some of them were actually created, while the creation of the others was already contemplated. The Torah and the throne of glory were created .... The creation of the Patriarchs was contemplated .... [The creation of] Israel was contemplated. ... [The creation of] Israel was contemplated .... [The creation of] the temple was contemplated .... The name of Messiah was contemplated" (*Gen. Rab.* 1.4).

"Torah preceded the creation of the world by two thousand years" (*Gen. Rab.* 8.2).

"Before I formed you in the womb I knew you, and before you were born I consecrated you . . ." (Jer 1:5).

"this man, delivered over by the predetermined plan and foreknowledge of God, you nailed to a cross by the hands of godless people . . ." (Acts 2:23).

". . . to those who are called according to His purpose. For those whom He foreknew, He also predestined . . . and these whom He predestined, He also called; and these whom He called, He also justified; and these whom He justified, He also glorified" (Rom 8:28–30).

"But when God, who had set me apart from my mother's womb and called me through his grace . . ." (Gal 1:15).

"He chose us in Him before the foundation of the world .... He predestined us to adoption as sons through Jesus Christ to Himself, according to the kind intention of His will .... In all wisdom and insight He made known to us the mystery of His will, according to His kind intention which He purposed in Him with a view to an administration suitable to the fullness of the times, the summing up of all things in Christ" (Eph 1:4–5, 8–10).

"Peter . . . to those who reside as aliens . . . who are chosen according to the foreknowledge of God the Father . . ." (1 Pet 1:1–2).

"[Jesus] was foreknown before the foundation of the world" (1 Pet. 1:20).

"Worthy are You, our Lord and our God . . . for You created all things, and because of Your will they already existed, and were created" (Rev 4:11).

THE SON OF GOD

". . . the Lamb who has been slain from the foundation of the world" (Rev 13:8).

So the question now arises, based on the data above, whether the thoroughly Jewish author of the Fourth Gospel actually suggested that Jesus Christ *literally preexisted* his birth as a personal being alongside God. It seems more likely that a notional (or ideal) preexistence, within the mind and plan of God, which could speak of things as already a reality, is being conveyed in John 8:58 and 17:5.

Furthermore, John 8:58 needs to be treated with care as it is positioned in the midst of one of the Fourth Gospel's distinctive misunderstanding motif, wherein Jesus is continually misheard by his dialogue partner(s) who take his sayings too literally.[12] After a lengthy dialogue concerning the paternity of "the Jews" who failed to believe, Jesus responds, "Your father Abraham rejoiced to see my day, and he saw it and was glad" (John 8:56).[13] The Jews misunderstand Jesus as saying that he has "seen Abraham" (John 8:57). Jesus answers by claiming to have been "before" Abraham (John 8:58), which effectively *ranks Jesus higher than Abraham*. John A. T. Robinson aptly cautions:

> To say that Jesus is 'before' him is not to lift him out of the ranks of humanity, but to assert his unconditional precedence. To take such statements at the level of 'flesh' so as to infer, as 'the Jews' do that, at less than fifty, Jesus is claiming to have lived on this earth before Abraham (8.52, 57), is to be as crass as Nicodemus who understands rebirth as an old man entering his mother's womb a second time (3.4). These are not assertions about the ego of the human Jesus, which is no more pre-existent than that of any other human being. Nor are statements about the glory that he enjoyed with the Father before the world was to be taken at the level of psychological reminiscence.[14]

When we look closely at the context surrounding John 17:5 we find some valuable clarity. Jesus petitions the Father to glorify him with the preexisting glory which was with God before the world was. In other words, Jesus is asking for something *to take place*, a glorification which he expects to come to pass shortly. However, the prayer continues to state that this

---

12. Brown, *Introduction to John*, 288–89; Culpepper, *Anatomy*, 86–87, 93, 104, 115, 117; Culpepper, *Gospel and Letters of John*, 135; Carter, *John*, 114.

13. See *4 Ezra* 3:14; *Gen. Rab.* 44.22.

14. Robinson, *Priority of John*, 384.

A SOCINIAN RESPONSE TO AN ARIAN VIEW

glory, which God has *already given* to Jesus, Jesus has similarly *already bestowed* upon the disciples (17:22).[15] The tension created by both the Jesus' request to be glorified and his subsequent statement that this glorification has already taken place (and furthermore passed onto the disciples) is resolved when we appreciate the fact that things which are fixed within God's plans are regularly spoken of as *having already taken place*, despite the fact that they clearly have not done so in the literal sense (see Gen 15:18; 28:4; 35:12; 2 Kgs 19:25; Matt 6:1; Rom 8:30; 1 Cor 2:7–8; 2 Cor 5:1). In sum, I recommend giving more emphasis to the Jewish context which speaks of the important aspects of God's plans as preexisting notionally (rather than literally) in addition to the customary way which speaks of these plans as having already come to pass. Upon doing so, the apparent problems of John 17:5 begin to disappear.

Dixon cites 1 Cor 8:6 as further evidence that Jesus, in his preexistent form, possessed an active role in creation. I recommend a few points worth considering as this passage is evaluated. Firstly, when Paul elsewhere calls Jesus *kyrios*, he quite naturally means *the exalted kyrios* (Phil 2:9–11). Secondly, when Paul elsewhere uses *dia* in reference to Jesus, his concern is always with the mediation of this exalted lord with Christians, not with the original creation (Rom 5:1; 1 Cor 15:57; 1 Thess 5:9). Moreover, Paul's insistence that "for us [Christians]" there is only one lord deliberately flew in the face of the Corinthian culture wherein the imperial cults, full of their own venerated lords, sought the locals' allegiance.[16] Additional indicators within the epistle which signify that believers now belong to Christ (1 Cor 3:23; 11:3; 15:25) mesh well with his exalted status as *kyrios*. Bruce Winter, noting that locals within Corinth sometimes used curse tablets evoking a variety of lords, proposes that it "would not have been difficult for a former pagan to draw the conclusion that Jesus, who had conquered the underworld in his death and resurrection, could substitute for the gods, especially Hermes of the underworld whose particular domain they had once believed was his."[17] These facts, among others, have persuaded a variety of scholars to see the "one lord Jesus Christ, through whom are all things, and we through him" as a description of *Christ's role in the mediation of the new*

---

15. Von Wahlde admits that if this verse is taken literally "the results could be quite other than is surely intended." *Gospel and Letters of John*, 2.735.

16. Dunn, *Beginning from Jerusalem*, 804–5.

17. Winter, *After Paul Left Corinth*, 177–78.

THE SON OF GOD

creation.[18] I too am persuaded by these arguments and I wish to offer them for Dixon's consideration.

For similar reasons, I suggest that the new creation is stressed in the Colossian hymn. How is the title "firstborn of all creation" to be understood (Col 1:15)?[19] Does "firstborn" indicate one who was first *in time* or one who is first *in rank*? Both definitions have support within the Hebrew Bible, but the deciding factor is found in the hymn's assertion that Christ is the firstborn from the dead *precisely so that he might become preeminent in all things* (Col 1:18).[20] This reading is strengthened by statements regarding Christ as the head of the body and the head of the church. While Col 1:16 indicates that "in him" all things were created, it seems unlikely that the hymn is praising Christ *as creator*. For one, the divine passive regularly indicates that God, rather than Jesus, is the unnamed creator.[21] Secondly, the prepositions associated with the created order ("in him," "through him," "for him") are certainty dissimilar from saying *by* him, as if Jesus did the creating himself. In fact, if all things have been created *for* (Gk. *eis*) him, then this suggests that creation finds its climax in the human Jesus (Col 1:20).[22] The hymn, drawing on Wisdom motifs (e.g., Ps 103:24 LXX), specifies that the female personification of God's creative action is now to be recognized as embodied in Christ, whose significance culminates in the cross and resurrection.[23] Lastly, I stress that metaphors of hymnic passages are not to be pressed in a meticulously literal manner, as hymns were to be read, sung, and interpreted appropriately within the confines of poetic form.[24]

I admire Dixon's attention to detail in addition to his quest to let the data "speak for itself." His presentation demonstrates a serious engagement with Christology over a prolonged period of time. I believe that this healthy dialogue will only bring about further fruitful conclusions, especially in regard to the questions which I raised in need of clarification. It is to that end that I offer this response.

---

18. E.g., Fitzmyer, *First Corinthians*, 343; Kuschel, *Born Before All Time?*, 289; Conzelmann, *1 Corinthians*, 144–45.

19. Barth and Blanke opt for "every creature." *Colossians*, 197.

20. BDAG, 894; Dunn, *Christology in the Making*, 189.

21. BDAG, 572; Barth and Blanke, *Colossians*, 198.

22. Cf. "The Christ who is *prōtotokos pasēs ktiseōs* . . . is the historical man Jesus." Sasse, "*kosmos, ktl.*"

23. Cf. Ps 89:27; Eph 1:10; O'Brien, *Colossians, Philemon*, 47.

24 Dunn, *Colossians and Philemon*, 88–93.

AN ARIAN REPLY

DANNY ANDRÉ DIXON

REPLY TO DUSTIN SMITH

Precision in Defining Jesus' Identity

SMITH CORRECTLY POINTS OUT that I have not precisely stated "who (or what) Jesus was as a divine being before the incarnation." But when he says that I do not provide any scriptural evidence to supplement my claim that Jesus is, at least, to be understood to be "a sentient individual," I would remind him that I spoke of what Jesus remembered of his preexistence when he said in John 8:58 that he existed before Abraham. I said: "Here Jesus reflects on his conscious existence, remembering his 'glory' shared with the Father before the world came into existence and recalling his being sent as God's Messiah." Certainly there is, in what I identified as "anamnesis" or "recalling" his past, a degree of evidence of a time of conscious awareness, which is how I characterized Jesus' comments in John 17:3–5. Smith's response to my comments suggests that I raise problems about Jesus' nature. I do not see this as a problem. I do not see, as Smith suggests that my position requires, that Jesus has more than one nature; therefore, I do not see that he has to be understood as two persons. I acknowledged that Jesus says he was given life by God (John 5:26; 6:57), and I see no reason why this living being who "became flesh" necessarily had to be divested of any memories that he previously had.

THE SON OF GOD

Smith lays out a catalogue of items within Jewish modes of discourse affirming "notional" or "ideal" preexistence in God's mind. Certainly I would not deny that God made (and makes) plans regarding what is to happen in the future. But this does not exclude the idea that Jewish writers saw patriarchal figures as preexistent, although Charlesworth regards the claim as "less common" than the notion that wisdom, Torah, or the nation Israel were preexistent.[1] For example, Smith cites *Pr. Jos.* 1:2 as one of several extrabiblical "passages in dialogue about the nature of preexistence." Charlesworth does regard the *Prayer* as "most likely to be situated within those first-century Jewish groups."[2] Note two points. First, there is the truth present in Charlesworth's cogent comment regarding that which "has survived of the Prayer of Joseph [as] direct speech by Jacob (not Joseph): 'I, Jacob, who is speaking to you.'" It would be difficult to consider the words of Jacob and *not* see sentient cognition of this divine entity. Here are the words of Jacob in full, including the portion excised by Smith:

> I, Jacob, who is speaking to you, am also Israel, an angel of God and a ruling spirit. Abraham and Isaac were created before any work. But, I Jacob, who men call Jacob but whose name is Israel am he who God called Israel which means, a man seeing God, because I am the firstborn of every living thing to whom God gives life (*Pr. Jos.*, Frag. A, 1–3).[3]

Jacob continues in a conversation speaking with Uriel, the angel of God:

> "[Am I not] Israel, the archangel of the power of the Lord and the chief captain among the sons of God? Am I not Israel, the first minister before the face of God?" And I called upon my God by the inextinguishable name (*Pr. Jos.*, Frag. A, 7–9).

That Jacob speaks as a preexistent entity flies directly in the face of Smith's observation.

Second, attention should be drawn to the word "created" (Gk. *proek-ktisis*) in the sentence from the *Pr. Jos.*, Frag. A, 2 where Abraham and Isaac are said to be "created before any work." Regarding this Smith has written:

> [The] term "created before" should be rendered literally as "pre-created." This seems to give the impression that Abraham and

---

1. Charlesworth, ed., "Prayer of Joseph," in *OTP* 2.713, emphasis added.
2. Ibid., 2.701.
3. Ibid., 2.713.

AN ARIAN REPLY

Isaac were, in some sense, pre-created, i.e., *with God from the beginning*. The divine passive "were pre-created" indicates that God was the active Creator. It would seem very strange to argue from this passage that these two patriarchs *literally existed* before the Genesis creation.

All in all, it seems that the preexistence spoken of in the Prayer to Joseph involves Abraham and Isaac as existing notionally and conceptually with God from the beginning, giving them a higher status worthy of the founding fathers of Israelite religion.[4]

The sum of Smith's argument regarding this text is that "it seems strange" that these persons would be literal persons existing before the Genesis creation. It would seem less strange if an entity in the literature is actually speaking to others in the same context. It would have been helpful to have included that in the argument.

I do think it was helpful for Smith (following Raymond Brown) to point out the misunderstanding motif in which Jesus is thought to be saying things that he was not particularly intending. It is in that light that Jesus says in John 8:57 that Abraham rejoiced to see Jesus' day and was glad. I make a *mild* grammatical argument in my response to Smith's main presentation to the effect that the language of John 8:58 would allow Jesus to be saying that he existed *before* Abraham came into existence, as certainly as Job said that Jobab had been his name before the verb indicating he was named Job. So Smith sees here an argument about rank in the word "before." The Jews were misunderstanding Jesus to be speaking inappropriately if they thought he was saying at an age of less than fifty he existed *before* Abraham. But even Raymond Brown says that "the readers are expected to understand."[5] The rendering I am arguing for ("I have been [in existence] before Abraham came into existence") and the utilization of the concept of *anamnesis* instead of *prolepsis* as a construct for interpretation, are reasonable, especially given literature with which the Jews were familiar (e.g., Jacob's comments about preexistence in the *Prayer of Joseph*).

The affirmation that Jesus makes, in plain language, is that he existed with God, that he had glory with God, and that he desired to have it *again*. It is proper for people to hear Jesus saying, "Give me the glory that I had with you *back* again," because he does not have it at the time he is speaking. We have seen in this debate, most recently with Jacob as the speaker in the

---

4. Smith, "Defining Jewish Preexistence."
5. Brown, *Introduction to John*, 288.

THE SON OF GOD

passage Smith cites (*Pr. Jos.*, Frag. A, 1–3, 9), that there were different divine figures present with God, Jesus included. At the very least, the language can be read that way. Most significantly, Smith leaves as relatively unchallenged my observation that the Son of Man figure, mentioned in the *Similitudes of Enoch* (*1 Enoch* 37–71), demonstrates a "preexistent Son of Man" in the mind of Second Temple Jews. Therefore, one should infer that he concedes the strength of this document (*1 Enoch*), during the Second Temple period, to reflect a Jewish allowance of understanding the presence of preexisting entities. As Erho has observed, "No scholar of early Judaism in the past forty years has ventured to date this document outside of the period 50 BCE to 100 CE."[6] Second Temple-Jewish literature significantly informed the writers of the New Testament documents, molding an understanding of the texts speaking of who and what Christ could have been understood to be.[7] Even if John were written as late as 100 CE, it was not as if the writer suddenly ceased to think according to Second Temple constructs. Jesus, as John presents him in John 17, speaks as one who existed, woodenly and literally, with the Father. He had glory, which he laid aside, when he became a man. Smith argues in John 17:22 that the disciples *now have* glory stored up for them, but when Jesus prays in John 17:5, he speaks of glory that he *does not presently have*. This problem is as easily, if not more easily, resolved by admitting Jesus had in mind two types of glory.

Conscious Existence as Creator in 1 Corinthians 8:6

I think that sometimes it is so very easy to miss what is contextually obvious. First Corinthians strikes me as a practical book written to a church with a host of problems. The church was beset with divisions brought about by an improper understanding of unity, which should have been based not so much in those who carried the gospel message as much as in the content of it. Consequently there were appeals to exalt the one who baptized another as opposed to following Christ (1 Cor 1:13–17), to appeal to individual superiority of knowledge and wisdom as opposed to seeking to immerse oneself in Christ (1 Cor 1:18–2:5). They needed to understand that God was the source of wisdom and that ministers within the faith were God's servants whose work with individuals would be revealed for what it was, "wood, hay,

---

6. Erho, "Similitudes of Enoch," 509.

7. "A date around AD 80 would satisfy the evidence," says George R. Beasley-Murray (*John*, lxxviii). Cp. Robinson, *Redating*, 307.

AN ARIAN REPLY

straw" or "gold, silver, costly stones," metaphors for the sort of disciple building that would be obvious at the tail end of one's ministry (1 Cor 3:10–15). Paul wanted the Corinthian readers to recognize his authority as an apostle of Christ sent to mold them into the image of Christ by imitating him and those who had already done so whom he had sent their way, namely, Timothy (1 Cor 4:1–17). Paul takes up a disciplinary tone addressing issues of immorality in the church (1 Cor 5:1–12; 6:12–20); Christians going to court against one another (1 Cor 6:1–11); confusion over matters of marriage, divorce, and remarriage (1 Cor 7:1–40); and matters of Christian behavior in a pagan world where believers were weak in faith and in understanding of even who Almighty God really is as compared with others who had superior knowledge of this matter (1 Cor 8:1–13). It is in this last context that Paul, speaking to believers who did have superior knowledge about God's nature, wants to advise the Christians about how to interact with other Christians with deficiencies in fundamental knowledge.

Christians who were mature knew that God was ruler over the universe, but some were prideful, or puffed up, about their knowledge (1 Cor 8:1–3). Consequently, they knew that there is no such thing as an idol in light of the knowledge that there is but one God the Father and one Lord Jesus the Messiah sent by God (1 Cor 8:4–6). Paul speaks specifically in the context of laying out how God brought about creation:

1. God exists alone as ruler in the world (v. 4).
2. God's sovereignty stands despite pretenders to his position (v. 5).
3. God is, then, the *source* of all creation from whom (Greek, *ek hou*, "out of whom," v. 6a) are all things.
4. Jesus is mediator, as Smith has correctly pointed out, but it is Paul's point that he is mediator in the sense of the "means through whom" the "all things" previously considered come about. Jesus is God's *agent*. The Greek *dia hou* is a prepositional phrase denoting "means through which" a thing is accomplished. "All things," meaning the created order, as well as "we," exist as members of creation (v. 6b). While it is not a primary point of the discussion to emphasize that Jesus is, in a sense, a secondary cause of creation, *it is an important point nonetheless*. Christ as the *dia hou* factor, "the means through whom" physical and spiritual identity come about, is a powerful incidental affirmation made in both 1 Cor 8:6 and Col 1:16, which uses nearly the same prepositional phrase (*dia autou*).

THE SON OF GOD

That Jesus is Lord over even those believed to be over the underworld goes without saying, and Paul's simple point is that knowledge of this tangent on who created the physical and spiritual universe can, even in itself, be a cause of division: Those who do not understand that there is no such thing as a person or "god" behind an idol will be caused to stumble in thinking that there is, if Christians can go in a marketplace and buy pagan-defiled goods and eat what is sold there (i.e., meat sacrificed to idols). Jesus is Lord because "all things come about through him, including our own existence." But neither knowledge about God the source of creation, nor his agent of creation Jesus the Lord and Christ—and what one does in the marketplace, given such knowledge—should be a cause of division in the Corinthian church.

Col 1:16–Agent of Creation ... Stated Again

Apparently Paul's point in 1 Cor 8:6 is to use creation language to establish how Christians with knowledge about the sublime nature of the one God and one Lord should treat one another. The apostle's point in Col 1:15 is establishing the preeminence of Christ in order to counter false philosophies, teachings about the superiority of angels (Col 2:6–15), and rogue legalistic Jewish influences in the church (Col :16). Believers have been transferred to Christ's kingdom (Col 1:13). They are redeemed and they are forgiven (Col 1:14). This is all possible through the preeminent Christ. The language is remarkably similar to 1 Cor 8:6, but the point is the same: Christ is the agent "through whom" (*dia autou*) all things are created. They are also created, Paul adds, "*for* him" (*eis auton*).

Firstborn of/over Creation

I do not have strong opinions about how to understand the term "firstborn" in Col 1:15. One who was chronologically firstborn could also have preeminence in everything in a Jewish family. So says Joseph of Manasseh (Gen 48:18), but David is firstborn because of his position (Ps 89:27). Jesus could be firstborn of all creation in a chronological sense, as the first of things created or brought into existence.[8]

---

8. For those who refer to Col 1:16, which says he is the creator of "all things," keep in mind that Eve is the "mother of all living" without being her own mother (Gen 3:20).

AN ARIAN REPLY
Final Thoughts

I can know who someone isn't without knowing who that person is without being logically inconsistent. I can look across the street and see that a person walking there is *not my brother* without knowing who they are. I can know, from biblical affirmation what Jesus is not (e.g., he is not an angel, according to Heb 1:5ff) without knowing precisely what he is; nor do I need to think that Scripture has revealed every detail about all the divine entities that may exist. So if I cannot speak beyond this—"God gave Jesus life in preexistent time, therefore he owes his origin to him"—that should be sufficient. I do not become confused when entities having important roles in Scripture are "never described or identified in any meaningful detail within the Bible."

I have never lost a moment's sleep wondering about the minute details of Enoch or Melchizedek. It is just such a lack of data that allowed Second Temple writers to speculate about them as being preexistent entities, and consequently they are important to *this* debate. Rather than think there is absolutely nothing about Jesus as a preexistent being, the identity of *Logos* of God or Word of God that became Jesus is not dissatisfying to me; and it is not that I do not have a penchant for reflection—I do not think Smith has shown how the miraculous birth from a virgin can be any more human than causing a preexistent entity to become human in birth. Enoch, Jacob, and others preexisted their human existence according to Second Temple-Jewish literature. This is problematic for a point of view that says no one could have imagined such. If I have not mentioned some things directly, perhaps I felt they were implied in other matters I did address. Smith says he appreciates my attention to detail; perhaps I missed some things over the course of the discussion that will better be served on another occasion in another forum.

I am grateful for Smith's participation in this debate. There is a sense in which he stands on the shoulders of others who have written and spoken before him, and he has expanded on their thought, lending clarification and focus to a number of the primary points of the Socinian christological position he has embraced. I have appreciated his kind regard, even in texts and calls between our posts, made in order to properly represent my view of these matters. "It's all good," as they say, and makes for an accurate and hopefully useful study tool for those who will read the discussion.

THE SON OF GOD
REPLY TO LEE IRONS

Arian? Jehovah's Witness?

If anyone else had mentioned this I would think that he or she was trying to prejudice the reader to avoid a fair discussion. But I had lunch yesterday, and was accosted—no, better to say *approached*—by a Spanish *Testigo de Jeova*—a kind Mexican American woman, a Jehovah's Witness, who came up to my Ford Escape while I was eating a lunch of chicken pot pie and grapefruit juice and listening to Rush Limbaugh. She wanted to talk to me about the kingdom of God and Armageddon and wanted me to tell her what I knew about those things. We didn't disagree much, so long as I was answering her questions. She assumed I agreed with her on every point, and there was much she said with which I did agree.

Even so, I *don't* believe Jesus to be Michael the Archangel, as the Jehovah's Witnesses do. I *don't* hold that their organizational structure is God's chosen faithful and discreet slave here on the earth. I *don't* believe one ought to neglect understanding that there is a sense in which we are a part of God's kingdom *now*. And on and on I could go. But I do agree with them that only the Father is God Almighty and that he had a special mission for his authorized Son of God—the Christ—to teach and preach about the eternal kingdom.

I also would not have banished Arius back in the fourth century, as we would have had a lot on which to agree. I prefer to just call myself a strict monotheist. That probably isn't good enough for Irons, though scholar that he is, he correctly represents Arianism connecting me with it. Irons and Basil of Caesarea both knew that there are two realities, creation and divinity with no hybrids, so Irons has decided that Arians, who do not believe Jesus is Almighty God, believe that he is of the created order. Maybe that is right, but I am content to say, biblically, that God gave Jesus life (says Jesus, John 5:26; 6:57).

Irons thinks I am contradicting myself to say that Jesus, as per Col 1:16 and Heb 1:3 created "all things," since he himself is part of the creation, and would, of necessity, have had to create himself. I actually think that is about as logical as saying that Eve, "the mother of all living" (Gen 3:20), was mother of herself. I do not even need to place the word "other," as in, "he created all *other* things," because I think it would be implied.

Irons refers to Ps 102:25–27, which reads one way in the Hebrew Masoretic text used in most Bibles. I know that the discussion involved is intricate on the matter, but the author of the book of Hebrews quotes the Septuagint text at Ps 102:25–27 in which the addressee, one called "Lord," is said to have laid the foundation of the earth, and the heavens are the work of his hands. Also what was created will perish and wear out as opposed to the Creator who is the same and whose years have no end. I would say that this is true from the point of the creation of things onward. The text says nothing about the origin of the Creator in the passage. I do know that Rev 1:18 says that Jesus was dead, but that God alone is immortal (1 Tim 6:16). Irons suggests that for one to be a son of God one has to have a divine nature. I do believe that in John 1:1 Jesus is adjectively "divine" without being the one who is named as God. "In the beginning was the Word [the one who became Jesus], and the Word was with God [the Father] and the Word was divine," but certainly the Word was not God the Father. I do not think Irons believes this, since he has cited Daniel Wallace to translate the second *theos* in John 1:1 as "divine" rather than "God" as in "and the Word was God."

Self-Consciousness as the Son of God

Possibly the crux of Irons's argument rests on three points. The first is what he calls the self-consciousness of Jesus as Son of God. For Irons, Jesus' awareness of his Sonship to the Father is very important to his argument. I think that, for all his argument about when Jesus is called Christ as set against how early he is called God's Son, the evidence given thus far, if carefully studied, will lead to a fair conclusion in anyone's mind. Second Samuel 7:12–16 on this issue is fundamental. The passage sets up an extremely important biblical precedent, namely that God's earthly anointed was his son. The dynasty of David became a significant theological line connecting Old and New Testaments. Whether it was Solomon as David's son recognized as God's son in that first passage or another king of Israel recognized as God's son in a royal psalm (importantly Pss 2 and 89), the term continues to function as the main designation of the relationship between God and his anointed king.

Jesus as the last one in the dynasty is most exalted, but that, in and of himself, does not make him God. He is called God's Son as regards his lineage in Luke 1:30–35, and the parallel nature of the terms "Christ" and "Son of God" are revealed through a fair analysis of the terms as mentioned in the Synoptic Gospels and in a careful consideration of what was said at the trial

THE SON OF GOD

of Jesus. While "son of" certainly has to do with one's nature as being that of the father named, that thought would not override the idea that God's Son is God's Messiah, and while that is a very important office in biblical theology, exalted as it is, it does not make one share in the identity of God. Jesus' self-awareness came because he remembered who he was and what would be the result if he stayed the course: He had glory coming his way, indeed glory that he had with the Father in preexistent time (John 17:3–5).

Creator

Jesus is creator because God wanted to use him in that role. God is the source out of which (Gk., *ek*) creation comes and Jesus is the means through which (Gk., *dia*) God accomplished that in preexistent time for him (John 1:1–2; 1 Cor 8:6, Col 1:16)

Aseity

Irons makes the statement that the Son, as a non-created entity, "has life in himself" in the same way that God has "life in himself" and he quotes John 5:26 just as I did. However, I did note that Jesus said that this was not an innate reality. Indeed he said, "the Father *has granted* the Son to have life in himself," so I will not have the text say otherwise.

Second Temple Perspectives

I think I understand why Irons devalues Second Temple-Jewish thought. I want to be careful here because I certainly share what I believe to be Irons's perspective that the Scripture alone has absolute authority. I know Irons to be a craftsman at exegesis, interpretation of the biblical text. So I know that he believes that one should understand words and thoughts in context. I would affirm that the New Testament nowhere articulates God to consist of multiple figures. Irons grandiloquently recognizes that a major reconceptualization of the very nature of God himself is revealed, "blazed out from the lightning strike of the incarnation, life, death, resurrection, and exaltation of the Son of God." But it is just that testimony of the record of the apostles' doctrine and preaching (*kerygma*) that Irons should see causes him problems.

AN ARIAN REPLY

Apostolic Preaching: What Was It?

I am tempted to appeal primarily to Jesus' personal ministry to discover what he believed about the nature of God. I might, for example want to go to Mark 12:28–29 and hear Jesus parley with a scribe who asks him this question: "Of all the commandments, which is the most important?" Of this, Kenneth Richard Samples said, "The Shema, which Jews continue to use today, consists of the prayerful reciting of Deut 6:4–9. *Shema* is Hebrew for 'hear,' and verse four appropriately begins as follows: 'Hear, O Israel: The LORD our God, the LORD is one.'"[9] Anthony Buzzard goes on to say of this that "Jesus as the founding teacher of the Christian religion was no less insistent on the Shema as the guide to true theology and faith" (Mark 12:28–34).[10]

R. T. France points out that: "Only Mark records Jesus' use of Deut 6:4 (the theological preamble) along with the ethical demand of Deut 6:5. It is the latter, of course, which is the point of the question: Dt. 6:4 is not in itself a 'command.'"[11] Jesus himself points out that *his* teaching was not the end-all of the message he wanted the world to hear. Rather the fullness would be revealed later: "I have much more to say to you [disciples], more than you can now bear. But when he, the Spirit of truth, comes, he will guide you into all truth" (John 16:12–13). The disciples began their preaching after the resurrection, which is, of course, Irons's marker for us from which point forward we will see the flash of revelation as to the nature of God. It is in the apostolic preaching that we are to learn all truth.

God Makes Jesus Lord and Christ (Acts 2:14–36)

It is in Acts 2 that the Holy Spirit arrives and the disciples begin to proclaim their message. What do they reveal on this the birthday of the church? Peter reveals that it was prophesied by Joel that the Holy Spirit would descend as it did on this Pentecost day. Peter makes a distinction between God and Jesus of Nazareth, "*a man accredited by God* to you by miracles, wonders and signs, which God did among you through him" (Acts 2:22). He speaks of Jesus as "*This man* [who] was handed over to you by God's set purpose and foreknowledge" and who was "put to death" on a cross (v. 23), whom God

---

9. Cited in Buzzard, *Jesus Was Not a Trinitarian*, 7–8.
10. Ibid., 8.
11. France, *Mark*, 479.

THE SON OF GOD

raised from the dead (v. 24). He is identified as the resurrected Christ (v. 31), Jesus whom God raised to life (v. 32), referred to as "my Lord" seated next to God until God makes that Lord's enemies his footstool (vv. 34–35). He is the one Israel should know that *God made to be* both Lord and Christ (v. 36). The message is clear: Jesus is a human being who was put to death, raised from the dead, and exalted to the right hand of God by God. As Bruce concludes,

> He claimed to be the Messiah, the Son of the Blessed (Mark 14:61). The Sanhedrin *rejected* His claim as blasphemous, and condemned Him to death. But God vindicated His claim as true, and brought Him back from death, exalting him at His own right hand as Lord and Messiah.[12]

A Prophet From Among Your Own People (Acts 3:12-26)

A short while later, the apostles Peter and John have an opportunity to preach to onlookers after a miraculous healing of a blind man. Peter declares that it was the God of Abraham, Isaac, and Jacob who glorified his servant Jesus, whom they handed over to be killed (Acts 3:13). Peter says they killed him, but that he was raised from the dead by God (Acts 3:15). He identifies Jesus as "a prophet like [Moses] from among your own people" (Acts 3:22), and as *Abraham's offspring*, a servant whom God raised up (Acts 3:25–26).

Descendant of David (Acts 13:16-41)

Paul and Barnabas preach in Pisidian Antioch announcing to the people that God had promised a *descendant of David* would come on their behalf (Acts 13:22–23). Salvation was promised to Gentiles to come through Jesus who was crucified, buried, and raised up from the dead by God (Acts 13:26–30, 36–37). It is through him that forgiveness of sins can be theirs (Acts 13:38).

---

12. Bruce, *Acts*, 73.

AN ARIAN REPLY

An Appointed Man (Acts 17:29-31)

God recognizes Gentiles as his offspring, and he has overlooked their spiritual ignorance. But he wants them to repent of their sins, for he will judge the world *through a man* he has appointed. The evidence? He raised him from the dead.

All of these passages recording the apostolic preaching reveal that Jesus was:

1. A man attested by God
2. A descendant of Abraham
3. A prophet from among their own people
4. A descendant of David
5. A crucified individual
6. A dead individual
7. A buried individual
8. A resurrected individual
9. An exalted individual

In summary, the apostolic preaching was of one who was a literal *human* descendant of *Abraham* and of *David*. He was *a human prophet* who was *crucified*, *dead*, and *buried*, and *resurrected* and *exalted* by God. Where in any of this is there mention of a person sharing in the identity of God? The silence is deafening.

What has proven to be offensive, then, and which Irons is quick to try to refute, is any notion that would make a mere mortal being equal with God. Like the Jews of old, we look for the stones for anyone, "a mere man," who would claim to be God (see John 10:32–33). When I point out the existence of Yahweh-functioning human or angelic figures, I am trying to interact with the present scholarly world. Of course, it annoys me that so often the language of scholars seems to require the biblical text to accommodate it. I am on the same page with Irons if he is saying that what the Scripture says is right. And it does not need to be backed up by any contemporary literature. Indeed, "Let God be true and every man a liar!" (Rom 3:4).

But I find it interesting that the Second Temple-Jewish literature, with which, as we have seen, Irons *is* conversant, does place in the expectation

THE SON OF GOD

of the Jews of the period the concept of men and of angels so exalted as to be seated next to God, to engage in the judgment prerogatives of God, and to even have the name of God, with some having this status in preexistence and later bringing it to earth. I will still maintain that biblical writers can be seen as speaking of an exalted man, not because it is in Second Temple Judaism, but because that is what the biblical data say is so about Jesus. The literature contemporary with the New Testament demonstrates that Jews could have conceived of the Messiah in such terms.

Enoch, the Son of Man Figure

Irons challenges my understanding of the Enochic Son of Man. Irons looks at three verses that I contend reveal "worship" of the exalted son of man in *1 Enoch*. Irons argues that it is not a case of a creature receiving divine worship, but of a transcendent angelic figure who represents God and receives prostration (not divine worship) as the representative of God. While one could say that the son of man figure is an angelic being, this does not preclude the notion that the son of man figure is Enoch himself. Enoch identifies himself in *1 En.* 71:5 as the son of man and is addressed as such by an angel a few verses later: "You, son of man, who art born in righteousness and upon whom righteousness has dwelt, the righteousness of the Antecedent of Time will not forsake you" (*1 En.* 71:14).[13] If Enoch is the son of man figure as suggested by this verse, we are presented with a divine being who was incarnate and later exalted to God's throne and worshiped by mankind. In *1 En.* 62:6 and 63:2 identical language, "bless" and "glorify," is used to articulate worship of the son of man figure and the worship of God. The notion of a late conversion for the worshipers is equally true in the worship of God (*1 En.* 63:1), so there is no distinction between the worship of the son of man figure and the worship of God.

Furthermore, Irons's observations do not really transcend my own. In his footnote 6, Irons presupposes intention in making his argument. It has been my consistent position that Jesus is *not* Almighty God. And in that light, he could not, in the most absolute sense, share in the identity of Yahweh. So as the king of Israel and Yahweh can, as says the King James Version, receive "worship," I take it no further than that. Jesus is God's anointed—indeed, his *final* messenger (Heb 1:1–3). And as the princes of Israel before him could appropriately receive prostration (*proskyneō* in the

13. ET: *OTP* 1.50.

AN ARIAN REPLY

LXX and *shachah* in the Hebrew at 2 Chr 29:20), so also could Jesus of Nazareth. I bear in mind that the eschatological end-point of all this is that Jesus will hand over the kingdom he has received (Cp. Acts 2:36; Dan 7:13; Mark 14:62) *back* to the Father who gave it to him, and God will become "all in all" (1 Cor 15:28). Then the Father will rise above any authoritative status he has given to the Messiah (Matt 9:5–8; 28:18; Phil 2:9–11).

As to this not being a matter of an angelic figure receiving divine worship, let it first be understood that an angel is "divine" in a strict sense as it may also rightly be called a created entity. And it is pointless to quibble over the words "prostration" and "worship" when the whole matter at hand is actually summed up in the concept of a person's "intentions." One falls prostrate before God in worship. One rightly "worships" by prostrating himself, so long as absolute deity is acknowledged. If the Apocalypse angel hesitates to receive John's prostration, why may it not be because he sensed what might be John's intention? And recall that it is an angel who requires obeisant behavior of Moses in Exod 3:5–6 (cp. Acts 7:30–33), yet he can call himself Yahweh since he is God's agent carrying God's name (Exod 23:21).

Yahoel

Irons challenges my understanding of Yahoel, and he asks regarding this angel, "In what sense is this figure bearing the divine name?" This is important if Irons, along with Bauckham, believes that bearing God's name places one in the divine identity. As I mentioned before, however, this reasoning would make the angel share in the identity of God, which I doubt either Bauckham or Irons wants to do. Irons's primary point seems to be that "The Creator-creature distinction is not compromised by the *Apocalypse of Abraham*'s depiction of Yahoel." I have no argument with him on this. I do not think it is compromised if I say Jesus is also God's vice-regent, temporarily placed in a position of authority. (See 1 Cor 15:23–23, where Paul affirms that Jesus will return the kingdom he was given in Dan 7:13 back to God who, in his own identity, will be "all in all.") I believe I am accurately representing who Jesus is in the New Testament depiction of him.

Melchizedek

Irons challenges my understanding of the Melchizedek figure. Melchizedek's ability to exercise divine prerogatives, the fact that he can be recognized as *elohim,* and even his passive involvement in atonement of the sons of light all indicate that he is an angelic *creature*, to be sure. And that figure is said not to violate the Creator-creature distinction. Again, I have no argument, but my agreement with Irons on this is not simply that Melchizedek is regarded as a mere angel. Angel or not, God is the one who dispenses prerogatives of authority. Melchizedek does so in the Qumranic literature. Jesus does so in the New Testament. I am merely saying that Jesus is not presented as being something other than what could have been expected by a typical informed reader of Second Temple-Jewish literature.

There is no explicit teaching that God consists of multiple figures. These readers would not see Jesus as being on the side of the Creator. Jesus participates in creation, but his role is that of an intermediate. If we are looking for a new interpretative flash of christological enlightenment, it is simply not in our New Testament materials. What *is* new is God's plan and willingness to work through a descendant of Abraham and messianic member of the Davidic dynasty to bring about the redemption of Jew and Gentile through Jesus the Messiah, as Paul indicates to his Ephesians readers:

> Surely you have heard about the administration of God's grace that was given to me for you, that is, the mystery made known to me by revelation, as I have already written briefly. In reading this, then, you will be able to understand my insight into the mystery of Christ, which was not made known to men in other generations as it has now been revealed by the Spirit to God's holy apostles and prophets. This mystery is that through the gospel the Gentiles are heirs together with Israel, members together of one body, and sharers together in the promise in Christ Jesus (Eph 3:2–6).

Summary

Irons fairly represents what I am trying to do with arguments about the Enochic Son of Man, the angel Yahoel, and Melchizedek as understood in the Qumran writings. It was understood that God was acting within his prerogative to exalt men and angels. It does not follow, however, that God's exalting such individuals is a marker that the ones exalted possess ontological equality with God or that they are partakers in "the divine identity." This has never been the understanding of agency in Jewish literature. Jesus should be seen, I would argue, as one who is not God, but is his supreme representative who should be treated as one standing in the place of God

AN ARIAN REPLY

with whatever rights and privileges God has for him. Jesus receives honor, for example, because the Father appoints that he should (John 5:23).

So long as one's intention is not to make Jesus equal to the Father, there is nothing blasphemous in this. Jesus was not self-consciously one with God in an ontological sense; oneness with God is to be understood, rather, in a sense of unity, a oneness that could be shared even by his human disciples/brothers (John 17:22–23; Heb 2:17). No secondary figures whom I mention ever claim to be the Son of God in a way that made them equal to God. But it is also true that Jesus never made such a claim. Certainly the Jews *thought* he was doing that, as seen in the passages Raymond Brown has identified as part of the misunderstanding motif (see note 5 above). But I would argue that there is not a single passage that can pass muster in which one can clearly determine that Jesus ever claimed, or allowed a charge to stand that he was claiming, to be God Almighty. I use that language. Irons and Bauckham use the language of sharing in the identity of God. I do not think either of them have fairly, or clearly, drawn out the implications of what that means. Irons will not go so far as to say that Jesus is Yahweh, although he admits the existence of at least two individuals who can be "identified" as God—namely an individual called the Father and an individual called the Son. This may be a legitimate strand of Trinitarianism, but it still reads like binitarianism to me.

Final Words to Lee Irons

I met Lee Irons when he was a sophomore on the campus of UCLA around 1987. I've watched him preach the gospel in daunting open-air fora as well as represent his theological positions from the solitude of a theological library. I've watched him marry, father, provide, and pastor. I've given him a bed when he needed one and enjoyed the hospitality of his family and home as well. He has always been a Christian gentleman and scholar whose love of books (the Scriptures first!), whose appreciation of the old hymns and spiritual songs, and whose almost idyllic picture that I have seen of his committed family, have burnt perpetual memories of him in my mind. I've watched him deal with rejection, criticism, and even unfair regard with perfect poise. I do not know that I'd have the patience in similar circumstances. We've joyfully argued theologically for hours on many a night. We even have a good rental car story to tell! He's more like a brother than the dear friend that he, of course, is as well. And here he has been a more than

THE SON OF GOD

competent opponent representing a particular strand of the Trinitarian tradition in this tripartite discussion on Christology.

May God bless this discussion and use it to aid others in building on the continuing understanding that I hope we all seek to have.

Part Three

A SOCINIAN VIEW
Jesus, the Human Son of God

DUSTIN R. SMITH

INTRODUCTION

WHILE THE AIM OF this book is to present three different views concerning Jesus Christ's identity, there is one thing on which the contributors concur. We all agree that Jesus was, has been, and will continue to be a polarizing figure. Although the seventeenth chapter of John's Gospel records Jesus praying that his followers "be one, even as we are," today there exists more confusion concerning this important figure than there was two thousand years ago (John 17:11; 21–22).

I grew up attending conservative Christian congregations. Each of these churches subscribed to the doctrine of the Trinity, wherein Jesus was taught as being, in some sense, both God and human. This was preached from the pulpit, proclaimed through worship lyrics, and drilled into the minds of those who attended Sunday school. However, it was not until I departed to college that I started reading the Bible for myself. I was attempting to take my faith into my own hands. As I read through the pages of Scripture, I continued coming across verses and passages which seemed, on the surface, to call into question my understanding of Jesus' identity. So I did what almost every curious teenager does when there is a burning question inside their head: I sought convincing answers. This pursuit, along with many others which resulted from my own personal study of the Bible,

THE SON OF GOD

eventually directed me to change majors, change schools, and ultimately change my mind on many of the doctrines with which I was raised.

My contribution to this book is the result of pursuing the question concerning the identity of Jesus which I have worked at as an academic and a personal quest for over ten years. Having worked with the original languages of the Bible, engaged with modern scholarly works, explored the history of Christian thought, and applied critical thinking, I am now convinced that Jesus the Messiah is *God's human agent* in the plan of redemption. Jesus is the Son of God, a person (or self) distinct from the only true God, Yahweh.

I have structured my initial presentation of Jesus' identity in what I consider a natural and logical progression of topics. I will begin by looking at the expectations of the Messiah from the Hebrew Bible while at the same time keeping an eye on how those texts were interpreted in the Second Temple period. From there I will look at the birth of the Messiah and examine some key data from the relevant texts, especially the two lengthy birth narratives located in Matthew and Luke. Subsequently, I will direct my attention to surveying the life and teaching of Jesus, particularly how both Jesus viewed himself and how others viewed him. From there, I will give attention to the importance of the suffering and death of the Messiah. Afterwards, Jesus' resurrection and exaltation will be given careful consideration. This chapter's study will end by drawing attention to relevant texts which describe the return of Jesus to consummate the kingdom of God upon the earth.

THE EXPECTATIONS OF THE MESSIAH

During the Second Temple period, the office of Israel's Messiah carried with it certain expectations. In particular, there were specific qualifications which would either justify one's claim to messiahship or exclude him altogether. By drawing on passages in the Hebrew Bible, Jews found a number of criteria which they deemed authoritative in describing the promised Messiah's identity.

The first passage I wish to examine is Gen 3:15. This passage details how the seed of the woman will victoriously crush the head of the serpent's offspring. Many of the Jewish Targums identified the woman's seed as the "King Messiah."[1] This messianic interpretation was later picked up by Jus-

---

1. *Ps.-J.*, *Neof.*, and *Frg. Tg.* on Gen. 3:15.

A SOCINIAN VIEW

tin Martyr and Irenaeus in the second century CE. The point which bears importance for this study is the fact that the expectation of the messiah was tied to Eve's *human* descendant.

Toward the end of Genesis there is an account where the patriarch Jacob gathers his children at this death bed in order to confer upon them personalized blessings. Beginning in Gen 49:8, Jacob promises his son Judah that his clan will receive praise, victory, and prostration. Judah is likened to a lion's cub, admired for his ferocity. Furthermore, he is prophetically promised that the scepter of kingship will certainly not depart from his tribe, indicating an enduring regime to be realized in his descendants (Gen 49:10). This passage was seized upon and interpreted messianically by many Jewish readers, especially at Qumran.[2] The *Genesis Pesher* (4Q252) is indicative of how Gen 49:8–10 was read in conjunction with other messianic texts:

> A scepter shall not be removed from the tribe of Judah. While Israel has the dominion, there will not lack someone who sits on the throne of David. For the *ruler's staff* is the covenant of royalty, the clans of Israel are the standards. Until *the Messiah of justice comes, the branch of David*. For to him and his seed has been given the covenant of royalty over the people for all everlasting generations (4Q252 5:1–4).[3]

The translator of the LXX similarly read the passage messianically by reworking the Hebrew of "scepter" into a single ruler.[4] In short, Gen 49:8–10 was widely read as an indicator that the coming messianic ruler would descend from Judah's tribe.

Balaam's oracle, recorded in Num 24:17, reports how a star shall come from Jacob and a scepter shall rise from Israel to subdue God's enemies. Rabbi Akiba's assertion that Balaam's "star" was pointing toward Simon bar Kosiba, otherwise hailed as Bar Kochba ("son of the star"), demonstrates that the messianic reading of this passage was highly regarded.[5] Similar readings are attested prior to Akiba. The LXX rendered the "scepter" as a

---

2. *T. Judah* 24.5; *4 Ezra* 11.37; 12.31–32; *Tg. Neof., Ps.-J.* on Gen 49:9–12; *Midr. Rab.* Gen. 97; 1QSb 5.20–29; 4QPBless. Bauckham rightly draws attention to the fact that the Qumran references combine the "lion of the tribe of Judah" with "the root of David" titles. *Climax of Prophecy*, 214.

3. Translation and italics are my own.

4. *ouk ekleipsei archōn ex Iouda*.

5. *j. Taan.* 68d.

THE SON OF GOD

human being,[6] a reading preferred and quoted by Philo of Alexandria.[7] The *Targum Onkelos* reads the oracle as "when a *king* shall arise out of Jacob and the *Messiah will be anointed* from Israel."[8] The author of the *Testament of Judah* likewise observed strong messianic overtones in Balaam's oracle:

> And after this there shall arise for you a Star from Jacob in peace: And a man shall arise from my posterity like the sun of righteousness.... This is *the Shoot of God Most High*; this is the foundation for the life of all humanity. Then he will illumine the scepter of my kingdom and from your root will arise *the Shoot*, and through it will arise the rod of righteousness for the nations, to judge and to save all that call on the Lord (*T. Jud.* 24.1–6).

Num 24:17 was widely regarded as a messianic passage indicating that the coming ruler would be a human ruler descended from Jacob.

It is almost certain that the "prophet like Moses" from Deut 18:15–19 was considered messianically in some circles. This passage describes how Yahweh will raise up a prophet like Moses who will come from "among your brothers." God will put his words into the mouth of this prophet, who will in turn speak as God's authorized spokesman. At Qumran, Deut 18:18–19 was placed alongside the messianic Num 24:17.[9] According to the author of 1 Maccabees, the expectation for this prophet was still active.[10] Overall, the anticipation provoked by Deut 18 envisaged an authoritative prophetic figure bearing the very oracles of God and coming from among the Jewish people.

One of the most influential texts within messianism was 2 Sam 7:12–16. The prophet Nathan informs King David that his dynasty, throne, and kingdom will endure forever. David's descendant, according to 2 Sam 7:12, "will come forth from you."[11] This effectively maintained the Davidic line of kings and the tribe of Judah's rulership. "Son of David," as I will shortly demonstrate, was a widely recognized messianic title during the Second

---

6. *anastēsetai anthrōpos ex Israēl*

7. *Mos.* 1:290; *Praem.* 95. Philo's reading should be considered weighty because he was disinterested in messianism.

8. Similarly, *Tg. Ps.-J.*; *Tg. Neof.*; and *Frg. Tg.*

9. 4QTestim (4Q175).

10. 1 Macc 4:46; 9:27; cf. 14:41: "the Jews and the priests were well pleased that Simon should be their governor and high priest forever until the faithful prophet should arise" (*heōs tou anastēnai prophētēn piston*). The use of *anistēmi* in regard to this prophet is dependent upon Deut 18:15–18 LXX where the verb occurs twice.

11. Unless otherwise indicated, all Scripture quotations are from the NASB.

A SOCINIAN VIEW

Temple period. It is highly noteworthy that God continues to reference David's seed when he says, "I will be a father to him and he will be a son to Me" (2 Sam 7:14).[12] Sonship therefore pertained to the role of kingship in addition to bearing a unique relationship with Israel's God.

The motif of kingly rule combined with the promise given to David's offspring took shape with another title, the "Branch of David." This is picked up by the prophet Jeremiah. In Jer 23:5 Yahweh declares that, "days are coming . . . when I will raise up for David a righteous Branch, and He will reign as king and act wisely." *Targum Jonathan* interpreted this passage as saying that God will raise up for David "the righteous Messiah." The oracle is nearly repeated in Jer 33:15–17, "In those days and at that time I will cause a righteous Branch of David to spring forth; and he shall execute justice and righteousness on the earth . . . David shall never lack a man to sit on the throne of the house of Israel." Although Jeremiah knew that the Davidic line of kings was temporarily suspended in 586 BCE, hope for a future king and Israel's restoration was nevertheless maintained. This offshoot (Branch) of David is identified in Jer 33:17 as a human figure. *Targum Jonathan* interpreted Jer 33:15 as "I will raise up for David the righteous Messiah." The prophet Zechariah moreover contributes to the expectation of the coming Branch of David in two passages.[13] One in particular records the prophet's oracle: "Thus says Yahweh of hosts, behold, a man whose name is Branch,[14] for he will branch out from where he is; and he will build the temple of Yahweh" (Zech 6:12). This figure was regarded by *Targum Jonathan* as the "man Messiah." In short, both Jeremiah and Zechariah describe the coming Branch as a human figure who will function in an authoritative position.

The Qumran document 4QFlor combines the Davidic Branch motif with both the promise of sonship expressed in 2 Sam 7:12–14 and the restoration envisioned in Amos 9:11:

> YHWH declares to you that he will build you a house. I will raise up your seed after you and establish the throne of his kingdom forever. I will be a father to him and he will be a son to me. This refers to the *Branch of David*, who will arise with the Interpreter of

---

12. 2 Sam 7:14b describes God's chastisement for those descendants of David who sin. The biblical chronicler regarded 7:14a as an indicator of the coming Messiah and omitted the statement concerning chastisement (1 Chr 17:11–14).

13. Zech 3:8; 6:12. In 3:8 *Targum Jonathan* interprets "Branch" with "the Messiah, and he will be revealed."

14. Literally: "sprout."

THE SON OF GOD

the law who will rise up in Zion on the last days, as it is written: I will raise up the hut of David which has fallen, this refers to the hut of David which has fallen, who will arise to save Israel.[15]

4QFlor overtly regards the human descendant of David as the messianic Branch, designated as the son of God. Along similar lines, 1QSa 2:11 looked forward to the moment "when God *begets* the Messiah."[16] These documents indicate that the Qumran Jews believed that the coming Messiah would be born in a manner which would involve God as the Father.

The hope of a messianic descendant from the line of David can be observed within the prophetic literature and the writings within the Hebrew Bible. Ps 18:50 declares that God gives salvation to His king, God's *mashiach*, to David and his seed forever. Similar words are expressed in Ps 89, wherein the psalmist encourages his readers, probably in the wake of the temple's destruction, by reminding them that David's seed and throne will endure forever (Ps 89:3-4, 28-29, 36-37). Yahweh promises in Ps 132:11 to confirm a sworn oath to David: "Of the fruit of your body I will set upon your throne," insisting on a lineal human descendant. Jeremiah likewise envisions a glorious future ("on that day") when the peoples will "serve Yahweh their God and David their king, whom I will raise up for them" (Jer 30:8-9). *Targum Jonathan* interprets this reference to David as "the Messiah, son of David, their king." Ezekiel states that Yahweh will set before Israel "one shepherd, My servant David," who will be a prince among them (Ezek 34:23-24).[17] The rabbis read Amos 9:11, where God promises to "raise up the fallen booth of David," as a reference to a single messianic figure.[18] In sum, the expectation for a Davidic descendant to be Messiah remained a strong conviction within Jewish circles.

The noteworthy "Son of Man" figure in Dan 7:13 evoked a variety of messianic readings. In this vision, Daniel witnesses what seems to be a human being (*bar enash*) described in deliberate contrast to four beasts. This

---

15. 4QFlor (= 4Q174) 1:10-13; cf. also the reference to the Branch (Shoot) in the Genesis Pesher and *T. Judah* 24.4-6, both cited above. Isa 11:1 demonstrates that the titles "Shoot" (*choter*) and "Branch" (*netser*) are synonymous. The Isaiah Pesher (4Q161 3:11-19) interprets the Shoot of Jesse (Isa 11:1) as the "shoot of David which will sprout in the final days."

16. Cf. 1QSa 2:14, 20 where the Messiah of Israel is clearly the one discussed.

17. Ezekiel later calls the coming servant David a "king" (Ezek 37:24-25). This passage was regarded as messianic by the Rabbis (*b. Sanh.* 98b) where the Messiah is called "the second David."

18. *b. Sanh.* 96b-97a.

A SOCINIAN VIEW

human figure approaches a distinct figure called the Ancient of Days (i.e., Yahweh). The Son of Man figure is subsequently given dominion, authority, and a kingdom, whereby all the peoples might serve him. The earliest interpretations of this Son of Man figure were messianic.[19] Rabbi Akiba notably suggested that the "thrones" set up in Dan 7:9 were discernible: "one is for him [God], the other for David" (*b. Sanh.* 38a). Akiba certainly had a candidate in mind, Simon bar Kosiba, whom Akiba regarded as the true son of David. Nevertheless, it seems fair to conclude that Dan 7:13 describes a human being receiving dominion and kingship from the Ancient of Days.

When the Hasmoneans took control of Israel in the second century BCE, some Jews reckoned their claim to kingship as a denial of the Davidic expectations. The *Psalms of Solomon* is one literary expression of such frustration. This document's expression of the coming Messiah draws on Ps 2 and Isaiah:

> See, Lord, and raise up for them their king, *the son of David*, to rule over your servant Israel in the time known to you, O God. Undergird him with the strength to destroy the unrighteous rulers, to purge Jerusalem from the gentiles who trample her to destruction; in wisdom and in righteousness to drive out the sinners from the inheritance; to smash the arrogance of sinners like a potter's jar; to shatter all their substance with an iron rod; to destroy the unlawful nations with the word of his mouth (*Ps. Sol.* 17:21–24).[20]

The first-century-BCE author of *Psalms of Solomon* seems to have regarded Isa 11:1–4 and Ps 2 as indicators of the coming warrior Messiah, who would be a descendant of David.

These passages from the Hebrew Bible and Jewish literature reflect the hopes and expectations concerning the coming Messiah. Notably, he is to be a legitimate member of the human race, from the seed of the woman, down through Jacob, Judah, and continuing in the seed of David. He will be a royal figure bearing authority from the one true God. It is striking that this promised descendant of David is never described in the Hebrew Bible as *already in existence*. Rather, the Messiah is a figure *yet to be born*, at which time God will be his Father and the Messiah will be God's son.

---

19. *4 Ezra* 13; *1 Enoch* 37–71 (esp. 46:1; 48:10; 52:4); *Num. Rab.* 13:14.
20. Drawing on Ps 2:2, 8–9; Isa 11:2, 4; 42:1–4.

THE SON OF GOD
THE BIRTH OF THE MESSIAH

The pages of the New Testament open in massive agreement with the promised expectation of a human Messiah. Matthew's Gospel begins with a lengthy attempt to place Jesus Christ in line with the Hebrew Bible's messianic hopes. The very first verse starts to build the case for the legitimacy of Jesus' messianic status: "The record of the *genesis* of Jesus Christ, son of David, son of Abraham" (Matt 1:1). This opening verse places considerable emphasis on the *genesis* of Jesus as the indicator of his coming into being at a specific moment.[21] The title "Son of David" connects Jesus with the lineal family tree of the ancient king. Furthermore, as the "Son of Abraham" Jesus remains firmly established as the human descendant in whom all of the Abrahamic promises will find their fulfillment. The passage continues with a lengthy list of genealogical names where Jesus' birth is traced all the way back to the patriarch Abraham. Of no small importance is the fact that Matthew uses the word "begat"[22] to connect one person to his son or daughter, using the standard Jewish formula "A begat B; B begat C."[23] Occasionally, the Matthean genealogy is even more explicit, stating that the person born came *out of* their respective mother.[24] The same preposition is used in Mat 1:16 to describe the birth of Jesus, who came *out of* Mary. This verse states that Joseph was the husband of Mary, out of whom Jesus was begotten.

Mat 1:18 sets forth how the begetting of Jesus took place: "Now the *genesis* of Jesus Christ was in this manner." The story notes how Joseph, upon realizing that Mary was pregnant, planned to send her away in secret. However, an angel of the Lord appeared to Joseph in a dream, unveiling an important truth. The angel said, "Joseph, son of David, do not be afraid to take Mary as your wife, for the child who has been *begotten in her* is from the holy spirit" (Matt 1:20). Mary goes on to give birth to the child Jesus (Matt 1:23).

Matthew's birth narrative demonstrates that he believed that Jesus was begotten, i.e., *brought into existence*, in the womb of Mary by the creative power of God's holy spirit. The late Raymond Brown noted that within this passage, "there is no suggestion of an incarnation whereby a figure who was

---

21. BDAG, 192.

22. *egennēsen*, used over forty times in this chapter, indicates the act when one becomes the parent of another (BDAG, 193).

23. Ruth 4:18–22; 1 Chr 2:10–15.

24. Cf. 1:3 (*ton Zara ek tēs Thamar*), 5 (twice), 6, 16, 18, and 20.

A SOCINIAN VIEW

previously with God takes on flesh."[25] Matthew rather faithfully follows the theology, inherited from the Hebrew Bible, concerning the expected Messiah to be born from the line of David.

The Gospel of Mark does not possess a birth narrative, choosing rather to jump right into the narrative portions of the story.[26] The Gospel, however, does indicate that Jesus was the son of Mary in Mark 6:3. This designation plainly links Jesus to his mother. Apart from this reference, there is no explicit reference to any traditions concerning his birth, with the possible exception being the title "Son of David" occasionally ascribed to him (Mark 10:47, 48; 12:35).

Luke's Gospel is similar to Matthew in that it begins with an extensive birth narrative.[27] Luke chooses to give the story from Mary's perspective rather than Joseph's. This story begins when God sends the angel Gabriel to the young Mary. She is greeted and informed that she will bear a child who is to be named Jesus (Luke 1:31). Gabriel then speaks of the child's grand destiny; "He *will* be great, he *will* be called the son of the Most High, and the Lord God *will* give him the throne of his father David, he *will* reign over the house of Jacob, and his kingdom *will* have no end" (Luke 1:32–33). This statement signifies that the child to be born will be both a descendant of David as well as the son of the Most High God, thus situating him firmly within the scope of messianic expectation. Mary responds to this wonderful announcement with some confusion, as she has yet to intimately know Joseph. Gabriel's answer carries with it crucial information: "Holy spirit will come upon you, and the power of the Most High will overshadow you; and *for that reason* the holy child shall be called the Son of God" (Luke 1:35). In one sentence, Gabriel very carefully indicates that Jesus' sonship is predicated on the miracle of his birth. In other words, it is precisely because he was miraculously begotten that Jesus can be called Son of God. This observation led Joseph Fitzmyer, among others, to argue that Luke does not teach an incarnational or preexistence theology.[28]

The book of Acts continues Luke's story of the early Christian movement. Within this document we find only a few statements regarding the

---

25. Brown, *Birth of the Messiah*, 141.

26. This is likely due to the fact that Mark was an apocalyptic document, attempting to urge its original audience to quickly respond to its message. Such a document would have little need to discuss the birth of Jesus or even his resurrection appearances, which are also omitted from Mark's conclusion.

27. Luke's genealogy traces Jesus' ancestry all the way up to Adam (3:23–38).

28. Fitzmyer, *Luke*, 351.

THE SON OF GOD

birth of Jesus. In the midst of the catena of citations found in Peter's initial sermon, Ps 132:11 is utilized to assert that Jesus was a descendant from the fruit of David's loins (Acts 2:30). Deut 18:15, where the prophet like Moses was to come "from among the people of Israel," is ascribed to Jesus in both Acts 3:22 and 7:37. Similarly, Paul's first sermon traces the origin of Jesus from King David: "From the seed of this man, according to promise, God has brought to Israel a Savior, Jesus" (Acts 13:23). The book of Acts depicts Jesus as descended from Israelite origins while drawing upon the Hebrew Bible in authoritative support of such claims.

The Apostle Paul likewise offers a few clues in regard to his understanding of Jesus' birth. The beginning of the Epistle to the Romans discusses what Paul considers the contents of the gospel of God, which were promised through the prophets (Rom 1:1–5). Paul remarks in Rom 1:3 that this gospel concerns God's son, who was *begotten* from the seed of David. In this packed verse, Paul combines son of God, son of David, and the act of Jesus *coming into being* by birth.[29] If the assertion made by most scholars is indeed correct that Rom 1:3–4 is a pre-Pauline formula, then it demonstrates that this view was previously preached by others and continued to be used authoritatively by Paul. Toward the end of the epistle, Paul cites Isaiah 11:10 in order to identify Jesus as the "root of Jesse" (Rom 15:12), i.e., the messianic figure descending from King David's father.[30]

Paul's Epistle to the Galatians contains a few further indicators regarding what Paul thought about the birth of Jesus. In the middle of the sustained argument of chapter three, Paul makes a bold exegetical move by arguing that the promises were spoken to Abraham and to *his seed* (Gal 3:16). He then carefully points out that the promises were not made to a plurality of seeds, but rather only to one, which he identifies as Christ. While this passage raises a variety of questions which can't be addressed in our current study, what can be said with certainty is that Paul regarded Jesus Christ as a *bona fide* descendant of Abraham, otherwise the argument would be nonsensical. Furthermore, Gal 4:4 states that, "when the fullness of time came, God commissioned his son, born of a woman, born under the Law." The phrase "born of a woman" denotes one who is born as a human being, "out of" a human mother.[31] The phrase "born under the Law" indicates

---

29. Dunn, *Romans 1–8*, 12.

30. Whitelam, "Jesse," 772.

31. Martyn, *Galatians*, 390; Betz, *Galatians*, 206. The expression also appears in Job 14:1; 15:14; 25:4; Matt 11:11, each indicating the normal act of birth.

A SOCINIAN VIEW

that Jesus was born as a Jew. The Davidic ancestry of Jesus continues to be emphasized in 2 Tim 2:8, "Remember Jesus Christ, risen from the dead, from the seed of David, according to my gospel." The connection between Jesus' Davidic lineage and the gospel formed in Rom 1:1–4 seems to be maintained here. In short, although Paul only makes a few scattered statements regarding the birth of Jesus, they nonetheless continue to emphasize his promised descent from such key figures as Abraham and David, while at the same time indicating that Jesus was indeed born.

The unknown author of Hebrews makes a few references which are relevant to our investigation. First, the opening chapter combines two messianic passages, Ps 2:7 and 2 Sam 7:14, as a critical component of the author's argument to distinguish Jesus from the angels (Heb 1:5). Both citations emphasize the sonship of Jesus in relation to the Father. Furthermore, the manner in which Jesus' sonship is argued is by stressing the *begetting* of the son ("today I have begotten you") and the act of *birthing* the son ("I will be a father to him and he will be a son to me"). Both Ps 2 and 2 Sam 7:14 were combined and interpreted messianically at Qumran, pointing toward the Branch of David.[32] The author of Hebrews seems to similarly combine these two texts in order to emphasize the son, Jesus, who was begotten by the Father.[33] Later in the author's argument, he declares what for him is plainly obvious: "it is evident that our Lord has sprung out of Judah" (Heb 7:14). The verb used here, *anatetalken*, is in the perfect active, indicating not only that Jesus descended from Judah but still endures in that state. The late F. F. Bruce noted that this passage echoes the messianic prophecy of Num 24:17, where the same verb appears in the LXX in reference to the rising star coming out of Jacob.[34] For the author of Hebrews, Jesus was begotten by the Father, superior to the angelic hosts, and belonging to the tribe of Judah.

Despite many popular readings, the Johannine literature significantly contributes to the discussion regarding Jesus' birth. Both the Gospel and

---

32. 4QFlor 1:10–11 cites 2 Sam 7:12–14 while 4QFlor 1:18–19 cites Ps 2:1–2. These passages continued to be linked by Jews on into the second century CE as evidenced by Rabbi Yudan in *Mid. Ps* 2 §9.

33. The most natural reading of Hebrews' argument is that Ps 2:7 and 2 Sam 7:14 are pointing to Jesus' birth by the Father. This way the title "Son of God," which characterized the Davidic king, overlapped with the moment Jesus came into existence upon being born.

34. Bruce, *Hebrews*, 143. Bruce also notes the messianic associations of the verb in Zech 6:12.

THE SON OF GOD

1 John describe Jesus as the "only begotten," using the word *monogenēs* (John 1:14, 18; 3:16, 18; 1 John 4:9). Although some prefer to translate this word as the "only one of its kind,"[35] when it is used in relation to the Father it can hardly mean anything other than an only begotten son.[36] Furthermore, since the *-genēs* component of *monogenēs* is derived from *genos* ("a descendant, family relatives, people, class, kind") it is almost certainly indicative of one who has been birthed.[37] The crowds in John 7:42 regard the promised Christ to come from the descendants of David. Additionally, it is virtually certain that the "one who was begotten from God" in 1 John 5:18 refers to Jesus Christ,[38] despite the scribal changes attempting to obscure this fact for obvious theological reasons.[39]

It is regularly argued that the Prologue of John (1:1–18) insists that Jesus existed prior to his birth in the form of the *logos*. However, the *logos* in John's Prologue functions as God's personified and personal utterance, not a conscious being alongside God.[40] Accordingly, when John 1:14 states that the *logos* became flesh, this indicates that God's personified speech was embodied in the human Jesus, allowing for the poetic and metaphorical overtones of the passage to take effect. If this is indeed the intention the phrase "the word became flesh," then this would again signify a reference to the human Messiah's birth.

The Johannine literature often describes Jesus as one who has "come into the world" (John 1:9; 3:17, 18; 6:14; 8:26; 9:39; 10:36; 11:27; 12:46; 16:28; 17:18; 18:37; 1 John 4:9). The idiom, however, was widely utilized by Jews to describe an individual's birth.[41] This is confirmed when we look at such examples as John 6:14, where "the prophet" (Deut 18:15–18), who

---

35. BDAG 658.
36. Barrett, *John*, 166.
37. BDAG 194.
38. Smalley, *1, 2, 3 John*, 303; Black, "Letters of John," 446.
39. TCGNT 650; Ehrman, *Orthodox Corruption*, 70–71.
40. This is the insistence of James Dunn: "We are dealing with personifications, rather than persons, personified actions of God rather than individual divine beings as such . . . if we translated *logos* as 'God's utterance' instead, it would become clearer that the poem did not necessarily intend the Logos in vv. 1–13 to be thought of as a personal divine being. In other words, the revolutionary significance of v. 14 may well be that it marks not only the transition in the thought of the poem from preexistence to incarnation, but also the transition from impersonal personification to actual person." *Christology in the Making*, 243.
41. See the references in "kosmos," *TDNT* 3.889; *4 Ezra* 7:21; *Lev. Rab.* 31:6.

A SOCINIAN VIEW

was to come from among the people of Israel, comes into the world. In John 16:21 the common birth of a child by a mother is described as the newborn "coming into the world."[42] Standing before Pilate, Jesus said, "For this I have been born, and for this I have come into the world" (John 18:37), indicating that Jesus' birth was the moment when he entered into the world.

The Apocalypse of John offers a few passages which are relevant for our inquiry into the birth of Jesus. In Rev 5:5, the angelic elder announces to the prophet that "the Lion from the tribe of Judah, the root of David, has triumphantly conquered." This passage links Jesus' lineage to the royal promise to Judah in Gen 49:8–10 and to the many messianic passages longing for a Davidic descendant. This theme is revisited in Rev 22:16 where Jesus announces, "I am the root and the descendant of David." From John's perspective, Jesus certainly descended from both Judah and King David.

THE LIFE AND TEACHINGS OF THE MESSIAH

I have argued thus far that Jesus is portrayed as the fulfillment of the messianic promises from the Hebrew Bible, where the coming figure is described as the human descendant of such pivotal figures as Abraham, Judah, and David. The New Testament contributes to this emphasis with its repeated insistence that Jesus was born as a human figure. In fact, many times his birth is described more explicitly as his *begetting*, the moment when he came into existence. His full humanity is articulated throughout all four Gospel accounts. The Synoptics call Jesus an *anthrōpos* a total of eleven times (three times in Matthew 3; two times in Mark; six times in Luke).[43] What may be surprising to some is the increased persistence regarding Jesus' humanity within the Fourth Gospel, which calls him an *anthrōpos* fifteen times—more than Matthew, Mark, and Luke combined![44] Furthermore, the Gospels describe Jesus with human traits. He grows, learns, and

---

42. It is also noteworthy that the child is spoken of as being begotten (*egennēthē*) at this juncture.

43. Luke also uses *anēr* of Jesus once. In the Book of Acts, Luke calls Jesus a man (*anēr*) in 2:22 and 17:31. On Acts 2:22, C. K. Barrett rightly notes that, "It is from this starting-point that the Christology of Acts proceeds, not from the notion of a divine being who by some kind of incarnation or kenosis accommodated himself to the human world. Luke never abandons his assertion of the manhood of Jesus." Barrett, *Acts*, 1.140.

44. John uses *anēr* of Jesus once. I owe these statistics to Robinson, *Priority of John*, 368.

THE SON OF GOD

matures in wisdom (Luke 2:40, 52).[45] Far from being omniscient, Jesus regularly asks others a variety of questions (Matt 15:34; 20:21, 32; Mark 5:9, 30–31; 6:38; 8:23; 9:21; Luke 8:45; John 11:37), requests to know individuals' names (Mark 5:9; Luke 8:30), and comes to conclusions based upon his own observations (Matt 8:10; Mark 11:13; Luke 7:9; John 11:17). Jesus even states that he does not know the date of his second coming, a time which only the Father knows (Matt 24:36).[46] As one who is fully dependent upon the Father, Jesus is taught and instructed by God (John 8:28).

One of the most fundamental aspects of Jesus' relationship to God is the role Jesus plays as the authoritatively commissioned agent. In the ancient world, the agent acts on behalf of the one who sent him. When one deals with the agent, it is as if one is dealing with the one who sent that person.[47] The principle of agency, which is taken for granted during the Second Temple period,[48] seems to be the most persuasive model for understanding Jesus' relationship to God. Quite frequently Jesus is depicted as the one who was sent by God, functioning as God's *shaliach* (Matt 10:40; Mark 9:37; Luke 4:43; John 4:34). To legitimate Jesus' authority as the one sent, the Gospel writers argue that Jesus came "in the name of God," thereby bearing God's authority (Matt 21:9; 23:39; Mark 11:9; Luke 13:35; 19:38; John 5:43; 12:13). Even the miracles and deeds which Jesus performs are done in the name of the Father (John 10:25). Since Jesus is God's messianic agent, he is able to exercise God's prerogatives, such as forgiving sins (Mark 2:7–10), working on the Sabbath (John 5:17), giving life (John 5:21), and enacting judgment (John 5:22.). As the prophet *par excellence* from Deut 18:15–18, where God promised to put His words into the mouth of the coming spokesman, Jesus can claim to speak the very words of God (John 3:34; 5:30; 7:16; 8:28; 12:49). In John's Gospel, where the "sending" language is profuse, God has placed his authoritative seal upon Jesus (John 6:27). On rare occasions, Jesus, functioning as the agent of the Father, is

---

45. Cf. "He *learned* obedience from the things which he suffered" (Heb 5:8).

46. ". . . but the Father alone" (Mark 13:32). The Matthew text was altered by scribes who removed the embarrassing reference to Jesus' ignorance in regard to the date. On this, see *TCGNT*, 51–52.

47. Thompson, "John, Gospel of," 377.

48. The common saying was "a man's agent is equivalent to himself" occurs frequently (*m. Ber.* 5:5; *b. B. Mes.* 96a; *b. Hag.* 10b; *b. Menah.* 93b; *b. Nazir* 12b; *b. Qidd.* 42b, 43a). Philo remarks that, "he who dishonors the servant, dishonors also the master" (*Dec.* 119). This motif is similarly expressed in *Gen. Rab.* 78, "the sender is greater than the one sent."

A SOCINIAN VIEW

declared to be *theos*.[49] However, since other agents were called *theos* and legitimately recognized as authoritative bearers of such title, it would be unwise to confuse the agent with the one who commissioned him.[50]

It must be admitted that the most common title used of Jesus within the New Testament is Son of God, occurring over forty times. This title carried with it all of the overtones regarding kingship, sonship, and messianism evoked from the Hebrew Bible. When Jesus was baptized by John, the voice from heaven spoke, "This is My beloved Son" (Matt 3:17). During the wilderness temptation narratives, the devil repeatedly attempted to dissuade Jesus from his vocation as Son of God (Matt 4:1–11; Luke 4:1–13). When Jesus encountered the demoniacs, they acknowledged him as Son of God (Matt 8:29). Matthew's climactic confession of Peter recognizes Jesus as "the Christ, the Son of the living God" (Matt 16:16). Martha's confession is similarly worded: "I have believed that you are the Christ, the Son of God" (John 11:27). The high priest demanded to know if Jesus was the Son of God (Matt 26:63). On the cross, the crowds questioned whether Jesus really was the Son of God (Matt 27:40, 43). The centurion, upon experiencing an earthquake at Jesus' death, famously admitted, "Truly this was the Son of God" (Matt 27:54). Mark's Gospel begins and John's Gospel concludes by labeling Jesus as the Son of God (Mark 1:1; John 20:17). The utter significance of this christological title must not be downplayed in any assessment of how the New Testament writers understood Jesus' identity.[51]

It should come as no surprise that Jesus frequently spoke about his identity. Within the Gospels, Jesus refers to himself most often as the Son of Man, the messianic human agent of judgment from Daniel 7:13.[52] At times, the phrase denoted a basic circumlocution ("me," "myself"), and it is very likely that Jesus deliberately used this phrase with such ambiguity. He used the title to indicate his authority (Matt 9:6; 12:8), his role as the coming judge (Matt 13:47; 16:27; 19:28; 24:27, 30, 37, 39, 44; 25:31), and the one on whom Israel's sufferings would be climaxed (Matt 12:40; 17:9; 22; 26:24, 45). Jesus sharpened the expectations of the messianic Son of Man by teaching that "the Son of Man did not come to be served, but to

---

49. I grant that Jesus is called *theos* in John 20:28 and Heb. 1:8 The other occurrences are considered dubious by most scholars.

50. BDB, 43; BDAG, 451; Exod 4:16; 7:1; 21:6; 22:8–9; Pss. 45:6; 58:1; 82:6; John 10:34; Philo, *Pot.* 1:161; *Mos.* 1:158; *Prob.* 1:43.

51. Bauer, "Son of God," 769–70.

52. Nickelsburg, "Son of Man," 137.

THE SON OF GOD

serve and to give his life a ransom for many" (Matt 20:28; Mark 10:45). My speculation is that Jesus saw himself as the Son of Man from Dan 7, wherein the many beasts were raging out of control. By combining Daniel's "Son of Man" with the reference in Ps 8:4–6, where God crowns the human figure with glory and majesty reminiscent of Adam's kingship in Gen 1:27–28, it is likely that Jesus regarded his own suffering and exaltation as the appropriate course of action to fulfill his vocation.

In regard to Jesus' relationship to God, the evidence is quite abundant. No less than forty times does Jesus address God as "My Father." As a good Jewish monotheist who without hesitation affirmed Judaism's *Shema* (Mark 12:28–34), Jesus identified the Father as "My God" ten times (Matt 27:46; Mark 15:34; John 20:17; Rev 3:2, 20). Since the Father was Jesus' God, he regularly claimed his unreserved subordination to Him by saying things like "the Father is greater than all," "the Father is greater than I," and so forth (John 10:29; 14:28; 20:17). Although Jesus served as the messianic agent, he nevertheless made a distinction between himself and the Father, calling him "the only true God" in John 17:3. As the Son of God, Jesus perfectly obeys the will of the Father (John 4:34; 5:30; 6:38; 7:28; 8:29). In fact, Jesus declared on multiple occasions that he is unable to do anything without the Father's help and guidance (John 5:19, 30; 12:49–50; 15:15). Time and time again, Jesus is depicted as the obedient son, acting as the authoritative agent of God.

THE DEATH OF THE MESSIAH

One of the most central tenets to Christianity is that Jesus suffered and died on the cross. It is my conviction that the New Testament writers understood that Jesus died completely and entirely. In other words, Jesus is described, without hesitation, as having been dead. He was 100 percent deceased on the evening of Good Friday. Since all human beings are susceptible to death, and Jesus Christ was a member of the human race, then consequently Jesus' death was like all others. Paul goes to great lengths to argue that it was *the human being* Jesus whose obedient death undid the sin of Adam (Rom 5:12–21). No New Testament text comes anywhere close to even hinting that Jesus only partially died. The death of Jesus is described in relation to the title "Son of Man" (Luke 24:7) as well as the title "Son of God" (Gal 2:20). When Jesus appeared to the prophet John, he emphasizes his death by stating, "I *became dead*, and behold I am alive forevermore"

A SOCINIAN VIEW

(Rev 1:18; cp. 2:8). The death of Jesus is one of the firmest pieces of historical data upon which scholars agree,[53] with only the most extreme denying its historicity. However, the conviction of the early Christians was that God raised Jesus from the dead on the third day.

THE RESURRECTION AND EXALTATION OF THE MESSIAH

The victory of Jesus Christ did not end when he was woken up from the grave. God furthermore exalted Jesus to a new position of grandeur and authority. Matthew's Gospel concludes with Jesus announcing that "All authority *has been given* to me in heaven and on earth" (Matt 28:18). Paul the Apostle likewise emphasizes that Jesus was highly exalted upon being resurrected from the grave (Phil 2:9). Psalm 110:1, where Yahweh addresses "my lord" and summons him to sit at the right hand, became the most preferred citation from the Hebrew Bible in regard to the exalted Jesus. The New Testament describes Jesus' exalted status and location as being at the right hand of God on twenty-two occasions. The author of Hebrews uniquely regards Jesus as the high priest, the one who intercedes between the people and God (Heb 8:1). As the exalted lord to God's right hand, it should not be a surprise that Jesus attains some of his highest christological titles, such as the Alpha and the Omega, the first and the last, the beginning and the end, etc. (Rev 22:13). However, these titles *were conferred onto Jesus*, who upon his exaltation was given a name above every name (Phil 2:9–11). James McGrath rightly notes that "God shares his own name and sovereign rule with Jesus as his supreme agent after the resurrection, and this is not an idea that was felt to be in conflict with monotheism."[54]

The exalted titles given to Jesus must be balanced with his sustained relationship in regard to God. Writers of the various New Testament epistles commonly regard God as "the God and Father of our lord Jesus Christ" (2 Cor 1:3; Eph 1:3; Col 1:3; 1 Peter 1:3; cp. Rev 1:6). Jesus is the exalted lord Messiah, but he still *has a God*. Dunn's comment on this fact is even clearer: "Jesus as Lord, still has God as his God!"[55] Even though Jesus is exalted to God's right hand, Jesus nevertheless maintains a subordinate position to

---

53. See esp. Meyer, "Jesus Christ"; Allison, "Jesus Christ," 290; Dunn, *Jesus Remembered*, 777–93; Ehrman, *How Jesus Became God*, 370.

54. McGrath, *Only True God*, 52.

55. Dunn, *New Testament Theology*, 62.

THE SON OF GOD

God (1 Cor 3:23; 11:3; Eph 4:4–6). In fact, 1 Timothy 2:5 highlights the exalted Messiah Jesus as the *human* mediator situated between the one God and humanity. In short, the resurrected Jesus is variously depicted as an exalted figure, but an exalted human being who maintains his subordinate status to God.

THE RETURN OF THE MESSIAH

One of the most foundational affirmations within the New Testament is the expectation of the return of Jesus to consummate the kingdom of God upon the earth. There are a few texts which accentuate Jesus as a human being in his role as the returning judge and king. Acts 17:30–31 records Paul preaching that people should repent because God has set a day in which he will judge the world through the *human Jesus*. It would seem that Luke still envisages Jesus as continuing in his human state after the exaltation. Furthermore, Paul's argument in the lengthy fifteenth chapter of 1 Corinthians contains a section which details the occasion of the believers' resurrection. In doing so, Paul evokes his Adam Christology which identifies Jesus as a human being, the second Adam (1 Cor 15:21).[56] At the *parousia* of the human Messiah, those who belong to him will be made alive via resurrection (15:22–23). Paul then narrates the next stage of the eschaton, where Jesus hands over the kingdom to the Father. Jesus will then forever live in subjection to the one who subjected all things (15:24–28). Richard Hays concludes that "it is impossible to avoid the impression that Paul is operating with what would later come to be called a subordinationist Christology."[57]

SUMMARY

My argument thus far has been to give full weight to texts which emphasize the humanity of Jesus. I have demonstrated that the Messiah promised from the Hebrew Bible comes from the line of human figures, such as Judah and David. Furthermore, the dominant interpretation of these passages within the Second Temple period expressed a royal human figure of David's line. The authors of the New Testament abundantly and without reservation declare that Jesus was truly born in a manner which, like all births from one's

---

56. Cf. 15:45, 47 ("second man").
57. Hays, *First Corinthians*, 266.

A SOCINIAN VIEW

mother, brings the child into existence. I regard the begetting of the Son of God as the point in history which anchors the beginning of Jesus' existence. In other words, Jesus did not exist one second prior to his begetting in the womb of Mary.

As an adult, Jesus functions as the human Messiah who represents the one true God as the authoritative agent. While functioning as the agent, Jesus can do and say things which uniquely belong to God. Since the principle of agency was well established in the Second Temple period, this reconstruction arguably makes the best sense of the data available. Jesus died completely for the sins of humanity and was raised up by God on the third day. He was subsequently exalted to God's right hand where he maintains his identity as the glorified second Adam. He is coming again to consummate God's kingdom upon the earth, bringing order to this creation and ultimately subjecting himself to the Father.

A TRINITARIAN RESPONSE TO A SOCINIAN VIEW

CHARLES LEE IRONS

IN HIS MAIN PRESENTATION, Dustin Smith articulates the view that Jesus was a mere man, a view called psilanthropism in the history of Christian theology.[1] It was a minority christological view whose first known advocate was Theodotus the Leather-Seller in the second century. But his views were not widely received, and he was excommunicated by Victor, the bishop of Rome (AD 189–198).[2] He is considered the founder of dynamic monarchianism, that is, the view that Jesus never had preexistence prior to his birth but was a mere man who was adopted as God's Son at some point in his life, whether at his birth or at his baptism. In the next century, a few subsequent individuals revived the views of Theodotus, such as Artemon and Paul of Samosata. Eusebius reports that a third-century book called "The Little Labyrinth" was written to combat the error of Theodotus and Artemon.[3] Whenever psilanthropism appeared, it was immediately challenged. Paul of Samosata was condemned by the Synod of Antioch in AD 268 for the same view and deposed from his office as bishop, fifty-seven years before the Council of Nicea (AD 325).[4] The view was revived later by the Socinians and Polish Anabaptists in the sixteenth century and articulated in the *Racovian Catechism*. All branches of Christendom—Roman Catholic, Eastern Orthodox, and Protestant—are united (in spite of their

1. From the Greek words *psilos* (mere) + *anthrōpos* (man).
2. *ODCC* 1345, 1602.
3. Eusebius, *Ecclesiastical History* 5.28; 7.30; *ODCC* 112, 986.
4. *ODCC* 1242.

A TRINITARIAN RESPONSE TO A SOCINIAN VIEW

intense disagreements on other points of theology) in condemning the Socianian view of Jesus as a mere man and its denial of the personal preexistence of the eternal Word before he became flesh. Psilanthropism was never a widely held view and whenever it did crop up, it was immediately and unanimously rejected by the church.

Smith has turned away from his conservative Christian upbringing in which he was taught (I believe, correctly) that Christ is both divine and human to the psilanthropic error that has been rejected by the church from the second century on. He has adopted a different view of Jesus because he thinks early Jewish literature mandates that the Messiah was to be an ordinary human and nothing more. But all he has shown is that the Messiah was to be human, which the Christian church, following Scripture, has always strongly affirmed. He has not shown that the Messiah was to be *merely* human.

The Christian church believes that "the Word became flesh" (John 1:14), that "he was manifested in the flesh" (1 Tim 3:16), that "Christ Jesus came in the flesh" (2 John 7), that he was "born of a woman" (Gal 4:4), that he "partook" of flesh and blood in order to be "made like" his brothers in every way, except without sin (Heb 2:14), and that he was sent "in the likeness of sinful flesh" (Rom 8:3). In all of these verses, what is affirmed is not that Jesus is an ordinary man but that he is the preexistent Son of God who became man. The difference is profound, and Smith's view fails to reckon with the force of these preexistence-incarnation texts.

Further evidence for the preexistence of Christ is found in John's Gospel. Jesus made an astonishing claim that scandalized the Jewish leaders and caused them to pick up stones to stone him to death: "Truly, truly, I say to you, before Abraham was, I am" (John 8:58). Elsewhere, Jesus claimed that he "descended from heaven" (John 3:13) and "came down from heaven" to do his Father's will (John 6:38). Later, in his high priestly prayer, he said to the Father, "I glorified you on earth, having accomplished the work that you gave me to do. And now, Father, glorify me in your own presence with the glory that I had with you before the world existed" (John 17:4–5).

Buzzard and Hunting attempt to explain these passages away by arguing that past tenses in the Hebrew Bible can be used proleptically, that is, a future event can be viewed as so certain in the mind or plan of God that it is described as if it had already occurred.[5] But the proleptic theory simply does not fit in any of these cases. It does not fit John 3:13; 6:38, for

---

5. Buzzard and Hunting, *Doctrine of the Trinity*, 167, 200–202.

THE SON OF GOD

in these verses Jesus is not looking ahead to a future, second coming from heaven, but is speaking of the fact that he has come "to do the Father's will" in his first coming. It does not fit John 17:5, which explicitly speaks of the glory that Jesus had with the Father "before the world was created." There is indeed a future aspect in which Jesus asks the Father to glorify him (referring either to the cross or the resurrection/exaltation, or both), but then he specifically requests to be glorified with the same glory he had with the Father before he came to earth. This is not a case of a past tense being used to refer to a future event but of a future event being compared to a past state. And the proleptic theory does not fit John 8:58, where Jesus says that he existed "before Abraham was," who lived in the past, not in the future. In each case, the context makes clear that these are not future events spoken of as if they were past but real past events.

In addition, we cannot ignore the early Christian confession of faith or hymn quoted by Paul in the second chapter of his letter to the Philippians. Paul exhorts us to have the same attitude in ourselves which was also in Christ Jesus, "who though he was in the form of God, did not count equality with God a thing to be grasped, but emptied himself, by taking the form of a servant, being born in the likeness of men" (Phil 2:6–7). Here it is affirmed of Jesus, prior to his human state, at the time when he "existed" (*hyparchōn*) "in the form of God," that instead of counting or regarding his equality with God as something to be grasped and used for his own advantage, he voluntarily emptied (*ekenōsen*) himself by "taking" (*labōn*) the form of a servant, "becoming" (*genomenos*) in the likeness of men. The contrast of moving from the present participle ("existing in the form of God") to the aorist verb ("emptied") and the two aorist participles that define how he emptied himself ("taking" and "becoming") implies that Christ was a divine, preexistent being who "became" a man. This text strongly affirms preexistence. Its early date (one or two decades after Jesus' resurrection) makes it all the more compelling.

Psilanthropism has enormous difficulty with these preexistence passages in John and Paul. Attempts to explain them away are unconvincing. The exegetical gymnastics needed to overcome their obvious meaning suggests that Scripture is being twisted to fit a preconceived dogma.

A TRINITARIAN RESPONSE TO A SOCINIAN VIEW
THE EXPECTATIONS OF THE MESSIAH

The large number of quotes from early Jewish literature gives the impression that Smith thinks Jewish messianic expectations are determinative for what Christians should believe about Jesus. While the examination of such literature is useful for shedding light on the historical, social, and religious context in which the New Testament was born, as a Protestant who holds to formal principle of the Reformation, *sola Scriptura*, I cannot follow Smith in elevating this early Jewish literature to such heights that it is capable of defining the qualifications for the Messiah. Right at the outset, then, I have a foundational objection to Smith's methodology.

But even if we set the question of methodology aside for a moment, there are two additional compelling reasons that Jewish messianic expectations cannot be treated as determinative for Christian Christology. First, Jewish messianic expectations were not uniform to begin with. The diversity of Jewish messianic expectation is a point on which scholars of early Judaism agree.[6] The Qumran community expected the prophet of Deuteronomy 18 and two messiahs, one priestly and one kingly.[7] These all seem to be human messianic figures. But *1 Enoch*, by contrast, shows no interest in a human Davidic messiah and looked ahead to a heavenly angelic messiah built upon the "Son of Man" figure in Dan 7.[8] Smith claims that the promised descendant of David "is never described in the Hebrew Bible as *already* in existence." But some Jews thought that the Messiah was already in existence, hidden in God's presence in heaven prior to creation.[9] Thus,

---

6. John J. Collins maps out four messianic paradigms in early Judaism. The first and most dominant messianic paradigm is the one Smith emphasizes: the messiah as Davidic king. But there are three other paradigms a well: the messiah as priest, as prophet, and as heavenly Son of Man. Collins, *Scepter and Star*. Another scholar writes: "The evidence from Qumran relating to messianic expectation has demonstrated once again just how varied were the beliefs of early Judaism." Knibb, "Messianism," 308.

7. "A prophet and the Messiahs of Aaron and Israel" (1QS IX.11; CD XII.23; XIV.19; XIX.10; XX.1).

8. "Lack of interest in the Davidic monarchy is a trait shared by the writings attributed to Enoch and to Daniel. The Similitudes of Enoch ... speak of a messiah (*1 En* 48:10; 52:4) but he is a heavenly figure." Collins, "Response," 62.

9. *4 Ezra* 13:26, 52; *1 Enoch* 48:3, 6; 62:7. Some have attempted to make the case against real preexistence in *1 Enoch*, arguing that the Son of Man is merely "given a name" before creation (48:3). However, a few verses later, we read that the Chosen One himself (not just his name) "was concealed in the presence of (the Lord of the Spirits) prior to the creation of the world" (48:6). Nickelsburg and VanderKam, *1 Enoch 2*, 170. ET: E. Isaac, "1 (Ethiopic Apocalypse of) Enoch," in *OTP* 1.35.

THE SON OF GOD

Jewish messianic expectations are not totally unified, and on the issue of preexistence they are mutually contradictory. At the end of the day, Smith is guilty of cherry picking the Jewish evidence to support a conception of the Messiah that he is already committed to on other grounds.

Second, even if we set aside *1 Enoch* as an outlier and limit the survey to Jewish texts that looked forward to a human messiah, another problem arises. These texts center upon the political hopes that the Jews had for a conquering military hero who would deliver them from Gentile oppression. Smith himself notes that the author of the *Psalms of Solomon* longed for a coming warrior messiah who would "smash the arrogance of sinners like a potter's jar" and "destroy the unlawful nations with the word of his mouth" (*Ps. Sol.* 17:23–24). But the Gospels emphatically reveal that Jesus viewed his mission as Messiah in quite different terms. He did not see himself as a military hero who would throw off the Roman imperial yoke, but as the Suffering Servant who came to lay down his life to save his people from their sins (Matt 1:21; 20:28). Were we to take the early Jewish messianic concept as normative, as Smith wants us to, we would be obliged to join the Jews in rejecting Jesus as a candidate for the office of Messiah.

I do not deny that early Jewish extra-biblical texts are helpful for providing us with a better sense of the Jewish matrix out of which the New Testament writings were born. But because they are mutually contradictory they cannot be taken as determinative for Christian Christology. We cannot rest our Christology on the messianic concepts of Jews, who (it is not irrelevant to note) rejected Jesus' claim to be the Messiah. What the Jews expected cannot be the touchstone of Christian theology. Jesus and the apostles rejected much that was current in the Jewish theology of their day. Instead, we look to the claims of Jesus himself and the apostolic testimony contained in the writings in the New Testament. If not, how can we claim to be Christians?

THE BIRTH OF THE MESSIAH

In this section, Smith moves from the Old Testament and Jewish literature to the birth narratives in Matthew and Luke. He argues that "the pages of the New Testament open in massive agreement to the promised expectation of a human Messiah."

Before examining the particular exegetical details of the birth narratives, I want to raise an objection to Smith's method, which is an argument

A TRINITARIAN RESPONSE TO A SOCINIAN VIEW

from silence. He takes the non-mention of Christ's preexistence in Matthew and Luke as evidence that they knew nothing of it. In effect, he uses Matthew and Luke as a club to overrule and reinterpret the preexistence Christology of the Gospel of John. But it is wrong to pit the Gospels against one another. Rather than seeing them as in conflict, they should be read as complementary. Using this logic, someone could just as easily take Mark, who lacks any mention of the virgin birth, as the standard and use Mark as a weapon against Matthew and Luke. Mark's Gospel could be taken to imply that Jesus was adopted as the Son of God at his baptism, not at his birth as Matthew and Luke teach (according to Smith). But this would be a faulty procedure. The absence of the virgin birth in Mark doesn't mean Mark knew nothing of the virgin birth or did not believe it. This argument from silence is dubious at best. I presume that Smith would agree with me that, rather than taking the absence of the virgin birth in Mark to suppress the witness of Matthew and Luke, we should take the latter two Gospels as providing additional information that complements Mark. Shouldn't we do the same with John's Gospel? Mark shows us that Jesus is the Son of God as far back as his baptism. Matthew and Luke push the divine Sonship of Jesus back to his birth. John takes us one step further back and shows us that he was the eternal Word in the Father's bosom (i.e., the Son) even before his birth. All four Gospels agree that Jesus is the Messiah, the Son of God, but they provide different yet complementary windows into the history of his Sonship.

Smith appeals to the following exegetical arguments from Matthew's account of the birth of Jesus. First, Smith appeals to the phrase "the *genesis* of Jesus Christ" (Matt 1:1) to deny preexistence. His argument is that the word *genesis* in Greek literally means "his coming into being at a specific moment," thereby implying that he did not exist prior to his birth. But the word *genesis* has a variety of meanings besides literal origin. Smith ignores the fact that the word *genesis* is part of a larger phrase, "the *book* of the *genesis* of Jesus Christ," which is an echo of Gen 2:4; 5:1 in the Septuagint. Therefore, as most commentators agree, the phrase means "the record of the *genealogy* of Jesus Christ," functioning as a header to the immediately following section (Matt 1:2–17).[10]

Second, Smith appeals to the repeated use of the word "begat" in Matthew's genealogy of Jesus to deny preexistence. In four cases the preposition

---

10. Hagner, *Matthew 1–13*, 9. The ESV, NASB, NKJV, NRSV, and RSV render *genesis* in Matt 1:1 as "genealogy."

151

THE SON OF GOD

ek is added (the four women in the genealogy), which Smith takes to mean that the "person born came out of their respective mother." But that is a wooden interpretation of the prepositional phrase. What it really means is that the father begot the individual named "by means of" the woman named. It is the *ek* of agency and could be translated "by" or "through," not the *ek* of source ("out of"). He then adds, "The same preposition is used in 1:16 to describe the birth of Jesus, who came out of Mary." But Smith misses the unexpected switch from the active form of the verb "begat" (used thirty-nine times in the genealogy prior to that point) to the divine passive, "was begotten [of God] by means of Mary."[11] The result is that Matthew, rather than showing how similar Jesus' birth was to other ordinary "merely human" members of the Davidic line, shows the dissimilarity and uniqueness of Jesus' birth. If the other members of the Davidic line had biological mothers and fathers, Jesus had a biological mother but no biological father. This does not make Jesus merely another "legitimate member of the human race," but the Son of God born as a man.

Third, Smith makes much of the fact that the Jews expected the messiah to be "the son of David" and therefore fully human. And yet Jesus is not "the son of David" by genetic descent but by adoption into David's line via Joseph the husband of Mary.[12] Smith seems to think that the humanity of Jesus is tied to his status as "the son of David." It is precisely at this point that one would expect to find a human father. Instead, we find not a human figure such as Joseph but, lo and behold, God as his Father. In Smith's own view, this disqualifies Jesus from being the Messiah! But the fact that the Messiah's Davidic credentials come via adoption rather than genetics makes sense from the standpoint of orthodox Christology: the role of the Davidic king as "God's son" (2 Sam 7:14; Ps 2:7; 89:27) was a typological foreshadow of the ontological Sonship of Christ. But it makes no sense from the standpoint of Smith's psilanthropic Christology.

Moving from Matthew's birth narrative, to Luke's, Smith places great weight on the phrase "for that reason" in the words of the angel to Mary: "The Holy Spirit will come upon you, and the power of the Most High will overshadow you; and *for that reason* the holy child shall be called the Son of God" (Luke 1:35). He argues (like Buzzard and Hunting[13]), that the miraculous (virgin) birth of Jesus is the basis or cause of Jesus' identity as

11. Hagner, *Matthew 1–13*, 12.
12. Ibid., 12–22.
13. Buzzard and Hunting, *Doctrine of the Trinity*, 70–71.

A TRINITARIAN RESPONSE TO A SOCINIAN VIEW

"the Son of God." Buzzard and Hunting use this argument in an attempt to prove that Luke had no concept of the preexistence of Christ. They reason that if Jesus became the Son of God at his birth, then he could not have been the Son of God before his birth. But the text does not say, "Therefore [because of his miraculous birth], the holy begotten [child] will *be* the Son of God," but "Therefore, the holy begotten [child] will *be called* (*klēthēsetai*) the Son of God." There is a big difference between "be" and "be called." Jesus' miraculous birth is not what causes him to be the Son of God but what causes people to call him such, to recognize that he is in fact the Son of God.[14]

Read this way Luke 1:35 actually points toward a higher Christology. It suggests that Luke's "Son of God" concept was not limited to a merely human messiah. For there was no Jewish expectation that Israel's merely human messiah would be born of a virgin, without a human father. In fact, much Jewish expectation would seem to have demanded a normal birth from a human father, since the messiah was expected to be the royal son of David through the paternal line. The fact that Jesus was born of a virgin, by the power of the Holy Spirit, however, was unexpected and irregular. But the irregularity was divinely intended. It was a pointer to his true identity—since he has no human father, God is his Father. It was fitting for one whose Father is God, when he becomes incarnate, to be born without the agency of a human father. The lack of a human father signals that he is the offspring of a divine Father.

There is another problem with this section of Smith's opening statement. There seems to be a dissonance in his thinking. On the one hand, Smith wants to say that being "a legitimate member of the human race" is a qualification for the office of Messiah. He repeatedly emphasizes the full humanity of Jesus as one who was "truly born in a manner which, like all births from one's mother, brings the child into existence." Smith apparently wants to emphasize how much Jesus is just like other men. On the other hand, he admits that Jesus is unique in several ways: (a) his birth was a miraculous birth from a mother who was a virgin, (b) he is called "the Son of God," (c) he was begotten not by a human father, but by God the Father. How are these things consistent with being an ordinary human like all other humans? I know of no ordinary human who has these three qualities.

---

14. The inferential use of *dio* with verbs like "call," "consider," "say" is found elsewhere in the Greek New Testament (Matt 27:8; Luke 7:7; Rom 4:22; 1 Cor 12:3; Eph 4:8; 5:14; Jas 4:6).

THE SON OF GOD

In sum, the birth narratives in Matthew and Luke do not teach that Jesus is a merely human Messiah. Rather, by focusing on the virgin birth, they teach that Jesus is the divine Son of God who took a true human nature into personal union with himself by being born of the virgin. That is the historic, orthodox interpretation of the birth narratives. It is superior to Smith's psilanthropic interpretation because it is consistent with the New Testament's preexistence-incarnation teaching.

THE LIFE AND TEACHINGS OF THE MESSIAH

In this section, Smith appeals to the concept of agency to explain the life of Jesus as Messiah. In response, I point out that the Jewish *shaliach* is of limited value for Christology, since there are too many differences between the Jewish *shaliach* and Jesus' role as the Son of God.[15] A *shaliach* is a human sent by another human to represent the latter and perform functions on behalf of the latter that the latter cannot perform due to physical distance. A *shaliach* is commissioned to perform a specific task that is limited in scope and duration; once the task is completed, the *shaliach* no longer has that delegated authority. All examples of God sending a human *shaliach* are prophets. But Jesus is more than a prophet, as the Gospels take pains to show (Matt 16:13–17 || Mark 8:27–29 || Luke 9:18–20).[16] The tasks that God gives to human *shaliachs* are all functions that are appropriate to a human being, not divine functions like forgiving sins, receiving worship, etc. There are certain things even God cannot do: he cannot command creatures to ascribe divine worship to another creature; he cannot grant creatures power to create; he cannot grant creatures power to forgive sins. The concept of agency is therefore of limited value. As I argued in my opening statement, it is more helpful and more true to the New Testament to view Jesus under the rubric of sonship. There is a fundamental difference between being God's "agent" and God's "Son." The New Testament may use language that formally sounds like agency ("sending," "obedience") but that language is not to be construed within the framework of human agency but within the framework of divine Sonship.[17]

---

15. Thompson, *God of Gospel of John*, 126–27.
16. Kingsbury, *Matthew as Story*, 76
17. Some theologians call the latter "divine-filial agency." Köstenberger and Swain, *Father, Son, and Spirit*, 121.

A TRINITARIAN RESPONSE TO A SOCINIAN VIEW

THE DEATH OF THE MESSIAH

Smith's claim that Jesus died "completely and entirely" cries out for further explanation. I assume this statement stems from Smith's peculiar anthropology which denies the traditional Christian belief that the human soul persists after death. On this view, then, the Messiah ceased to exist for three days—a fairly shocking statement to Christian ears. Did not Peter say that the soul of Jesus was not abandoned in Hades (Acts 2:27 quoting Ps 16:10)? The notion that the Messiah "died completely and entirely" is not only shocking, but raises additional questions. If the Messiah died "completely and entirely," did God re-beget his Son on the third day? If so, would not the resurrected Jesus be a new person created out of nothing, unrelated to the Jesus who died? Smith speaks of "the victory of Jesus Christ" when he rose again. But if he ceased to exist completely, then how could "he" have victory over death? It would seem, rather, that death had gotten complete and total victory over him.

THE RESURRECTION AND EXALTATION OF THE MESSIAH

Smith quotes James McGrath: "God shares his own name and sovereign rule with Jesus as his supreme agent after the resurrection, and this is not an idea that was felt to be in conflict with monotheism." It is true that exalted secondary figures in early Judaism functioned as agents of God and did so in a way that was not in conflict with monotheism. But the New Testament attributes to Jesus things that go far beyond anything that Jewish literature ever attributed to its human or angelic agents, especially creation, aseity, and divine worship. Smith also points out that even in his exaltation, the Messiah is still subordinate to God. I agree, but I interpret the subordination differently. Smith would clearly take this to be an ontological subordination, a creature subordinate to the Creator. I take it to be a personal subordination based on his identity as the eternal Son of God sent by the Father and obedient to the Father.

THE RETURN OF THE MESSIAH

In this section Smith introduces us to an important facet of his beliefs about Jesus, namely, "the expectation of the return of Jesus to consummate the

THE SON OF GOD

kingdom of God upon the earth." Although he does not call it this, it is known as chiliasm and fits in with his overall Jewish emphasis on Jesus as the Davidic Messiah of Israel's hopes. The Church of God General Conference believes in "the final restoration of Israel as the Kingdom of God under the kingship of Christ."[18] Jesus is no spiritual Messiah destined to reign over a spiritual kingdom. In this view, he will literally reign over a restored Israel from the literal throne of David in Jerusalem.

This literalistic interpretation of the kingdom of the Messiah places it entirely in the future, over against the New Testament's strong "already/not-yet" eschatology. New Testament scholars agree that there is both a present and a future aspect of the kingdom that Jesus brought.[19] He inaugurated it in his death and resurrection and he will consummate it at his return. This means that the kingdom is indeed something spiritual, at least in its present form prior to his return. The spiritual nature of the kingdom comports with the higher conception of Jesus as the divine Son of God. He is not a mere human who inaugurated a mere earthly, political kingdom. He is the divine Son of God who laid down his life to save his people from their sins (Matt 1:21)—not to save Israel from the Romans and set up an earthly kingdom.

CONCLUSION

In sum, Smith's psilanthropic Christology labors under a host of difficulties. I grant that Smith has shown that Jesus is the Messiah and that he is a true man. Thus far, we agree. What he has failed to show is that Jesus is God's Son only in a functional or messianic sense and that he is a mere man. When one takes stock of all the biblical evidence, one can only conclude that psilanthropism has too many serious liabilities to represent a serious claim upon the Christian conscience. It is impossible for me as a Christian to join Smith in adopting such low, Judaizing views of the person of Christ.

---

18. COGGC Statement of Faith; http://www.abc-coggc.org. Accessed August 14, 2014. See Buzzard, "Gospel of the Kingdom."

19. Ladd, *Theology of the New Testament*, 54–67.

AN ARIAN RESPONSE TO A SOCINIAN VIEW

DANNY ANDRÉ DIXON

INTRODUCTION

As I read through Dustin Smith's essay I amazed at how often I found myself nodding in agreement with what he said about who the Messiah was expected to be. Recently, a Sunday school class that I attended considered the John 6:16–21 pericope—where Jesus' disciples are rowing across the Sea of Galilee to Capernaum. After three or four hours of trying to get to the other side, the disciples see Jesus approaching them and are fearful because they think he is a ghost (Gk., *pneuma*; cp. Matt 14:26). The lesson plan for the Sunday's lesson considered Jesus' approaching the boat walking on the water and declaring to the disciples, "Do not fear, it is I" (ASV at John 6:20), and the class materials veered toward establishing that the "I am" statement there (*Egō eimi*) was a proof that Jesus was the great I AM of Exod 3:14, which, I am to understand is a set and closed concept in that denomination. I expressed some reasons for my opinions otherwise, and found myself in a conversation with an elder in the church, a friend of many years whose sons I have had the privilege of teaching in high school. He wanted to know what I was. "A strict monotheist would about cover it," I said. He wanted to know what made me different than a Jew. I replied that the Jews do not believe that the Messiah has come. So he asked if I were something between a Jew and a Christian. I replied that because "Christ" is essentially the same

THE SON OF GOD

thing as what a Hebrew-speaking Jew would call "Messiah," and because I believed that Jesus is in fact that promised Messiah who was to come, that I therefore would consider myself a follower of Messiah—a Christian.

The whole conversation which continued for some minutes after the worship hour ended caused me to think about my perspective on who the Jewish community had expected Jesus to be. I also wondered about the inspired revelation of the informed community of faith as the disciples wrote Scripture about the advent of their Lord and Christ, his ministry on the earth, and his present status as mediator between God and man (1 Tim 2:5) seated at God's right hand (cp., for example, Ps 110:1 and a host of verses such as 1 Cor 15:23–28 and Heb 1:3). In a scholarly fashion, Smith has carefully and systematically traversed the ground covering these matters. And as little as I have to disagree with most of his presentation, I will address some of the highlights following his outline. In a word, I ultimately would have to challenge Smith's claim that Jesus could not be both a preexisting being and be born as a human.

THE EXPECTATION OF THE MESSIAH

Even a casual reading of Smith's presentation reveals a deep and thorough study into ancient Jewish nonbiblical and biblical texts regarding the expectation of the Messiah. Quotations of rabbinic Jewish expectation pepper his essay throughout from Genesis to Revelation. While I would be inclined to disagree that Gen 3:15 was intended by the original writer to be prophetic,[1] Smith's analysis adequately treats other biblical texts and rabbinic understandings regarding the Messiah's human lineage, particularly in Jacob's prophetic announcement that once there came to be a king in Israel, ultimately the scepter would remain as a dynasty in the descendants of Judah (Gen 49:8–10). And even if I did not agree with Smith that Num 24:17 was also a messianic passage, that it was considered so by Jewish scholars of the time is significant. And Smith's thoroughness in considering the then-contemporary Targums addressing this is appropriate.

"The Prophet" of Deut 18:15–19 gets due attention, and could have received more in a consideration of the crowd's speculation as to Jesus' identity in John 7, especially when some affirm, "This is really the prophet"

---

1. There is no New Testament passage that directly quotes Gen 3:15. But would anyone deny the presence of an *allusion* to it in Rom 16:20 ("The God of peace will soon crush Satan under your feet")?

AN ARIAN RESPONSE TO A SOCINIAN VIEW

(John 7:40), and others say, "This is the Christ" (v. 41). Also, the oblique references, without quoting Scripture, to the messiah's being descended from David and coming from Bethlehem (v. 42), reinforce Smith's description of Jewish messianic expectations of the time. I even concur with Smith's consideration of 2 Sam 7:12 and the "kingdom [that] will endure forever" in the dynasty of David which "effectively maintained the Davidic line of kings and the tribe of Judah's rulership." The "son of God" language, in which the king in the Davidic line is, in effect, God's son in that dynasty plays out in Jesus' being God's Son in that sense. And even "Son of David" was a widely recognized messianic title during the Second Temple period. I will return to this admission shortly. The "Branch of David" prophecy (Jer 23:5; 33:15), Qumranic Jewish expectation of God begetting the Messiah, the raising up and establishing of David, the Son of Man figure, even the denial of Hasmonean rulers as legitimate because they were *not* of the Davidic line—all bespeak the expectation of a literal descendant of David to be the one who would be Israel's Messiah.

THE BIRTH OF THE MESSIAH

Smith spends much space discussing the "record of the *genesis*" of Jesus. Whether the word means "birth," "lineage," "genealogy," or "beginning," or "origin," the lexicons make a case, albeit a convoluted one, that Jesus' *genesis* means his "birth" into this world or his origin as it relates to historical incidents surrounding that event. Smith's treatment of these matters is thorough, as he examines the birth narratives in Matthew and Luke, as well as references in Acts, Romans, Galatians, even Hebrews. He demonstrates that Jesus would be born, that he would be an Israelite, born of a woman, be of David's ancestry, and be begotten by God. Smith (appropriately) does overkill in stressing Jesus' physical birth. But he does not want to carry the argument as far as it could go. For while it is important for him to affirm that Jesus' birth would have to be absolutely human and literal on his mother's side, he does not want to take it so far as to argue that his father was also human. This is very important: in creating this human being (Jesus), God has deviated from the normal course of human birth and caused a son to be born via miraculous intervention. Smith does not hold to a liberal view that Jesus' father was a man who impregnated Mary. He would probably agree

THE SON OF GOD

with Dunn who writes, primarily to establish that "there is no sign of any Christology of preexistence"[2]:

> In his birth narrative however Luke is more explicit than Matthew in his assertion of Jesus' divine sonship from birth (1:32, 35; note also 2:49). Here again it is sufficiently clear that *a virginal conception by divine power* without the participation of any man is in view (1:34). But here too it is sufficiently clear that it is a begetting, a becoming which is in view, the coming into existence of one who will be called, and will in fact be the Son of God, not the transition of a pre-existent being to become the soul of a human baby or the metamorphosis of a divine being into a human foetus.[3]

So Jesus' beginning, on this earth, is miraculous. But it is also natural because it came about through a woman in the direct lineage of David through Mary. Perhaps we should also recognize the legal appropriateness of Jesus being the Messiah, since his mother was married to Joseph, also in David's line, even though that had nothing to do with the conception (Matt 1:18). While such a detailed line of argumentation is absent from Smith's presentation, the idea of Jesus as a preexistent entity is rejected outright mainly because the birth of Jesus has to be so very *human*, directly from the seed of David. However, Smith *must* admit that the birth of Jesus is not human enough. To take the passages in the biblical prophecy as to Jesus' coming literally, there is no room for the miraculous. Human beings do not get born, they do not even come into existence, simply by a human mother. It puzzles me why the equally extant understanding of entities existing in the heavenly realm and being born human is so odious in the biblical understanding of Jesus' identity. Patrick Navas has effectively written regarding this heavenly/miraculous vs. exclusively earthly/human dichotomy:

> Some have argued that the "came-down-from-heaven" language is simply a reference to how God brought the man Jesus into existence through the virgin birth (a heavenly/miraculous birth as opposed to an exclusively earthly/human one) and subsequently sent him forth into the world (Matt 1:18; and Luke 1:35), and that the language need not demand a literal notion of a personal, pre-human, heavenly existence. This may be true. However, according to John 3:13, Jesus similarly said, "No one has ascended into heaven except he who descended from heaven [*ek tou ouranou katabas*], the Son of Man." Essentially the same language is used of

---

2. Dunn, *Christology in the Making*, 51.
3. Ibid., 50–51.

AN ARIAN RESPONSE TO A SOCINIAN VIEW

"the angel of the Lord" in Matt 28:2 whom we know did actually live in the heavenly realm before coming to the earth: "And behold there was a great earthquake, for an angel of the Lord descended from heaven [*angelos gar kuriou katabas ex ouranou*] and came and rolled back the stone and sat on it" (Matt 28:2). It seems clear that the angel dwelled in the realm called "heaven" (with God or where God dwells) and left this realm ("wherever" that is) to come to the earth. The language Jesus used of himself is essentially identical. Thus it would only seem natural to conclude that the Son of God lived in the heavenly dimension, "like the angel of the Lord" clearly did—before he was born in the earth as a human being.[4]

What we have here is essentially a difference of opinion as to whether we should see a passage as literal or figurative. Jesus, in John 3:13, claims prehuman existence. He says he descended from heaven. I cannot anticipate how Smith will address this in his reply. But it is not beyond God's miraculous power for a preexistent entity to make an advent to earth by God's causing a woman to become pregnant and giving birth to that entity.

JOHN 1:1–18

Smith affirms that the *Logos* in John's Prologue (John 1:1–18) is God's "personified and personal utterance," and "not a conscious being alongside God." The language of the first few verses of John 1, however, suggests the presence of the *Logos* "with" God and the *Logos* is also described as being "divine," which is the only logical possibility in the text grammatically as "God" (*Theos*) has already been identified in the verse as meaning the Father.[5] Whether "utterance" should be taken as the only one of about an English yard of definitions for the word *Logos* is debatable.

JOHN 8:58

I mentioned this in my response to Irons, but the translators of the NASB have as a legitimate alternate reading, "before Abraham came into being *I have been.*" This is very much like the Greek reading from the beginning of the *Testament of Job*, which I mentioned in my first presentation: The Greek here is remarkably similar grammatically to the pseudepigraphal *T.*

---

4. Navas, *Divine Truth or Human Tradition*, 357 n55.
5. Wallace, *Greek Grammar*, 266–69.

THE SON OF GOD

Job 2:1: "For I have been Jobab [*Egō gar eimi Iōbab*] before the Lord named me Job [*prin ē onomasai me ho Kyrios Iōb*]." This is to say that the concept of a person having existed before human birth was a concept not unknown to the Second Temple-period mind.

JOHN 17:5

Near his ministry's end Jesus prayed, "Father, glorify me in your presence with the glory I had with you before the world was." This is a clear reference to Jesus' presence with his Father.

COLOSSIANS 1:15

Jesus is called God's "firstborn" here and is presented in the following verses as being the one through whom God created all things. "First-born" glosses the Greek word *prōtotokos*. The conceptual background of this passage is Wisdom texts like Prov 8. This is not to say that Prov 8 is speaking of Christ *per se*, but to point out that the language is very similar to that language. Barron writes:

> The Septuagint version of Pro 8:22 uses *archē*, translated either "first" or "beginning" with Wisdom being "the *archē* of God's ways." Here "God's ways" refer to his creative activities (cf. Job 26:14; 40:19). The thought of "first" parallels Col 1:15's use of *prōto-*. Similarly, Pro 8:24 finds Wisdom to have been "born," translated from *genna*, while the same is of Christ with *tokos*, meaning "born."[6]

PSALM 2:7 AND 2 SAMUEL 7:12–16

This is a minor point, but Smith acknowledges that these two passages are messianic. In fact they are both quoted as such in the first chapter of Hebrews. The language of these passages has little or nothing to do with physical birthing. 2 Sam 7:14 sets forth the language that would be repeated in various Old Testament passages (e.g., Ps 89:26). Ps 2:7 is better seen as a coronation psalm that would be read at the inauguration of the monarch, who would be viewed as having been adopted by God. I chose the *American*

---

6. Barron, *God and Christ*, 48.

AN ARIAN RESPONSE TO A SOCINIAN VIEW

Standard Version margin reading, not because I have some penchant for archaic speech, but because of the word choice for the translation of the Greek word *genesis*—"generation"—in verse 18. If this translation is correct, the passage speaks of Jesus' literal "beginning," which was as a person for the first time, *in this world*.

THE LIFE AND TEACHINGS OF THE MESSIAH

I agree that Jesus was a man *only* during his sojourn on the earth, and he had human limitations, normal human progressions in physical and mental growth. I also agree with all Smith has to say regarding agency and Jesus' prerogative, assigned to him by God, to perform work on God's behalf. Nor do I think Smith has exceeded any implications in acknowledging that Jesus is "Son of God." I do think, however, that based upon the contextual application present in 2 Sam 7:12–16 and Ps 2 to acknowledge the then-crowned king in David's dynasty as God's "son," as well as the New Testament applications to Jesus in Hebrews 1, that Son of God should be seen as an equivalent designation for God's Messiah.

THE DEATH OF THE MESSIAH/THE RESURRECTION AND EXALTATION OF THE MESSIAH

It could be a topic worth discussing, but the question whether Jesus was individually multipartite ("May your whole spirit, soul, and body be kept blameless" [1 Thess 5:23], or "Fear him who is able to destroy both body and soul in *gehenna*" [Matt 10:28]) does not make a difference one way or the other for the present study.

Also, according to 1 Tim 2:5, the resurrected, and therefore exalted, Jesus serves a mediatorial role as an exalted human. "There is one God, and one mediator between God and humans, the human Christ Jesus."

THE RETURN OF THE MESSIAH

Regarding Jesus' designation, prophetically, as the "Son of Man" in Dan 7:13, being given a kingdom, dominion, and authority, I know I would have different perspectives regarding Smith's premillennial point of view, but they are not at issue in this study; that the passage was widely understood as being prophetic of the Messiah *is* the point at issue, and Smith is correct on that. However, a statement like "the kingdom of God is at hand," spoken by John the Baptist in Matt 3:1 and imitated by Jesus in Mark 1:15, seems to indicate that the promised kingdom of God was thought by Jesus, as he told his disciples on one occasion, to be imminent within the lifetimes of some of those standing nearby, who would not taste death before the coming of the kingdom (Mark 9:1). And I take Dan 7:13 to be fulfilled in Peter's announcement to Israel in Acts 2:36 that God had made the Jesus they had crucified both Lord and Messiah.

1 Cor 15:23ff seems to me to suggest that Jesus is reigning now, spiritually, in one phase of his kingdom rule that was to be simultaneous with the rule of his enemies *until* they would be subjected. But again, that is another debate for another day.

SUMMARY

I have a history that has caused me to reconsider many things theologically. It is doctrinally significant to try to understand who is the Absolute and Supreme deity (1 Tim 6:15). Jesus is God because he is God's agent, but he is not Almighty God if he has had a beginning. Smith and I agree on the wording of the preceding although we differ on what I would consider minor details regarding the life Jesus has had (whether preexistent or one beginning at approximately 6 BC [according to Dustin, p. 177]). The ministry of Jesus demonstrated how God would walk around in human flesh were he here. There has not been much on which to clash in this presentation. As presented and as his position stands, Dustin Smith and I seem to have differences of opinion that should not preclude acceptance of one another (Rom 14:1), and that should be the cause of much fruitful conversation in the future.

A SOCINIAN REPLY

DUSTIN R. SMITH

I AM GRATEFUL FOR THE opportunity to interact with Dixon's and Irons's responses to my initial essay. Their objections have given me an opportunity to clarify points which were either unclear or in need of further explanation. I intend to accomplish both of these tasks in this essay, and furthermore, I will direct my response to the weightier objections raised by both Dixon and Irons. In reading their responses, I have had the opportunity to think more critically regarding my position—an expected outcome from scholarly discourse.

If I had to summarize the major distinction of my position it would come down to the nature of preexistence. I consider it of no small importance to establish this point thoroughly in order that the evidence be able to breathe the air of contextual data, thoughts, and concepts regarding the elusive conception of "preexistence."[1] In his article on preexistence in the *Dictionary of the Later New Testament & Its Developments*, David Capes helpfully notes that "the pre-existent state may be described as ideal (existence in the mind or plan of God) or actual (existence alongside and distinct from God)."[2] Capes's two categories of preexistence—"ideal" and "actual" (which I have previously identified as "notional" and "literal")—adequately set the stage for the debate. I have argued that the New Testament's concept of preexistence is best understood as notional ("ideal") rather than literal

---

1. It is extremely unfortunate that the majority of the standard resource dictionaries fails to offer articles on this monumental subject.

2. Capes, "Preexistence," 956. The older study by Robert G. Hamerton-Kelly articulates the two options as "either in the mind of God or in heaven." *Pre-Existence*, 11.

THE SON OF GOD

("actual"). My reasons for coming to this conclusion are numerous. For one, Jewish preexistence was surely notional, within God's foreknowledge and purposes.[3] Secondly, a virtual consensus exists today among scholars that the most fundamental background for the idea of preexistence in the New Testament is the Jewish tradition (rather than Platonic).[4] The implications are clear. If Jesus only preexists in God's mind and plan, then his physical existence chronologically begins at the moment of his begetting in the womb of Mary. The New Testament regularly speaks of preexistence in the same cultural and conceptual framework in which the Jews operated. Jesus was foreknown from the foundation of the world (1 Pet 1:20), existing in God's foreknowledge. Regarding the Jewish understanding of foreknowledge, the article in the *International Standard Bible Encyclopedia* is helpful:

> The term foreknowledge is an expansion of the idea of God's "counsel" or plan, regarding it as an intelligent prearrangement, the idea of foreknowledge being assimilated to that of foreordination. The same idea is found in [1 Pet 1:20]. Here the apostle speaks of Christ as a lamb "foreordained" by God before the foundation of the world.... It has the idea of a purpose which determines the course of the Divine procedure.[5]

Apart from 1 Pet 1:20, I observed that Christ is spoken of within the matrix of Jewish notional preexistence in Acts 2:23 ("the man Jesus was delivered over according to God's predetermined plan and foreknowledge"); Rom 8:29-30 ("God foreknew and foreordained believers to be conformed to the image of his Son"); Eph 1:4-5 ("God chose us in Christ before the foundation of the world . . . God predestined us to adoption as children through Jesus Christ"); Rev 13:8 ("the Lamb has been slain from the foundation of the world"). More general statements about God's plans and foreknowledge are evidenced in 1 Pet 1:1-2 and Rev 4:11. I contend that this evidence deserves further consideration by my dialogue partners.

---

3. I noted in my previous essays a sampling of examples from Jewish literature: Jer 1:5; *b. Pes.* 54a; *b. Ned.* 39b; *Tg. Zech.* 4:7; *Prayer of Joseph* 1:2; *T. Moses* 1:14; *Gen. Rab.* 1.1, 4; 8.2. See also 2 Kgs 19:25 ("Long ago I did it, from ancient times I planned it. Now I have brought it to pass"); *2 Bar.* 4:2-7 ("this [temple] building . . . was already prepared from the moment I decided to create Paradise . . . now it is preserved with me").

4. Hurtado, "Pre-existence," 743. Capes offers a similar line: "Because Second-Temple Judaism provides an adequate conceptual base, the view is that the background for a preexistence christology is found in Judaism." Capes, "Preexistence," 956.

5. Hodge, "Foreknow," 1130.

A SOCINIAN REPLY

I understand the value of responsibly researching the way in which Jewish preexistence was conveyed within these texts (and the nonbiblical sources). Since there is an abundance of evidence which demonstrates that Jews often spoke of a manner of preexistence which was notional, bound up in God's predetermined purpose, then this must be a grid through which we read similar passages in the New Testament. It will simply not do to ignore these contextual clues and resort to a so-called "plain meaning of the text," which is subjective to each interpreter in his or her time. What is of extreme importance is the necessity to read these texts regarding Jesus as a Jew would, in other words, within its Jewish context (rather than with our modern, Western eyes).[6] Failure to take seriously the notional preexistence expressed by the plethora of texts creates a problem when applied to Jesus, where he exists prior to his coming into existence. This is, I respectfully suggest, both confusing and contradictory.[7] How can persons physically exist before they are begotten? This, I argue, is impossible. My respectable dialogue partners attempt to resolve this conundrum by arguing that Jesus' begetting was not actually the time when he came into existence. This leads to a downplaying of the birth of Jesus, a redefining of regular "begetting" language, and a weakening of the humanity of Jesus. Those Christologies which articulate that Jesus literally preexisted his birth are forced to ignore the genealogies and birth narratives in Matthew and Luke, reject the messianic expectation laid as the foundation within the Hebrew Bible, and replace Jewish concepts with postbiblical Greek philosophy. I regard these objections as weighty and in need of serious consideration.

Irons seems to have misunderstood my position by his repeated claim that I supposedly paint Jesus as being "a mere man." I wish to respond by stating that this designation is an unfair representation of both my Christology and of my initial essay. I argued that Jesus is the Christ, a noteworthy messianic title depicting the promised king of God's kingdom. Furthermore, Jesus was sinless, despite the fact that he was tempted like every other human being. Additionally, Jesus is the only individual who has been raised to eternal life. After his resurrection, God highly exalted him and placed him at his right hand. God has invested his name and authority upon Jesus—his

---

6. James D. G. Dunn echoes my point here: "Jesus was a Jew and must be understood within the terms provided by Judaism and its sacred scriptures." See Dunn, "Christology (NT)," 989; Dunn, *Christology in the Making*, 6.

7. Cf. John Hick et al, who confess their hope to "release talk about God and about Jesus from confusions, thereby freeing people to serve God in the Christian path with greater integrity." *Myth of God Incarnate*, x–xi.

THE SON OF GOD

principal agent and beloved son. According to the Prologue of John, Jesus is the incarnation of the very Word which both created all things and reflects God's will. Since no other human being, living or dead, can come close to any of these accolades (much less their combination), I contend that it is a gross misunderstanding to suggest that Jesus was a mere man. Writing toward the end of the first century CE, Luke is comfortable describing Jesus as "a *man* attested to you by God with miracles and wonders and signs *which God performed through him* in your midst" (Acts 2:22). Certainly this description is much more than a mere man! For one who is miraculously begotten, sinless, resurrected to eternal life, seated at God's right hand, invested with God's authority, expected to return as the messianic king, and the living embodiment of God's creative speech is nevertheless the *second Adam*, the second human being (1 Cor 15:45, 47).

Irons furthermore suggests that the incarnation of the preexisting Son is *clearly taught* in the following passages: John 1:14; 2 John 7; Gal 4:4; Rom 8:3; 1 Tim 3:16; and Heb 2:14. I suggest that this line of thinking uncritically appraises these texts and the intentions of their original authors. I will now offer what seems to me to be the most plausible explanation for these disputed texts.

The famous John 1:14 indicates that the *Logos* became flesh and tabernacled among us. I have already offered a fuller treatment of my reading of this text in my response to Danny Dixon, so I will only offer a summary here. I contend that the *Logos* is God's creative and self-expressive utterance. It is both powerful, in that it is said to be the means through which God ordered the Genesis creation (Gen 1:3, 6, 9, etc.), and it is personal, in that it is appropriately personified with poetic masculine pronouns throughout the Johannine Prologue (John 1:3, 4, 10, 11). Since this manner of personifying God's attributes can similarly be observed in the profusely poetic Prov 8 and Wis 6, where God's Wisdom is depicted as a female figure, it seems appropriate to read the opening of the Fourth Gospel along similar lines. I also note that God's *davar/logos* is never described as a conscious being alongside God in either the Hebrew Bible or Second Temple-Jewish literature. It is sometimes personified, yes, but a poetic and metaphorical personification of God's speech is significantly different from a conscious, separate being. To put it differently, there is a significantly important difference between the Qumran Jews saying that "everything shall come into being by God's plan" (*b'mahashbat*) (1QS 11:11) and the Platonist philosopher turned Christian, Justin Martyr, writing, "For not only among the Greeks

A SOCINIAN REPLY

did the Logos prevail to condemn these things through Socrates, but also among the non-Hellenic peoples by the Logos himself, who assumed human form and became man, and was called Jesus Christ."[8] This leads me to regard John 1:14 as indicating that the *Logos*, God's personified utterance, became embodied in the human Jesus, who as such speaks God's words to human beings on earth.[9] There is no indication within the Prologue that a preexistent "Son" is in view. Colin Brown has challenged this interpretation: "It is a common but patent misreading of the opening of John's Gospel to read it as if it said: 'In the beginning was the *Son*, and the *Son* was with God, and the *Son* was God' (John 1:1)."[10] One is forced to redefine the Jewish concept of God's *davar/logos* in order to make a doctrine of "a preexisting being who becomes human" fit awkwardly into the Prologue of John.

Second John 7, arguably the central verse of the entire epistle, confers the label of "the deceiver and the antichrist" to those who refuse to confess "Jesus Christ coming in the flesh." How is this confessional phrase to be interpreted? One might conclude that this is referencing a preexisting being who takes on flesh. However, this is not the best reading of this passage for a number of reasons. For one, the designation "Jesus Christ" is generally recognized as the given human name (Matt 1:21, 25; Luke 1:31) combined with the messianic title *Christos*.[11] The "Christ" is never mentioned as a preexisting figure in the Hebrew Bible or within Second Temple-Jewish literature. Another problem with the incarnational interpretation is that phrase concerning Jesus' flesh (*en sarki*) which is most appropriately translated "as a human being." If a preexistent being was coming into the flesh, one would expect the preposition *eis*. One must also place this passage within the overall context of the epistle, which seems to be battling some form of docetic understanding of Jesus, a Christology which marginalizes flesh as evil in favor of spirit. The elder responds to this christological controversy, not by claiming that the Son who preexisted came down and became a man, but rather by utterly stressing Jesus' full humanity.[12] After all is said and

---

8. Justin Martyr, *First Apology*, 5. On the influence of Heraclitus, Stoic philosophy, Philo, and Middle Platonists upon Justin Martyr's Logos theology, see Hillar, *From Logos to Trinity*, 138–69.

9. I also noted in my response to Dixon the much neglected parallels in Philo where Moses is twice depicted as the embodiment of God's Torah (*Moses* 1.162; 2.4). This is hardly describing incarnation of a preexisting person.

10. Brown, "Trinity and Incarnation," 89, italics are his.

11. Meyer, "Jesus Christ," 773.

12. See the comments by Holladay, *Critical Introduction*, 522–24. The supposed

THE SON OF GOD

done, it seems like a reading which stresses Jesus Christ as a fully-fledged human being, a *bona fide* member of the human race, is the interpretive path of least resistance.

The Pauline passages Gal 4:4 and Rom 8:3 are closely related, so it seems appropriate to deal with them together. The former is used in Paul's comment concerning the timing and circumstances of Jesus' birth: "When the fullness of time came, God sent for his Son, born of a woman, born under the law . . . ." The verb employed here (*exapostellō*) is used in the LXX (with God as the subject) in two primary ways: to describe when God sends someone *from heaven* and to describe the commissioning of a human messenger *on earth*.[13] Since the majority of these instances fall into the category of God commissioning someone on earth, it is likely that this is how Paul's Galatian readers would have understood his words.[14] It is also highly doubtful that these readers would have had an "incarnation" frame of reference out of which to conclude that the Son descended from heaven and became human.[15] Furthermore, the following phrase "born of a woman" is only used elsewhere to refer to the traditional act of a mother birthing her child.[16] It never indicates nor hints at any manner of incarnational thought or theology. Since the two phrases "born of a woman, born under the law" are clearly actions which occurred simultaneously (rather than in chronological order),[17] this strengthens the likelihood that the previous statement concerning "God sending forth his Son" was similarly intended by Paul to be understood as having occurred at the same time. If this is the case, the

---

connection with the christological dilemma observed in 1 John sheds light upon my reading. According to 1 John 2:22, the "antichrist" is the one who denies that Jesus is *the Christ*, a denial which is something quite other than a denial of conscious preexistence of the Son. It seems that 2 John was composed to combat the rising docetic tendencies by reaffirming that Jesus Christ was truly human. Brown may even be correct by suggesting that there is "insufficient context in II John to enable us to surmise what the author means by this formula." R. Brown, *Epistles of John*, 686.

13. See the data collected in Dunn, *Christology in the Making*, 38–39.

14. Cf. James D. G. Dunn's insistence that "the much more established theme of the sending of a prophet has to be considered." Dunn, *Theology of Paul*, 278. The verb is also used of Paul's own commissioning in Acts 22:21.

15. Kuschel, *Born Before All Time?*, 273; Dunn, *Christology in the Making*, 42; Williams, *Galatians*, 111.

16. Job 14:1; 15:14; 25:4; Matt 11:11. Dunn reminds us that this phrase was a typical Jewish circumlocution for "the human person . . . the human condition." Dunn, *Galatians*, 215; cp. Osiek, *Galatians*, 46.

17. Longenecker, *Galatians*, 171.

A SOCINIAN REPLY

commissioning of Jesus to redeem those under the Law occurred precisely at his birth, where the circumstances of his birth ("of a woman," "under the law") are Paul's characteristic way of unpacking the initial statement.[18] I suggest that the most natural way that Paul's original recipients would have understood Gal 4:4 is along the lines of other prophetic servants who were commissioned from their birth (see Isa 49:1, 5; Jer 1:5; Gal 1:15).

The closely related passage Rom 8:3 also indicates that "God sent his own Son in the likeness of sinful flesh." In this passage Paul utilizes the verb *pempō* with the same mind-set as we observed in Gal 4:4, in a manner which expresses a messenger's or prophet's authority (Matt. 11:2; 14:10; Luke 4:26; 20:13; John 20:21). The reference to sinful flesh, in context, is clearly a description of Jesus who knew the same mortality and experienced human weakness. To imply that Paul was teaching that God sent his Son from heaven to become flesh both anachronistically imports a postbiblical theology into this text and misses the influence that *sarx* has had as the dominating theme spanning back to Rom 7:5.[19] The sense here, however, concerns God's initiative in the act of sending the Son in favor of humanity in the face of the impossibility and incompetence of the law.[20] After careful scrutiny, neither Gal 4:4 nor Rom 8:3 are indicative that Paul believed in a preexistent Son who became incarnate at his birth. What is much more likely is that Paul's "sending" language in these two passages is characteristic of its normal lexical convention which involved the commissioning of an agent for a specific purpose.[21]

An interesting and notorious history belongs to 1 Tim 3:16. Theologically motivated scribes who were not comfortable with the text merely stating "He who was manifested in the flesh," chose to alter the Greek to read "*God* was manifested in the flesh."[22] All modern textual critics admit this corruption occurred and agree that the relative pronoun is the origi-

---

18. Longenecker (*Galatians*,166) points out that J. B. Lightfoot made the same observation back in 1890. Dunn (*Galatians,* 216–17) observes that Paul has paralleled Gal 4:4–6 with his earlier 3:13–14 in a manner which indicates that the Son's redemption was achieved by his death, not by incarnation. See also Martyn, *Galatians*, 407–408.

19. Cf. N. T. Wright's comments on *sarx*: "Jesus' humanity was indeed the genuine article; it was not a cover for a smuggled-in Docetism in which Jesus was not actually human but only seemed to be." Wright, "Romans," 578; cp. Wright, *Paul and the Faithfulness of God*, 898–900.

20. Kuschel, *Born Before All Time?*, 300–301.

21. Dunn, *Theology of Paul*, 278; Dunn, *Christology in the Making*, 45.

22. Ehrman, *Orthodox Corruption*, 77–78.

nal reading.[23] With that being said, it is also important to note that the designation "Son" is nowhere to be found in this hymn. The use of *sarx* in this passage is the only occurrence located in the Pastorals. Luke Timothy Johnson helpfully notes that the rather simple phrase *en sarki* predominantly expresses an ordinary human existence (Rom 2:28; 7:5, 18; 8:3; Gal 2:20; 4:14; Eph 2:11; Phil 1:22; 3:3; Col 1:24; Phlm 16).[24] In other words, the hymn seems to be indicating that Jesus was manifested as a purely human individual, not entering the human race from above. It seems highly unlikely that this passage was intended to mean something wholly other than the simple statement made earlier in the epistle, "for there is one God, and one mediator between God and humans, the human Messiah Jesus (2:5)."[25] When the six lines of the text are placed in parallel, the hymn appears to contrast Christ's pre-Easter earthly ministry with his post-Easter exaltation, similar to what we find in 1 Pet 3:18.[26] This "two-stage" formula also appears in 2 Tim 2:8, and along with 1 Tim 3:16 these passages show absolutely no indication of a (third) preexistent stage in the person of the Son.

The comment in Heb 2:14 that Jesus partook of blood and flesh is easier to discern. The verse begins with a temporal clause, "Therefore, since the children have shared in blood and flesh," meaning human nature (which is susceptible to corruption).[27] The author connects the experience of Jesus with that of the aforementioned children, using the adverb *paraplēsiōs* ("similarly, in just the same way"). Stated differently, the author associates the manner in which Jesus embraced the human condition with the same way that every other human has traditionally done so. Jesus was as we are. This is hardly the language of a preexistent Son who assumed human nature. If it is, how does that square with the author's statement in 2:17 that Jesus was *like his brethren in all aspects*? How can the "children" be brothers and sisters of a preexistent Son of God? On the whole, there seems to be

---

23. *TCGNT*, 573–74.

24. Johnson, *Timothy*, 233; Dunn, *Theology of Paul*, 62–72.

25. I. Howard Marshall, who admits that preexistence "does not appear to be a point of emphasis," highlights 1 Tim 2:5 as the similar thought in mind regarding 3:16 where JesusJesus' "human experience is therefore probably uppermost in mind." See Marshall, *Pastoral Epistles*, 524. William D. Mounce is similarly hesitant to see preexistence. See Mounce, *Pastoral Epistles*, 227.

26. Jeremias, *Timotheus und Titus*, 23; Gundry, "Form, Meaning," 209; Dunn, "Timothy and Titus," 808.

27. Craddock, "Hebrews," 40.

A SOCINIAN REPLY

no indication of incarnational theology present here unless the interpreter decides to force it clumsily upon the text.

While these six passages are often highlighted as proof that Jesus was the preexistent Son of God who became man, such a reading must begin with that presupposition from the outset. I respectfully suggest that this presupposition is both unwarranted and impossible, since Yahweh was unaccompanied at the time of creation (Isa 44:24). Since the incarnation, in its full and proper sense, is not something directly presented in scripture but rather is a construct of a handful of passages mixed with postbiblical Greek philosophy, this presupposition must be abandoned and appropriately labeled as anachronistic.[28]

The symbolism which saturates the Fourth Gospel is regularly read too literally, resulting in confusion over Jesus' metaphoric statements.[29] A selection of passages (John 3:13; 6:38; 8:58; 17:5) are read by both Irons and Dixon in a way which argues for literal preexistence. Having already treated 8:58 and 17:5 in my reply to Dixon, it is necessary to give attention to the remaining two texts at this juncture.[30] John 3:13 records Jesus saying that "no one has ascended into heaven except for the one who came down from heaven, the Son of Man." My contention is that the symbolism expressed in this passage gets entirely missed if it is passed over by a woodenly literal reading. The preceding verse depicts Jesus positing a question: How can Nicodemus, if he doesn't demonstrate belief when he is told "earthly things," believe if he is told "heavenly things?" The contrast here between the things of the earth and the things of heaven in the Fourth Gospel is more a matter of polarizing one's *religious identity and traits* rather than citing differing *locations*. The word "earthly" (*epigeios*) in John 3:12 also appears in a similar contrast with the things "from above" (*anōthen*) in James 3:15, where demonic wisdom is described as "earthly" rather than "from above." The same theme appears earlier in the document in Jas 1:17, "Every good thing given and every perfect gift is from above, coming down from the Father." "Godly wisdom" is also said to be "from above" in Jas 3:17, where it is described with all of its positive characteristics. One does not get the sense

---

28. Wiles, "Christianity without Incarnation?," 3. I can still recall the conversation I had in 2009 with the late Dr. Eugene Carpenter, scholar in residence at Bethel College (Mishawaka, Indiana), when he admitted to me privately that the doctrine of the incarnation was not biblical but was the church's best attempt at resolving the meaning of a few key texts.

29. Koester, *Symbolism*, 9.

30. See pp. 102-5 above.

THE SON OF GOD

in James that the contrast with "things from above" and "from the earth" is merely a description of locations but rather concerning wisdom *from God* which is characterized in all of its affirmative aspects. Similar contrasts can be observed in the Synoptic account regarding the time when Jesus questions the chief priests and elders about John's baptism (Matt 21:23–27; Mark 11:27–33; Luke 20:1–8). For Jesus to ask if the baptism was "from heaven or from humans" is clearly a distinction in religious identity, not location. These examples, I suggest, create a grid through which we can understand the metaphorical contrast between earth and heaven in John 3:11–13. Therefore, to say that Jesus "descended from heaven" is unlikely to signify that he literally dropped from the sky. A much more probable case is that he is the perfect gift from God (Jas 1:17), characterized by godly traits rather than demonic (Jas 3:15, 17), bearing in his person the authority from heaven (Matt 21:23). It is also prudent to note that the Fourth Evangelist is almost certainly polemically pointing to Jesus as the true and authoritative revealer of the heavenly Father, which rules out other options available in Judaism's variegated expressions.[31] Since the opponents in the Fourth Gospel, "the Jews," surely considered Jesus to be a deceiving messianic pretender, there is a strong emphasis in stressing that Jesus *truly is God's authorized Messiah*, i.e., that he has "descended from heaven." In sum, I suggest that attempts to push the words of John 3:13 too literally both ignores the metaphoric symbolism which is so prevalent in the document and fails to take seriously the Jewish context regarding how persons or objects "from heaven" are characterized by a heavenly identity and description.

A lot of the same can be stated in regard to John 6:38, "I have come down from heaven." This long passage begins with the metaphor of bread from heaven, an allusion to God sustaining the Israelites during the wilderness wanderings (John 6:31). Jesus gives a quotation from Psalm 78 where the psalmist recalls how God "opened the doors of heaven; He rained down manna upon them to eat and gave them grain from heaven. Man did eat the bread of angels; He sent them provision in abundance" (Ps 78:23–25).

The sense expressed by the psalmist is that God provided for the needs of the Israelites. It is probably of no small significance that the food "from heaven" is described as being "sent." Just as the manna was provided to sustain God's people in Exodus, the Fourth Evangelist identifies Jesus as

---

31. Figures hailed as revealers of God's secrets included Enoch (*1 Enoch* 14:8–25; 39:3–8; 70–71; *2 Enoch* 3–23), Abraham (*T. Abr.* 10–15; *Apoc. Ab.* 15–29), Adam (*Life of Adam and Eve* 25–29), Levi (*T. Levi* 2–8), Baruch (*2 Baruch* 76), and Isaiah (*Asc. Isa.* 7–10).

A SOCINIAN REPLY

the current manifestation of God's "bread from heaven." The text continues with Jesus stating that "My Father is the one who *is giving you* the true bread out of heaven" (John 6:32). This language of "giving" is reminiscent of the aforementioned Jas 1:17. Of course, the Jews grumbled at Jesus' assertion, and misunderstood his statement by taking it literally. The misunderstanding theme is dominant in the Fourth Gospel, exhibited when Jesus says something provocative and his dialogue partner(s) interpret it literally (which is always the incorrect interpretation). If this is the case, then why do so many modern interpreters assume that Jesus *literally came down out of heaven*? If we continue reading the passage, would we be correct if we assumed that Jesus' flesh literally descended from the clouds above (John 6:51)? Are we to literally eat Jesus' flesh and drink his blood (John 6:53)? Attempts to press the language in such a strictly literal manner seem to be misguided and unconvincing. A much more persuasive reading recognizes that Jesus is *truly a gift from God* and is expressed here through the symbolism of food, which both sustained the Israelites in the past and offers the life of the age in the present (John 6:54).

The Christ hymn in Phil 2:6–11 is cited by Irons as proof of personal preexistence of the Son. While space does not allow for a full treatment of this passage (about which entire volumes have been written), I feel that a few comments will demonstrate that Paul was speaking of neither incarnation nor preexistence. The hymn has a specific purpose established in Phil 2:5, which is to provide a moral model for Paul's Philippian audience to believe, adapt, and imitate.[32] The readers were to possess the mind of humility within their Christian community "which was also in Christ Jesus." In other words, Paul expects that the humility exhibited by Christ Jesus was something to be emulated and reasonably lived out. If this is the case, then a reading of Phil 2:6–7 which insists that a preexistent being (usually God) decided to become a man and die on the cross fails to offer a plausible model to imitate. How are believers to emulate the assumption of humanity? I suggest that this interpretation is problematic enough to warrant an examination of readings which insist that Paul describes the earthly career of "Christ Jesus," a designation which *never* indicates personal preexistence.

There are a number of scholars who concluded that there is no preexistence in Phil 2.[33] Even Martin Luther interpreted "the form of God" as

---

32. Barclay, "Jesus and Paul," 499.

33. Robinson, *Cross*, 57, 103–5; Talbert, "Problem of Pre-existence"; Borsch, *Son of Man*, 250–56; Robinson, *Human Face*, 162–69; Bartsch, *Konkrete Wahrheit*;

THE SON OF GOD

Christ's manhood rather than a preexistent divine person.[34] Paul draws on "servant" imagery from Isa 52:13—53:12 in his description of Christ Jesus as the one who took the servant's role and poured himself out to death.[35] Jesus here is depicted as one who always submitted to the will of God, even to the point of martyrdom. Colin Brown explains that the statements concerning Jesus' humility "each apply to the whole of Christ's life, all of them culminating in the cross."[36] The sustained argument of Philippians also strengthens my interpretation regarding the humility of the human Jesus, as his example is emulated by both Paul (Phil 2:17; 3:4–7) and Epaphroditus (Phil 2:25–30), who both poured out their lives in service of others. Paul even expected his original audience to "have this attitude" (Phil 3:15) and to "join in following my example" (Phil 3:17). The fact that both Paul and Epaphroditus demonstrated humility as selfless human beings strongly suggests that Phil 2:6–11 regards the humility of the human Jesus. I regard this interpretation as far more persuasive than one which presupposes personal preexistence.

I am disappointed that my employment of Jewish texts in an attempt to recreate plausible historical contexts was so effortlessly dismissed. Any text, biblical or extra-biblical, needs to be placed into its proper context. This methodology underlies any responsible interpreter's reading of historical texts. One cannot dismiss the scaffolding around the building as unimportant. I find it rather amazing that Irons waves the *sola scriptura* flag in defense of his position, seeing how the consensus of Church historians is that the Trinity was a slowly developing doctrine over the course of the first five centuries. Scholars who have attempted to acutely define the specifics regarding how "a preexisting being can become human" are regularly puzzled, forcing them to resort to unpersuasive lingo concerning a "mystery [which] can only be described in terms of paradox."[37] What Charles Wesley deemed "mystery all! The Immortal dies!" is the unfortunate result of such a linguistic contradiction.[38]

Murphy-O'Connor, "Phil. 2:6–11"; Howard, "Phil 2:6–11"; Dunn, *Christology in the Making*, 114–21; Kuschel, *Born Before All Time?*, 250–5; C. Brown, "Ernst Lohmeyer's Kyrios Jesus"; Osiek, *Philippians, Philemon*, 65–67; McGrath, *Only True God*, 50–51.

34. See the citation in Robinson, *Human Face*, 165 n91.
35. Isa 53:12 says that he poured out his soul unto death (i.e., Jesus' soul died).
36. C. Brown, "Empty," 549.
37. Beyreuther and Finkenrath, "Like," in *NIDNTT* 2.504–5.
38. Lyrics from "And Can It Be That I Should Gain," by Charles Wesley, 1738.

A SOCINIAN REPLY

I admit that the variegated Jewish expectations and hopes were not always unified on every point regarding Christology. However, Irons's citation of *4 Ezra* as evidence for preexistence should be called into question since that document was composed after the destruction of the second temple. This means that *4 Ezra* could not have historically influenced the historical Jesus, the apostle Paul, or the earliest traditions of Jesus (Q and Mark).[39] If it turns out that *4 Ezra* is a second-century-CE composition, then it would be ruled out as a possible influence even on the Gospel of John.

Both of my dialogue partners fail to be persuaded by what seems to me to be a fairly obvious conception of Christology in the birth narratives of Matthew and Luke. Irons argues that the "non-mention of Christ's preexistence in Matthew and Luke" is an argument from silence. I respectfully disagree. Both Matthew (1:18, 20) and Luke (1:35) clearly demonstrate that Jesus came into existence.[40] If a person begins to exist at a specific moment in time, then by definition they could not have personally existed at any moment prior. If Jesus was brought into existence in 6 BCE, then he did not have any conscious existence prior to that date. The "begetting" language employed by both Matthew and Luke, by anchoring Jesus' beginning in time, categorically screens out any manner of literal, conscious preexistence of the Son.[41]

Irons's position forces him to abruptly downplay the relevance of the Jewish category regarding agency and the commissioned *shaliach*, despite the rather obvious parallels. Scholars are in agreement that the person who is sent acts as the sender's authorized agent,[42] entrusted with a task.[43] The Jewish principle of agency was employed in a wide variety of situations. For example, the *shaliach* could arrange a betrothal (*m. Qidd.* 2.1), a divorce (*m. Git.* 4.1), or a simple business transaction (*t. Yebam.* 4.4). The Jewish

---

39. Of course, we should not assume that every Jew would have had access to these extra-biblical texts.

40. *Gennaō*: "coming into being at a specific moment." BDAG, 192.

41. I would also draw attention to the other passages which describe Jesus' birth which I noted in my initial presentation, especially those in Paul and John.

42. Davies and Allison, *Matthew 8–18*, 153–54.

43. See esp. Rengstorf, who notes that the one who is sent "embodies in his existence as such the one who sends him" ("*apostellō*," 401). Erich von Eicken and Helgo Lindner observe much of the same, "since the envoy has full powers and is the personal representative of the one sending him, a close connection is established between the sender and the recipient." "Apostle," 127.

THE SON OF GOD

agents sent to court or belonging to the Jerusalem Sanhedrin were called the *sheluhim* (*m. Git.* 3.6; *m. Yebam.* 16.7). Furthermore, we can observe in all four Gospel accounts that Jesus Christ both believed the concept of agency and subsequently taught it to his disciples:

> He who receives you receives me, and he who receives me receives Him who sent me (Matt 10:40).

> Whoever receives one child like this in my name receives me; and whoever receives me does not receive me, but Him who sent Me (Mark 9:37).

> Whoever receives this child in my name receives me, and whoever receives me receives Him who sent me; for the one who is least among all of you, this is the one who is great (Luke 9:48).

> The one who listens to you listens to me, and the one who rejects you rejects me; and he who rejects me rejects the One who sent me (Luke 10:16).

> Truly, truly, I say to you, he who receives whomever I send receives me; and he who receives me receives Him who sent me (John 13:20).

The Fourth Gospel, upon close observation, carries with it this Jewish principle of agency. While this Gospel does not call Jesus an apostle (as does Heb 3:1), Betz has nevertheless pointed out that John presumes "the concept and terminology of sending."[44] Marianne Thompson argues in her article on the Gospel of John in hearty agreement with Betz: "Jesus is presented in the Gospel against the backdrop of the Jewish concept of agency and, furthermore, against the understanding that there is one chief agent through whom God acts.... Because Jesus is the chief agent of God, *when one confronts him, one confronts God.*"[45] Jesus declared repeatedly that he was commissioned to carry out the will of God, not his own (John 4:34; 5:30; 6:38, 39). Jesus is also depicted as being sent in order to carry out the works of God (John 4:34; 5:36; 9:4). Similarly, the teaching (John 7:16), commandment (John 12:49), and word (John 14:24) do not belong to Jesus but rather to God who commissioned him. The Fourth Gospel makes sure that there is no confusion regarding the roles of both the sender and the one sent, for Jesus identifies his sender as "the only true God" (John 17:3).

---

44. Betz, "Apostle," 311.
45. Thompson, "John, Gospel of," 377, italics are mine.

A SOCINIAN REPLY

At the conclusion of the Gospel, Jesus extends his ministry to his disciples via the mode of authoritative commissioning, "Just as the Father has sent me, I also send you" (John 20:21). It seems, based upon the evidence in the Gospel of John, that Thompson's observation is on point: "As Son, Jesus can function as the unique delegate (*saliah*) on his Father's behalf and, indeed, the 'Father has given all things into the Son's hands' (3:35)."[46] Therefore I reckon that the principle of Jewish agency is the obvious backdrop against which the New Testament's "sending" language is employed of Jesus' relationship to God.

Before coming to a close I would like to respond to the points which Irons insists that God cannot do (assumptions for which Irons offers no scriptural evidence). The suggestion that "God cannot command creatures to ascribe divine worship to another creature" is misinformed according to 1 Chron 29:20 and Rev 3:9. The next proposal which states that "God cannot grant creatures the power to create" seems to ignore Isa 51:16, where Yahweh intends to put his creative words into the mouth of an agent so as to plant the heavens and found the earth.[47] Lastly, there is plenty of evidence that God has granted creatures the power to forgive sins, such as evidenced by the Israelite high priest and within such texts as 4Q242; Matt 9:8; and John 20:23. It is not surprising that the observation that God hands over his unique prerogatives to the Messiah fits nicely within the principle of agency (see John 13:3).

In conclusion, I regard my position of the human Jesus as unscathed by the rebuttals of my respective opponents. My hope and desire is that I have faithfully allowed the evidence to speak for itself regarding the Bible's christological descriptions of the one mediator between God and humans, the man Messiah Jesus.

---

46. Ibid., 378. She concludes by stating that Jesus "represents God to human beings in such a way that the Gospel can say that to encounter Jesus is to encounter God, to have seen him is to have seen the Father (12:45; 14:7–9) or to know and receive him is to have known and received the Father (8:19; 12:44; 13:20; 17:8; cf. 15:23)." Peder Borgen closes his study on God's agent similarly: "Similarities have also been found between John and rabbinic *halakah* about agency." Borgen, "God's Agent," 75.

47. Watts, *Isaiah 34–66*, 212. See also 4Q 521.

BIBLIOGRAPHY

Aland, Kurt, ed. *Synopsis of the Four Gospels.* Stuttgart: United Bible Societies,1972.
Allison, Dale C. "Jesus Christ." In *NIDB*, vol. 3, 261–93.
Armstrong, Karen. *A History of God.* New York: Ballantine, 1993.
Aschim, Anders. "Melchizdek and Jesus: 11QMelchizedek and the Epistle to the Hebrews." In *The Jewish Roots of Christological Monotheism: Papers from the St. Andrews Conference on the Historical Origins of the Worship of Jesus,* JSJSup 63, edited by Carey C. Newman, James R. Davila, and Gladys S. Lewis, 129–47. Leiden: Brill, 1999.
Ash, Anthony Lee, and Clyde M. Miller. *Psalms.* The Living Word Commentary on the Old Testament. Austin, TX: Sweet, 1980.
Ashton, John, ed. *The Interpretation of John.* Issues in Religion and Theology 9. Philadelphia: Fortress, 1986.
Barclay, John M.G. "Jesus and Paul." In *DPL*, 492–503.
Barclay, William. *Jesus as They Saw Him.* Grand Rapids: Eerdmans, 1962.
Barth, Markus, and Helmut Blanke. *Colossians: A New Translation with Introduction and Commentary.* Translated by Astrid B. Beck. AB 34B. New Haven, CT: Yale University Press, 1994.
Barrett, C.K. *A Critical and Exegetical Commentary on the Acts of the Apostles,* vol. 1. ICC. London: T&T Clark, 2004.
———. *The Gospel According to John: An Introduction with Commentary and Notes on the Greek Text.* 2nd ed. Philadelphia: Westminster, 1978.
Barron, David. *God and Christ: Examining the Evidence for a Biblical Doctrine.* ScripturalTruths.com, 2009.
Bartsch, Hans-Werner. *Die konkrete Wahrheit und die Lüge der Spekulation: Untersuchung über den vorpaulinischen Christushymnus und seine gnostische Mythisierung.* Theologie und Wirklichkeit 1. Frankfurt-Main: Peter Lang, 1974.
Bauckham, Richard. *The Climax of Prophecy: Studies in the Book of Revelation.* Edinburgh: T&T Clark, 1993.
———. *Jesus and the God of Israel: God Crucified and Other Studies on the New Testament's Christology of Divine Identity.* Grand Rapids: Eerdmans, 2008.
Bauer, David R. "Son of God." In *DJG*, 769–75.
Bavinck, Herman. *Reformed Dogmatics, Vol. 2: God and Creation,* edited by John Bolt. Translated by John Vriend. Grand Rapids: Baker Academic, 2004.
Beale, G. K., and D. A. Carson, eds. *Commentary on the New Testament Use of the Old Testament.* Grand Rapids: Baker Academic, 2007.

BIBLIOGRAPHY

Beasley-Murray, George R. *John*. WBC 36. 2nd ed. Nashville, TN: Thomas Nelson, 2000.

Betz, Hans Dieter. "Apostle." In *ABD*, vol. 1, 309–11.

———. *Galatians*. Hermeneia. Philadelphia: Fortress, 1979.

Beyreuther, E. and G. Finkenrath, "Like," in *NIDNTT*, vol. 2, 504–5.

Black, C. Clifton, "First, Second, and Third Letters of John." In *New Interpreter's Bible*,.vol. 12, 363–469. Nashville: Abingdon: 1998.

Boccaccini, Gabriele, ed. *Enoch and Qumran Origins: New Light on a Forgotten Connection*. Grand Rapids: Eerdmans, 2005.

Bock, Darrell L. *Blasphemy and Exaltation in Judaism: The Charge against Jesus in Mark 14:53–65*. Grand Rapids: Baker, 1998.

———. "What Did Jesus Do that Got Him into Trouble? Jesus in the Continuum of Early Judaism–Early Christianity." In *Jesus in Continuum*, edited by Tom Holmén, 171–210. WUNT I/289. Tübingen: Mohr Siebeck, 2012.

Borgen, Peder. "God's Agent in the Fourth Gospel." In *The Interpretation of John*, edited by John Ashton, 67–78. Philadelphia: Fortress, 1986.

Borsch, Frederick H. *The Son of Man in Myth and History*. Philadelphia: Fortress, 1967.

Bowman Jr., Robert M. and J. Ed Komoszewski. *Putting Jesus in His Place: The Case for the Deity of Christ*. Grand Rapids: Kregel, 2007.

Box, G. H., with J. I. Landsman. *The Apocalypse of Abraham*. Translations of Early Documents Series I: Palestinian Jewish Texts, Pre-Rabbinic. London: SPCK, 1919.

Brown, Colin. "Empty." In *NIDNTT*, vol. 1, 548–53.

———. "Ernst Lohmeyer's Kyrios Jesus." In *Where Christology Began: Essays on Philippians 2*, edited by Ralph P. Martin and Brian J. Dodd, 6–42. Louisville: Westminster John Knox, 1998.

———. "Trinity and Incarnation: In Search of Contemporary Orthodoxy." In *Ex Auditu* 7 (1991) 83–100.

Brown, Raymond E. *The Birth of the Messiah: A Commentary on the Infancy Narratives in Matthew and Luke*. Garden City: Doubleday, 1977.

———. *The Epistles of John: A New Translation with Introduction and Commentary*. AB 30. Garden City: Doubleday, 1982.

———. *The Gospel According to John: A New Translation with Introduction and Commentary*. AB 29. Garden City: Doubleday, 1966.

———. *An Introduction to the Gospel of John*. ABRL. New York: Doubleday, 2003.

———. *An Introduction to New Testament Christology*. New York: Paulist, 1994.

Bruce, F. F. *The Book of Acts*. NICNT. Grand Rapids: Eerdmans, 1979.

———. *The Epistle to the Hebrews*, NICNT. Grand Rapids: Eerdmans, 1964.

———. *The Gospel of John: Introduction, Exposition, and Notes*. Grand Rapids: Eerdmans, 1983.

Bullinger, E.W. *Figures of Speech Used in the Bible*. Grand Rapids: Baker Book House, 1898.

Buzzard, Anthony F. "The Gospel of the Kingdom in the Prophets: The Unfulfilled Dream of Messianic Government." *Journal from the Radical Reformation* 4.3 (1995) 3–30.

———. *Jesus Was Not a Trinitarian: A Call to Return to the Creed of Jesus*. Morrow, GA: Restoration Fellowship, 2007.

Buzzard, Anthony F., and Charles F. Hunting. *The Doctrine of the Trinity: Christianity's Self-Inflicted Wound*. Lanham: International Scholars, 1998.

Capes, David B. "Preexistence." In *DLNT*, 955–61.

Caragounis, Chrys C. "*bēn*." In *NIDOTT*, vol. 1, 672–77.

BIBLIOGRAPHY

Carter, Warren. *John: Storyteller, Interpreter, Evangelist.* Peabody: Hendrickson, 2006.
Ciampa, Roy E., and Brian S. Rosner. *The First Letter to the Corinthians.* PNTC. Grand Rapids: Eerdmans, 2010.
Charlesworth, James H., ed. *The Old Testament Pseudepigrapha.* 2 Vols. New York: Doubleday, 1983.
Collins, Adela Yarbro, and John J. Collins. *King and Messiah as Son of God: Divine, Human, and Angelic Messianic Figures in Biblical and Related Literature.* Grand Rapids: Eerdmans, 2008.
Collins, John J. "Enoch and the Son of Man: A Response to Sabino Chilà and Helge Kvanvig." In *Enoch and the Messiah Son of Man*, edited by Gabriele Boccaccini, 216–37. Grand Rapids: Eerdmans, 2007.
———. "Response: The Apocalyptic Worldview of Daniel." In *Enoch and Qumran Origins: New Light on a Forgotten Connection*, edited by Gabriele Boccaccini, 59–66. Grand Rapids: Eerdmans, 2005.
———. *The Scepter and the Star: Messianism in Light of the Dead Sea Scrolls.* 2nd ed. Grand Rapids: Eerdmans, 2010.
Conzelmann, Hans. *1 Corinthians.* Translated by James W. Leitch. Hermeneia. Philadelphia: Fortress, 1975.
Craddock, Fred B. "The Letter to the Hebrews." In *New Interpreter's Bible*, vol. 12, 1–173. Nashville: Abingdon, 1998.
Cranfield, C. E. B. *The Epistle to the Romans.* 2 Vols. ICC. Edinburgh: T&T Clark, 1975.
Cross, F. L., and E. A. Livingstone. *The Oxford Dictionary of the Christian Church.* 3rd ed. Oxford: Oxford University Press, 1997.
Culpepper, R. Alan. *Anatomy of the Fourth Gospel: A Study in Literary Design.* Philadelphia: Fortress, 1987.
———. *The Gospel and Letters of John.* Nashville: Abingdon, 1998.
Dana, H. E., and J. R. Mantey. *A Manual Grammar of the Greek New Testament.* Toronto: The Macmillan Company, 1955.
Davies, W. D., and Dale C. Allison. *The Gospel According to Saint Matthew 1–7.* ICC. London: T&T Clark, 1988.
———. *The Gospel According to Saint Matthew 8–18.* ICC. London: T&T Clark, 1991.
———. *The Gospel According to Saint Matthew 19–28.* ICC. London: T&T Clark, 1997,
DelCogliano, Mark, and Andrew Radde-Gallwitz. *St. Basil of Caesarea: Against Eunomius.* The Fathers of the Church 122. Washington, DC: The Catholic University of America Press, 2011.
Donaldson, Terrence L. "Son of God." In *NIDB*, vol. 5, 335–41.
Dunn, James D.G. *Beginning from Jerusalem: Christianity in the Making, Vol. 2.* Grand Rapids: Eerdmans, 2009.
———. *Christology in the Making.* Philadelphia: Westminster, 1980.
———. "Christology (NT)." In *ABD*, vol. 1, 979–91.
———. *Did the First Christians Worship Jesus? The New Testament Evidence.* London: SPCK, 2010.
———. *The Epistle to the Galatians.* BNTC. Peabody: Hendrickson, 1993.
———. *The Epistles to the Colossians and to Philemon.* NIGTC. Grand Rapids: Eerdmans, 1996.
———. "The First and Second Letter to Timothy and the Letter to Titus." In *New Interpreter's Bible*, vol. 11, 775–880. Nashville: Abingdon, 2000.
———. "Incarnation." In *ABD*, vol. 3, 397–404.

BIBLIOGRAPHY

———. *Jesus Remembered: Christianity in the Making*, Vol. 1. Grand Rapids: Eerdmans, 2003.

———. *New Testament Theology: An Introduction*. Nashville: Abingdon, 2009.

———. *Romans 1–8*. WBC 38A. Nashville: Thomas Nelson, 1988.

———. *The Theology of Paul the Apostle*. Grand Rapids: Eerdmans, 1998.

Ehrman, Bart. *How Jesus Became God: The Exaltation of a Jewish Preacher from Galilee*. New York: HarperOne, 2014.

———. *The Orthodox Corruption of Scripture: The Effects of Early Christological Controversies on the Text of the New Testament*. New York: Oxford University Press, 1993.

Emerson, R.W. *Nature; Addresses, and Lectures*. Boston and Cambridge: James Munroe and Company, 1849.

Erho, Ted M. "Historical-Allusional Dating and the Similitudes of Enoch." *JBL* 130:3 (2011) 493–511.

Fitzmyer, Joseph A. *The Dead Sea Scrolls and Christian Origins*. Grand Rapids: Eerdmans, 2000.

———. *First Corinthians: A New Translation with Introduction and Commentary*. AB 32. New Haven, CT: Yale University Press, 2008.

———. *The Gospel According to Luke I–IX: Introduction, Translation, and Notes*. AB 28. Garden City: Doubleday, 1981.

Fossum, Jarl. "Son of God." In *ABD*, vol. 6, 128–37.

France, R. T. *The Gospel of Mark*. NIGTC. Grand Rapids: Eerdmans, 2002.

García Martínez, Florentino, and Eibert J. C. Tigchelaar, *The Dead Sea Scrolls: Study Edition*. 2 Vols. Grand Rapids: Eerdmans, 1998.

Garland, David E. *Luke*. ZECNT. Grand Rapids: Zondervan, 2011.

Gasque, W. Ward, and Ralph P. Martin, eds. *Apostolic History and the Gospel: Biblical and Historical Essays Presented to F.F. Bruce on His 66th Birthday*. Grand Rapids: Eerdmans, 1970.

Gathercole, Simon J. *The Preexistent Son: Recovering the Christologies of Matthew, Mark, and Luke*. Grand Rapids: Eerdmans, 2006.

Gundry, Robert H. "The Form, Meaning and Background of the Hymn Quoted in 1 Timothy 3.16." In *Apostolic History and the Gospel: Biblical and Historical Essays Presented to F.F. Bruce on His 66th Birthday*, edited by W. Ward Gasque and Ralph Martin, 203–22. Grand Rapids: Eerdmans, 1970.

Haag, H. "*bēn*." In *TDOT*, vol. 2, 145–59.

Hagner, Donald A. *Matthew 1–13*. WBC 33A. Dallas: Word, 1993.

———. *The New Testament: A Historical and Theological Introduction*. Grand Rapids: Baker Academic, 2012.

Haight, Roger. *Jesus, Symbol of God*. Maryknoll, NY: Orbis, 2002.

Hamerton-Kelly, Robert G. *Pre-Existence, Wisdom, and the Son of Man: A Study of the Idea of Pre-Existence in the New Testament*. SNTSMS 21. Cambridge: Cambridge University Press, 1973.

Hanson, A. T. *The Image of the Invisible God*. London: SCM, 1982.

Harnack, Adolf. *History of Dogma*. Vol. 1. Translated by Neil Buchanan. New York: Dover, 1961.

Hays, Richard. *First Corinthians*. Interpretation. Louisville: John Knox, 1997.

Heiser, Michael S. "Deuteronomy 32:8 and the Sons of God." *BSac* 158 (Jan–Mar 2001) 52–74.

BIBLIOGRAPHY

Hengel, Martin. *Between Jesus and Paul*. London: SCM, 1983.
———. *The Son of God*. London: SCM, 1976.
Hick, John. *The Myth of God Incarnate*. London: SCM, 1977.
Hillar, Marian. *From Logos to Trinity: The Evolution of Religious Beliefs from Pythagoras to Tertullian*. Cambridge: Cambridge University Press, 2012.
Hodge, Caspar Wistar. "Foreknow." In *ISBE*, vol. 2, 1128–31.
Hodge, Charles. "Religious State of Germany." *The Biblical Repertory and Princeton Review* 18:4 (1846) 514–46.
Holladay, Carl R. *A Critical Introduction to the New Testament: Interpreting the Message and Meaning of Jesus Christ*. Nashville: Abingdon, 2005.
Howard, George. "Phil 2:6–11 and the Human Christ." *CBQ* 40 (1978) 368–87.
Hurtado, Larry W. *How on Earth Did Jesus Become God? Historical Questions about Earliest Devotion to Jesus*. Grand Rapids: Eerdmans, 2009.
———. *Lord Jesus Christ: Devotion to Jesus in Early Christianity*. Grand Rapids: Eerdmans, 2003.
———. "Pre-existence." In *DPL*, 743–46.
Jeremias, Joachim. *Die Briefe an Timotheus und Titus*. Das Neue Testament Deutsch 9. Göttingen: Vandenhoeck & Ruprect, 1975.
———. *The Prayers of Jesus*. Translated by C. Burchard et al. Naperville, IL: Allenson, 1967.
Johansson, Daniel "'Who Can Forgive Sins but God Alone?' Human and Angelic Agents, and Divine Forgiveness in Early Judaism." *JSNT* 33:4 (2011) 351–74.
Johnson, Luke Timothy. *The First and Second Letters to Timothy: A New Translation with Introduction and Commentary*. AB 35A. New York: Doubleday, 2001.
de Jonge, M., and A. S. Van der Woude. "11Q Melchizedek and the New Testament." *NTS* 12:4 (1966) 301–26.
Kerrigan, Jason. *Restoring the Biblical Christ: Is Jesus God?* Vol. 1. Denver: Outskirts, 2007.
Kingsbury, Jack Dean. *Matthew as Story*. Philadelphia: Fortress, 1986.
Knibb, Michael A. "Messianism in the Pseudepigrapha in the Light of the Scrolls." In *Essays on the Book of Enoch and Other Early Jewish Texts and Traditions*, SVTP 22, 307–26. Leiden: Brill, 2009:
Koester, Craig. *Symbolism in the Fourth Gospel: Meaning, Mystery, Community*. 2nd. ed. Minneapolis: Fortress, 2003.
Köstenberger, Andreas J. "John." In *Commentary on the New Testament Use of the Old Testament*, edited by G. K. Beale and D. A. Carson, 415–512. Grand Rapids: Baker Academic, 2007.
Köstenberger, Andreas J. and Scott R. Swain. *Father, Son, and Spirit: The Trinity and John's Gospel*. NSBT 24. Nottingham: Apollos, 2008.
Kuschel, Karl-Josef. *Born Before All Time? The Dispute over Christ's Origin*. Translated by John Bowden. New York: Crossroads, 1992.
Ladd, George Eldon. *A Theology of the New Testament*. Revised by Donald A. Hagner. Grand Rapids: Eerdmans, 1993.
Lee, Aquila H. I. *From Messiah to Preexistent Son: Jesus' Self-Consciousness and Early Christian Exegesis of Messianic Psalms*. WUNT II/192. Tübingen: Mohr Siebeck, 2005.
Lewis, Jack. "The Jewish Background of the New Testament," *Restoration Quarterly* 4 (1961) 209–15.
Lightfoot, Neil R. *Jesus Christ Today*. Grand Rapids: Baker Book House, 1976.

BIBLIOGRAPHY

Longenecker, Richard. *Galatians*. WBC 41. Nashville: Thomas Nelson, 1990.

Manzi, Franco. *Melchisedek e l'angelologia nell'Epistola agli Ebrei e a Qumran*. Rome: Pontifical Biblical Institute, 1997.

Marcus, Joel. "Mark 14:61: 'Are You the Messiah-Son-of-God?'" *NovT* 31:2 (1989) 125–41.

Marshall, I. Howard. *A Critical and Exegetical Commentary on the Pastoral Epistles*. ICC. London: T&T Clark, 1999.

Martin, Ralph P., and Brian J. Dodd, eds. *Where Christology Began: Essays on Philippians 2*. Louisville: Westminster John Knox, 1998.

Martyn, J. Louis. *Galatians: A New Translation with Introduction and Commentary*. AB 33A. New Haven, CT: Yale University Press, 1997.

McCready, Douglas. *He Came Down from Heaven: The Preexistence of Christ and the Christian Faith*. Downers Grove, IL: InterVarsity, 2005.

McGrath, James. *John's Apologetic Christology: Legitimation and Development in Johannine Christology*. SNTSMS 111. Cambridge: Cambridge University Press, 2001.

———. *The Only True God: Early Christian Monotheism in Its Jewish Context*. Urbana and Chicago: The University of Illinois Press, 2009.

———. "A Rebellious Son? Hugo Odeberg and the Interpretation of John 5.18." *NTS* 44 (1998) 470–73.

Meyer, Ben. F. "Jesus Christ." In *ABD*, vol. 3, 773–96.

Michel, Otto. "Son." In *NIDNTT*, vol. 3, 636–37.

Morris, Leon. *The Gospel According to John*. NICNT. Grand Rapids: Eerdmans, 1971.

Mosser, Carl. "The Earliest Patristic Interpretations of Psalm 82, Jewish Antecedents, and the Origin of Christian Deification." *JTS* 56 (April 2005) 30–74.

Mounce, William D. *Pastoral Epistles*. WBC 46. Nashville: Thomas Nelson, 2000.

Murphy-O'Connor, Jerome. "Christologia Anthropology in Phil. 2:6–11." *RB* 83 (1976) 25–50.

Navas, Patrick. *Divine Truth or Human Tradition?: A Reconsideration of the Orthodox Doctrine of the Trinity in Light of the Hebrew and Christian Scriptures*. Bloomington, IN: AuthorHouse,   2011.

Nickelsburg, George W. E. "Enoch, First Book of." In *ABD*, vol. 2, 508–16.

———. "Son of Man." In *ABD*, vol. 6, 137–50.

Nickelsburg, George W. E., and James C. VanderKam. *1 Enoch 2: A Commentary on the Book of 1 Enoch Chapters 37–82*. Hermeneia. Minneapolis: Fortress, 2012.

O'Brien, Peter T. *Colossians, Philemon*. WBC 44. Waco: Word, 1982.

Ohlig, Karl-Heinz. *One or Three? From the Father of Jesus to the Trinity*. Translated by Richard Henninge. Frankfurt am Main: Peter Lang, 2002.

Osiek, Carolyn. *Galatians*. New Testament Message 12. Wilmington: Michael Glazier, 1984.

———. *Philippians, Philemon*. Abingdon New Testament Commentaries. Nashville: Abingdon Press, 2000.

Parry, Donald W., and Emmanuel Tov. *The Dead Sea Scrolls Reader*. Leiden: Brill, 2004.

Phillips, W. Gary. "An Apologetic Study of John 10:34–36." *BSac* 146 (Oct–Dec 1989) 405–19.

Rengstorf, Karl Heinrich. "*apostellō*." *TDNT*, vol. 1, 398–423.

Robinson, H. Wheeler. *The Cross in the Old Testament*. London: SCM, 1956.

Robinson, John A. T. *The Human Face of God*. Philadelphia: The Westminster, 1973.

———. *The Priority of John*. Philadelphia: Fortress, 1985.

———. *Redating the New Testament*. London: SCM, 1976.

BIBLIOGRAPHY

Rowe, C. Kavin. "Romans 10:13: What is the Name of the Lord?" *HBT* 22 (2000) 135–73.

Sasse, Hermann. "*kosmos, ktl.*" *TDNT*, vol. 3, 867–98.

Seow, Choon-Leong. *A Grammar for Biblical Hebrew*. Rev. ed. Nashville: Abingdon, 1995.

Silva, Moisés. *Biblical Words and Their Meaning*. Grand Rapids: Zondervan, 1983.

Smalley, Stephen S. *1, 2, 3 John*. WBC 51. Waco: Word, 1984.

Smith, Dustin. "Defining Jewish Preexistence—Part 5," Dustin Martyr Blog, October 7, 2014. https://dustinmartyr.wordpress.com/2014/10/07/defining-jewish-preexistence-part-5/.

Talbert, Charles H. "The Problem of Pre-existence in Phil. 2:6–11." *JBL* 86 (1967) 141–53.

Thayer, Joseph H. *Greek-English Lexicon of the New Testament*. Peabody: Hendrickson, 2009.

Thompson, Marianne Meye. *The God of the Gospel of John*. Grand Rapids: Eerdmans, 2001.

———. "John, Gospel of." In *DJG*, 368–83.

Tilling, Chris. *Paul's Divine Christology*. WUNT II/323. Tübingen: Mohr Siebeck, 2012.

"Truth 'Once for All Delivered' or a Living Theology." *The Biblical World* 35.4 (April 1910) 219–22.

Van de Water, Rick. "Michael or Yhwh?: Toward Identifying Melchizedek in 11Q13." *JSP* 16.1 (2006) 75–86.

Van der Horst, Pieter W. "Review of *The Only True God: Early Christian Monotheism in Its Jewish Context* by James McGrath." *JSJ* 41 (2010) 413–14.

VanderKam, James C. *The Dead Sea Scrolls Today*. Grand Rapids: Eerdmans, 1994.

Von Eicken, Erich and Helgo Lindner. "Apostle." In *NIDNTT*, vol. 1, 126–37.

Von Wahlde, Urban C. *The Gospel and Letters of John*. Vol. 2. Grand Rapids: Eerdmans, 2010.

Wallace, Daniel B. *Greek Grammar Beyond the Basics*. Grand Rapids: Zondervan, 1996.

Watts, John. *Isaiah 34–66*. WBC 25. Waco: Word, 1987.

Westcott, B. F. *The Epistle to the Hebrews*. Grand Rapids: Eerdmans, 1980.

Whitelam, Keith W. "Jesse." In *ABD*, vol. 3, 772–73.

Wiles, Maurice. "Christianity without Incarnation?" In *The Myth of God Incarnate*, edited by John Hick, 1–10. London: SCM, 1977.

Williams, Rowan. *Arius: Heresy and Tradition*. Rev. ed. Grand Rapids: Eerdmans, 2001.

Williams, Sam K. *Galatians*. ANTC. Nashville: Abingdon, 1997.

Winter, Bruce. *After Paul Left Corinth*. Grand Rapids: Eerdmans, 2001.

Wise, Michael O., Martin Abegg Jr., and Edward Cook. *The Dead Sea Scrolls: A New Translation*. San Francisco: HarperSanFrancisco, 1996.

Witherington, Ben, III. *The Christology of Jesus*. Minneapolis: Fortress, 1990.

Wright, N. T. *Jesus and the Victory of God*. Minneapolis: Fortress, 1996.

———. "The Letter to the Romans." In *New Interpreter's Bible,* vol. 10, 393–770. Nashville: Abingdon, 2002.

———. *Paul and the Faithfulness of God*. 2 Vols. Minneapolis: Fortress, 2013.

INDEX OF ANCIENT SOURCES

OLD TESTAMENT/ HEBREW BIBLE

Genesis

1:3	168
1:6	168
1:9	168
1:26-27	42, 65
1:27-28	142
2:4	151
2:18-25	65
3:15	98, 128, 158
3:20	114
5:1	151
6:2	91
14	90
15:18	105
28:4	105
33:7	43
35:12	105
48:18	112
49:8-10	98, 129, 139, 158
49:8	129
49:10	129

Exodus

3:5-6	121
3:14	15, 20, 157
4:16	68, 141
7:1	68, 141
8:10	37
9:14	37
21:6	141
22:8-9	69, 141
23:20-21	34
23:21	44, 90, 92, 121

Numbers

24:17	98, 129, 130, 137, 158
25:1-13	51

Deuteronomy

1:17	69
4:35	37
4:39	37
6:4-9	117
6:4	66, 117
6:5	117
18	130, 149
18:15-19	158
18:15-18	130, 138, 140
18:15	136
18:18-19	43, 130
18:18	98
21:18-21	52
21:18	39
29:29	82, 83
32:8	91
32:39	79
32:43	19

INDEX OF ANCIENT SOURCES

Ruth
2:10	43
4:18-22	134

1 Samuel
2:2	37
21-22	68
24:8	89
28:13	72

2 Samuel
7:12-16	24, 115, 130, 162, 163
7:12-14	131, 137
7:12	98, 130, 159
7:14	6, 23, 38, 45, 131, 137, 152, 162
7:22	37
9:6	89

1 Kings
22:19-22	28

2 Kings
19:19	37
19:25	105, 166

1 Chronicles
2:10-15	134
17:11-14	131
17:20	37
28:5	44
29:20	34, 43, 71, 179
29:23	44

2 Chronicles
9:8	44
19:6-7	69
29:20	121

Nehemiah
9:6	37

Job
1:6	28, 91
2:1	28, 91
10:13	100
14:1	136, 170
15:14	136, 170
23:14	100
25:4	136, 170
26:14	162
27:11	100
38:7	91
40:19	162

Psalms
2	42, 115, 133, 137, 163
2:1-2	137
2:2	133
2:7-8	42
2:7	6, 38, 45, 49, 137, 152, 162
2:8-9	133
7	76
7:7-8	76, 91
8:4-6	142
8:4	72
8:5	72
8:6	17, 91
16:10	155
18:50	132
29:1	91
33:6	99
45:1	69
45:6-7	69
45:6	141
58:1	141
78	174
78:23-25	174
82	58, 59, 60, 69, 75, 76
82:1	68, 76, 91
82:2	75
82:6	27, 58, 59, 60, 141
83:18	37
86:8	37
86:10	37
89	115, 132
89:3-4	132
89:6-7	91
89:26-27	6, 38

INDEX OF ANCIENT SOURCES

89:26	162
89:27	106, 112, 152
89:28-29	132
89:36-37	132
96:5	14
97:7	91
102:25-27	15, 32, 86, 114, 115
103:24	106
106:28-31	51
110	90
110:1	9, 17, 25, 26, 30, 42, 49, 51, 143, 158
132:11	98, 132, 136
136:5	99
138	72
138:1	73, 91
145:13	18
148:2	28
148:5	28

Proverbs

2:1	100
3:19-20	99
8	99, 162, 168
8:22-31	14
8:22	162
8:24	162

Isaiah

6:6-7	77, 79
11:1	98, 132, 133
11:2	133
11:4	133
37:20	37
42:1-4	133
42:8	19
43:25	79
44:24	37, 99, 173
45:5	37
45:6	37
45:21-22	19
45:21	37
45:22	37
45:23	18, 19
46:9	37
49:1	171
49:5	171
49:7	89
51:16	179
52:7	77, 91
52:13-53:12	176
53	45
53:12	45
61:2	75, 76, 91

Jeremiah

1:5	40, 103, 166, 171
10:6	37
10:7	37
10:11	14
10:16	14
23:5	131, 159
30:8-9	132
30:9	98
33:15-17	131
33:15	159
33:17	98, 131
51:19	14

Ezekiel

34:23-24	132
34:23	98
37:24-25	132

Daniel

2:46	43
4:34	18
7	149
7:9	133
7:13-14	17, 30, 42, 81
7:13	9, 121, 121, 132, 133, 141, 163, 164
7:14	18

Joel

2:27	37
2:32	19, 21

Amos

9:11	131, 132

INDEX OF ANCIENT SOURCES

Zechariah

3:8	131
6:12	98, 131, 137

APOCRYPHA

1 Maccabees

4.46	130
9.27	130
14.41	130

Baruch

3.23-4.1	101

Sirach

1.1	100
3.6-16	39
24.23	101
33.8	99
48.9-10	41
50	100

Wisdom of Solomon

6	99, 168
9.1	99
9.9	100

PSEUDEPIGRAPHA

1 Enoch

12.4	42
14.8-25	174
37-71	69, 110, 133
39.3-8	174
39.6	69
39.12	71
45.3	70
46.1	133
48.2-3	69
48.3	149
48.4	70
48.5	70, 71, 87, 88, 89
48.6	69, 149
48.10	70, 133, 149
49.4	70
51.3	70
52.4	133, 149
52.6	71
55.4	70
61.3	71
61.8	70
61.9	70, 71
61.11	71
61.12	71
62.3	72
62.6-9	88
62.6	70, 71, 87, 88, 120
62.7	149
62.9-11	88
62.9	70, 71, 87
63:1	120
63.2	71, 120
69.24	71
69.27	70
70-71	174
71.5	120
71.14	69, 120

2 Baruch

4.2-7	166
76	174

2 Enoch

3-23	174

3 Enoch

10	81

4 Ezra

3.14	104
11.37	129
12.31-32	129
13	133
13.26	149
13.52	149
14.9	41

Ascension of Isaiah

7-10	174

INDEX OF ANCIENT SOURCES

Apocalypse of Abraham

1.1	90
7.10	90
7.21	138
8.3	90
9.3	90
10.3-4	73
10.3	44, 89
10.6	89
10.8	44, 73
15-19	174
17	90
17.8	73
17.13	73
17.15	73

Ezekiel Tragedian

68-86	41

Jubilees

12.4	99
30.18	51

Life of Adam and Eve

25-29	174

Prayer of Joseph

1.1-3	108, 110
1.2	102, 108, 166
1.7-9	108
1.9	110

Psalms of Solomon

17.21-24	133
17.23-24	150

Sibylline Oracles

5.414-416	81

Testament of Abraham

10-15	174
11.4-12	41
12.4-11	41
13.1-4	41

Testament of Job

2.1	28, 80, 161
3.5	81

Testament of Judah

24.1-6	130
24.4-6	132
24.5	129

Testament of Levi

2-8	174

Testament of Moses

1.14	102, 166

NEW TESTAMENT

Matthew

1:1	134, 151
1:2-17	151
1:3	134
1:5	134
1:6	134
1:16	134, 152
1:18	38, 98, 134, 160, 177
1:20	38, 98, 134, 177
1:21	150, 156, 169
1:23	134
1:25	169
3:1	164
3:17	5, 7, 38, 141
4:1-11	141
4:8-9	81
5:17	13
6:1	105
6:9	39
8:5-13	68
8:29	141
9:2-3	77
9:2	79
9:3	9, 28
9:5-8	121
9:6	39, 141

INDEX OF ANCIENT SOURCES

Matthew *(cont.)*

9:8	28, 33, 39, 77, 79, 81, 179
9:13	13
10:28	163
10:34-35	13
10:40	140, 178
11:2	171
11:11	136, 170
11:27	5, 8, 10, 23, 81
12:8	141
12:12	27
12:40	45, 141
13:37-43	81
13:47	141
14:10	171
14:26	157
15:34	140
16:13-17	154
16:16	5, 6, 24, 25, 141
16:20	25
16:27	141
17:5	5
17:9	141
17:22	141
19:28	141
20:21	140
20:28	13, 142, 150
20:32	140
21:9	140
21:23-27	174
21:23	81, 174
21:37	5, 23
22:41-46	7
23:39	140
24:27	141
24:30	141
24:36	6, 40, 60, 61, 140
24:37	141
24:39	141
24:44	141
25:31	141
26:24	141
26:45	141
26:62-66	5
26:63-66	9
26:63	6, 24, 141
27:8	153
27:40	141
27:43	141
27:46	142
27:54	5, 141
28:2	161
28:18	17, 33, 54, 81, 121, 143

Mark

1:1	6, 24, 141
1:11	5, 7, 38
1:15	164
2:7-10	140
2:7	9, 13, 77, 92
5:9	140
5:30-31	140
6:3	135
6:5	33
6:38	140
8:23	140
8:27-29	154
8:29	5, 24
8:45	140
9:1	164
9:7	5
9:21	140
9:37	140, 178
10:45	13, 142
10:47	135
10:48	135
11:9	140
11:13	140
11:27-33	174
12:6	5, 23
12:28-34	117, 142
12:28-29	117
12:35-37	7
12:35	135
13:32	6, 40, 60, 61, 140
14:36	7, 26
14:53-66	51
14:61-64	5, 9
14:61	6, 24, 118
14:62	121
15:39	5
15:34	142

INDEX OF ANCIENT SOURCES

Luke

1:30-35	115
1:31	135, 169
1:32-33	135
1:32	38, 160
1:34	160
1:35	38, 40, 98, 101, 135, 152, 160, 177
2:40	140
2:49	160
2:52	140
3:22	5, 7, 38
3:23-38	135
3:38	65, 82
4:1-13	141
4:26	171
4:43	140
5:21	9
5:32	13
7:1-10	68
7:2-10	68
7:3	68
7:7	153
9:18-20	154
9:20	5
9:35	5
9:48	178
10:16	178
10:22	5, 7, 10, 23
12:49	13
12:51	13
13:35	140
19:10	13
19:38	140
20:1-8	174
20:13	5, 23, 171
20:41-44	7
22:67-71	5, 9
22:67	25
22:70	25
23:47	5
24:7	142

John

1:1-18	98, 138, 161
1:1-14	82, 168
1:1-13	138
1:1-3	11, 40
1:1-2	116
1:1	20, 34, 37, 60, 65, 82, 98, 100, 115, 169
1:2	11
1:3	11, 14, 15, 31, 56, 66, 82, 85, 100, 168
1:4	168
1:6	40, 82
1:9	13, 138
1:10	14, 31, 56, 85, 168
1:11	168
1:12	26, 65
1:14	11, 82, 98, 100, 101, 138, 147, 169
1:18	86, 98, 138
3:4	104
3:11-13	174
3:12	173
3:13	11, 146, 147, 160, 161, 173, 174
3:16	98, 138
3:17	13, 138
3:18	98, 138
3:19	13
3:31	11
3:34	101, 140
3:35	81, 179
4:34	140, 142, 178
5	79
5:17	79, 140
5:18	8, 27, 39, 52, 53
5:19	39, 78, 79, 142
5:20	79
5:21	78, 79, 140
5:22-23	19
5:22	78, 140
5:23	78, 123
5:26-27	82
5:26	15, 32, 56, 57, 65, 82, 85, 107, 114, 116
5:30	39, 140, 142, 178
5:36	178
5:43	140
6:14	13, 138
6:20	157
6:27	140
6:31	174

195

INDEX OF ANCIENT SOURCES

John *(cont.)*

6:32	175
6:38	11, 142, 147, 173, 174, 178
6:39	178
6:42	11
6:51	40, 175
6:53	175
6:54	175
6:57	32, 65, 82, 107, 114
6:62	11
7	158
7:16-17	101
7:16	140, 178
7:28	142
7:29	11, 40
7:40	159
7:41	159
7:42	138, 159
8:10	140
8:19	55, 179
8:26	138
8:28	140
8:29	142
8:30	140
8:40	98
8:41	27
8:42	11
8:52	104
8:56	104
8:57	104, 109
8:58-59	8
8:58	11, 28, 40, 79, 102, 104, 107, 109, 147, 148, 161, 173
9:4	178
9:39	138
10:25	140
10:29	142
10:30-36	8, 28
10:30-33	27
10:30	10, 29, 58
10:31	58
10:32-33	119
10:32	58
10:33	8, 53, 58
10:34-36	58
10:34	141
10:35	60
10:36	8, 11, 36, 40, 138
10:38	59
10:39	59
11:17	140
11:27	6, 13, 24, 138, 141
11:37	140
12:13	140
12:44	179
12:45	179
12:46	13, 138
12:47-50	101
12:49-50	142
12:49	140, 178
13:3	179
13:20	178, 179
14:7-9	179
14:7	55
14:9	55, 86
14:9-10	10, 29
14:10	101
14:24	101, 178
14:28	142
15:15	142
15:23	179
16:12-13	117
16:28	11, 13, 41, 138
17	110
17:1	12
17:3-5	79, 80, 107, 116
17:3	37, 45, 66, 142, 178
17:4-5	12, 147
17:5	40, 54, 102, 104, 105, 110, 148, 162, 173
17:6	101
17:8	179
17:11	127
17:16	101
17:18	13, 138
17:21-23	29
17:21-22	127
17:22-23	123
17:22	105, 110
17:24	12
18:37	13, 98, 138, 139
19:7	9, 28, 53, 59
19:9	59
20:17	39, 44, 141, 142
20:21	171, 179

INDEX OF ANCIENT SOURCES

20:23	39, 179
20:28	141
20:31	6, 24

Acts

2:14-36	117
2:21	19, 44
2:22	117, 139, 168
2:23	103, 117, 166
2:24	118
2:27	45, 155
2:30	136
2:31	118
2:32	118
2:36	33, 54, 118, 121, 164
3:12-26	118
3:13	118
3:15	45, 118
3:22	118, 136
3:25-26	118
7:30-33	121
7:37	136
10:25	43
13:16-41	118
13:22-23	118
13:23	137
13:26-30	118
13:33	38
13:36-37	118
13:38	118
17:29-31	119
17:30-31	144
17:31	139
20:28	61
22:21	170

Romans

1:1-5	136
1:1-4	38, 137
1:3-4	136
1:3	98, 136
1:4	17, 33
1:23	45
1:25	18
2:28	172
3:4	119
3:25	21
4:22	153
5:1	105
5:12-21	142
7:5	171, 172
7:18	172
8:3	147, 168, 170, 171, 172
8:15	26
8:17	42
8:28-30	103
8:29-30	166
8:30	105
10:13	19, 21, 44
14:1	164
15:12	136
16:20	158

1 Corinthians

1:13-17	110
1:18-2:5	110
2:7-8	105
3:10-15	111
3:23	105, 144
4:1-17	111
5:1-12	111
6:1-11	111
6:12-20	111
6:14	45
7:1-40	111
8:1-13	111
8:4-6	111
8:4	111
8:5	111
8:6	14, 31, 56, 66, 85, 105, 111, 112, 116
11:3	105, 144
12:3	153
15:4	45
15:20	45
15:21	144
15:22-23	144
15:23-28	42, 158
15:23	121, 164
15:24-28	144
15:25	105
15:27	17, 31, 56
15:28	121
15:45	42, 144, 168

INDEX OF ANCIENT SOURCES

1 Corinthians (cont.)
15:47	144, 168
15:57	105

2 Corinthians
1:3	143
4:4	10
4:14	45
5:1	105
5:17	21

Galatians
1:13-14	51
1:15	103, 171
2:20	21, 142, 172
3:16	136
4:4	98, 136, 146, 168, 170, 171
4:6	26
4:14	172

Ephesians
1:3	143
1:4-5	103, 166
1:8-10	103
1:10	106
1:20-22	17
2:11	172
2:18	26
3:2-6	122
3:19	30
4:4-6	144
4:8	153
5:14	153
6:12	69

Philippians
1:22	172
2	80, 175
2:5-11	12, 31, 55
2:5-8	54
2:5	13, 175
2:6-11	175, 176
2:6-7	148, 175
2:7	50
2:9-11	18, 80, 105, 121, 143
2:9-10	20
2:9	45, 81, 143
2:10-11	18
2:10	19
2:17	176
2:25-30	176
3:3	172
3:4-7	176
3:6	51
3:17	176
3:21	17

Colossians
1:3	143
1:13	112
1:14	112
1:15-16	17, 66
1:15	10, 29, 31, 32, 106, 112, 162
1:16	14, 16, 31, 56, 85, 111, 112, 114, 116
1:17	15
1:18	106
1:19	10
1:24	172
2:6-15	112
2:9	10, 30
2:16	112
3:10	21

1 Thessalonians
5:9	105
5:23	163

1 Timothy
1:15	13
1:17	45
2:5	43, 66, 144, 158, 163, 172
3:16	147, 168, 171, 172
6:15	17, 33, 164
6:16	115

2 Timothy
2:8	172

INDEX OF ANCIENT SOURCES

Titus
2:13	21, 35

Philemon
1:16	172

Hebrews
1:1-14	13, 94
1:1-3	120
1:1-2	37
1:2-3	17
1:2	14, 31, 56, 85
1:3	10, 15, 30, 85, 86, 114, 158
1:5	24, 38, 95, 97, 113, 137
1:6	13, 19
1:8	141
1:10-11	86
1:10	32, 85
1:11-12	15, 32
1:12	32
2:5-18	13
2:14	147, 168
2:8	31
2:9	72
2:14	172
2:17	123, 172
3:1	178
5:5-8	13
5:8	140
7:3	13
7:14	137
8:1	143
10:5-7	13
10:5	13
13:8	15, 32

James
1:17	40, 173, 174, 175
3:15	40, 173, 174
3:17	40, 173, 174
4:6	153

1 Peter
1:1-2	103, 166
1:3	143
1:20	103, 166
3:18	172

2 Peter
1:1	21, 35
1:4	30
3:10-13	33

1 John
2:22	170
3:1-2	65
4:2	12
4:9	13, 98, 138
5:18	138

2 John
1:3	55
1:7	12, 147, 168

Revelation
1:6	143
1:18	115, 143
2:8	143
3:2	142
3:9	43, 179
3:20	142
4:11	43, 103, 166
5	43
5:5	139
5:9	43
5:12-14	19
5:13	43
13:8	104, 166
19:10	18, 34
22:3	19
22:8-9	18
22:13	143
22:16	139

DEAD SEA SCROLLS

CD
12.23	149
14.9	149
19.10	149
20.1	149

INDEX OF ANCIENT SOURCES

1QS
9.11 — 149
11.11 — 99, 168

1QSa
2.11 — 132

1QSb
5.20-29 — 129

4Q147 — 6

4Q161
3.11-19 — 132

4Q174 — 38, 131, 132
1.18-19 — 137

4Q175 — 130

4Q242 — 179

4Q246 — 6

4Q252
5.1-4 — 129

4Q280 — 129

4Q400-407 — 73

4Q401 — 78

4Q521 — 81, 179

11Q13 — 60, 77, 90, 91, 92
2.11-12 — 75

RABBINIC WRITINGS

b. B. Mes
96a — 140

b. Hag
10b — 140

b. Menah
93b — 140

b. Nazir
12b — 140

b. Ned
39b — 102, 166

b. Pes
54a — 102, 166

b. Qidd
42b — 140
43a — 140

b. Sanh
38a — 133
96b-97a — 132
98b — 132

b. Qidd
42b — 44
43a — 44

INDEX OF ANCIENT SOURCES

j. Taan
68d	129

m. Ber
5.5	140

m. Git
3.6	178
4.1	177

m. Qidd
2.1	177

m. Sanh
9.6	51

m. Yebam
16.7	178

t. Yebam
4.4	177

y. Ta'anit
4.5	9

Genesis Rabbah
1.1	103, 166
1.4	103, 166
8.2	103, 166
44.22	104
78	140
97	129

Leviticus Rabbah
31.6	138

Midrash Psalms
2	137

Numbers Rabbah
13.14	133

Targum Fragment
Num 24:17	130

Targum Jonathan
Jer 33:15	131
Zech 3:8	131

Targum Neofiti
Gen 49:9-12	129
Num 24:17	130

Targum Ps.-Jonathan
Gen 49:9-12	129
Num 24:17	130

Targum of Zechariah
4.7	102, 166

GRECO-ROMAN WRITINGS

Josephus
Antiquities
6.257	68

Livy
History of Rome
1.16	3
5.24	3

Philo
Conf.
63	39

Congr.
1.12-13	100

Dec.
118	39
119	140

INDEX OF ANCIENT SOURCES

Det. Pot.

54	99
124	100
161	141

Fug.

109	99

Leg.

2.82	100

Praem.

95	130

Prob.

1.43	141

Somn.

1.229	100

Spec.

1.54-55	51
2.253	51

Vit. Moses

1.155-6	81
1.158	141
1.162	100, 169
1.280	130
2.4	100, 169

EARLY CHRISTIAN WRITINGS

Athanasius

Against the Arians

1.5	4, 84
1.14	58
1.20-21	10
1.36	15, 86
1.39	60
1.58	15, 86

Circular to the Bishops of Egypt and Libya

14	15

Basil of Caesarea

Against Eunomius

2.16-17	10
2.31	85

Alexander of Alexandria

Epistle

	85

Eusebius

Ecc. History

5.28	146
7.30	146

Praep.

9.29.4-6	81

Gregory of Nyssa

Oratio Catechetica Magna

3	58
3.2	46
3.17-20	61
4.15	61

Hermas

Similitudes

5.6.4	81

Irenaeus

Against Heresies

1.7.2	45

Leo

Tome

	62

INDEX OF ANCIENT SOURCES

Tertullian
Against Hermogenes
3   45

INDEX OF AUTHORS

Abegg Jr., Martin, 76, 77, 91
Aland, Kurt, 24
Allison, Dale C., 81, 97, 143, 177
Armstrong, Karen, 46
Aschim, Anders, 77
Ash, Anthony Lee, 68, 69

Barclay, John M. G., 175
Barclay, William, 100
Barth, Markus, 106
Barrett, C. K., 138, 139
Barron, David, 66, 162
Bartsch, Hans-Werner, 175
Bauckham, Richard, 13, 15, 16, 19, 30, 31, 50, 71, 72, 74, 75, 76, 87, 88 121, 123, 129
Bauer, David R., 141
Bavinck, Herman, 15, 32
Beasley-Murray, George R., 82, 110
Betz, Hans Dieter, 137, 178
Beyreuther, E., 176
Black, C. Clifton, 138
Bock, Darrell L., 9, 30, 51, 52
Borgen, Peder, 39, 179
Borsch, Frederick H., 175
Bowman Jr., Robert M., 78
Box, G. H., 90
Brown, Colin, 169, 176
Brown, Raymond E., 6, 8, 60, 104, 109, 123, 134, 135, 170
Bruce, F. F., 82, 83, 118, 137
Bullinger, E. W., 80

Buzzard, Anthony F., 117, 147, 152, 153, 156

Capes, David B., 165, 166
Caragounis, Chrys C., 37
Carter, Warren, 100, 104
Ciampa, Roy E., 21
Charlesworth, James H., 108
Collins, Adela Yarbro, 78
Collins, John J., 69, 78, 149
Conzelmann, Hans, 106
Cook, Edward, 76, 77, 91
Craddock, Fred B., 172
Cranfield, C. E. B., 17
Culpepper, R. Alan, 104

Dana, H. E., 81, 82
Davies, W. D., 81, 97, 177
DelCogliano, Mark, 10, 85
Donaldson, Terrence L., 37
Dunn, James D. G., 8, 10, 12, 42, 80, 98, 99, 101, 105, 106, 136, 138, 143, 144, 160, 167, 170, 171, 172, 176

Ehrman, Bart, 46, 138, 143, 171
Emerson, R. W., 3, 184
Erho, Ted M., 110
Finkenrath, G., 176
Fitzmyer, Joseph A., 6, 106, 135
Fossum, Jarl, 37
France, R. T., 7, 117

García Martínez, Florentino, 73, 76

INDEX OF AUTHORS

Garland, David E., 25
Gathercole, Simon J., 11, 13, 80
Gregory of Nyssa, 46, 58, 61
Gundry, Robert H., 172

Haag, H., 37
Hagner, Donald A., 12, 151, 152
Haight, Roger, 101
Hamerton-Kelly, Robert G., 165
Hanson, A. T., 46
Harnack, Adolf, 102
Hays, Richard, 144
Heiser, Michael S., 91
Hengel, Martin, 13, 14
Hick, John, 167
Hillar, Marian, 169
Hodge, Caspar Wistar, 166
Hodge, Charles, 21
Holladay, Carl R., 169
Howard, George, 176
Hurtado, Larry W., 9, 12, 16, 18, 38, 67, 72, 166
Hunting, Charles F., 147, 152, 153

Jeremias, Joachim, 8, 81, 172
Johansson, Daniel, 9
Johnson, Luke Timothy, 172
de Jonge, M., 92

Kerrigan, Jason, 31
Kingsbury, Jack Dean, 154
Knibb, Michael A., 149
Koester, Craig., 173
Komoszewski, J. Ed, 78
Köstenberger, Andreas J., 28, 59, 154
Kuschel, Karl-Josef, 106, 170, 171, 176

Ladd, George Eldon, 7, 24, 156
Landsman, J. I., 90
Lee, Aquila H. I., 8, 11, 12, 16
Lewis, Jack, 66
Lightfoot, Neil R., 72, 171
Lindner, Helgo, 177
Longenecker, Richard, 170, 171

Manzi, Franco, 77
Marcus, Joel, 6, 9, 24, 51
Marshall, I. Howard, 172

Martyn, J. Louis, 137, 171
McCready, Douglas, 11, 12, 15
McGrath, James, 39, 46, 52, 67, 71, 74, 102, 143, 155, 176
Meyer, Ben. F., 143, 169
Michel, Otto, 37
Miller, Clyde M., 68, 69
Morris, Leon, 82
Mosser, Carl, 67
Mounce, William D., 172
Murphy-O'Connor, Jerome, 80, 176

Navas, Patrick, 160, 161
Nickelsburg, George W. E., 69, 70, 89, 141, 149

O'Brien, Peter T., 106
Ohlig, Karl-Heinz, 101
Osiek, Carolyn, 170, 176

Phillips, W. Gary, 59, 60
Rengstorf, Karl Heinrich, 177
Robinson, H. Wheeler, 175
Robinson, John A. T., 101, 104, 110, 140, 175, 176
Rowe, C. Kavin, 19

Sasse, Hermann, 106
Seow, Choon-Leong, 72
Silva, Moisés, 20
Smalley, Stephen S., 138
Smith, Dustin R., 109

Talbert, Charles H., 175
Thayer, Joseph H., 32
Thompson, Marianne Meye, 140, 154, 178, 179
Tilling, Chris, 71

Van de Water, Rick, 77
Van der Horst, Pieter W., 53
VanderKam, James C., 69, 70, 89, 92, 149
Von Eicken, Erich, 177
Von Wahlde, Urban C., 105

Wallace, Daniel B., 20, 25, 115, 161
Watts, John., 179

INDEX OF AUTHORS

Westcott, B. F., 72, 82
Whitelam, Keith W., 136
Wiles, Maurice, 173
Williams, Rowan, 4
Williams, Sam K., 170

Winter, Bruce, 105
Wise, Michael O., 76, 77, 91
Witherington, Ben, 8
Wright, N. T., 16, 38, 39, 171

INDEX OF SUBJECTS

Adam, 41, 42, 65, 82, 142, 174n31
Adam Christology, 12, 42, 80, 144
Agency, principle of, 43–44, 67–68, 72n20, 74–75, 77, 90–95, 96, 121–122, 140–143, 145, 154–155, 163, 171, 177–179
Almighty God, 27, 65, 74, 111, 120, 164
Anabaptists, 146
Anamnesis, 79–80, 107, 109
Angel(s) viii, xiv, 6, 14, 18, 19, 28, 34, 42–44, 47, 55, 60, 66, 67, 72–75, 87–95, 97, 108, 112, 114, 119–122, 134, 135, 139, 149, 152, 155, 161
Apocalyptic, 135n26
Apotheosis, 4, 16–17
Arianism, x, xiv, xv, 52, 84–86, 95, 114
Arius, xi, xiv, 4n3, 84n1, 95, 114
Aseity, 15–16, 32–33, 55, 56–57, 93, 116, 155

Beget, begotten, 40, 42, 46, 58n8, 82n50, 86, 95, 98, 101, 132, 134–139, 145, 152–153, 155, 159, 160, 166–168, 177
Binitarianism, 34, 38, 50, 77, 123
Blasphemy, 5, 8–9, 11, 18, 21, 27–28, 39, 51–53, 58–60, 67, 78, 79, 93, 118, 123

Christ, see Jesus Christ

Christology, vii, viii, xi, xiii–xv, 13, 16, 31, 41, 46, 54–55, 60, 67, 84, 94–95, 96, 106, 124, 139n43, 144, 149–154, 156, 160, 167, 169, 177
Christological monotheism, 16n30
Councils, ecumenical, 4
   Chalcedon, 45, 60–61, 62n16
   Nicaea, xi, 146
Creator-creature distinction xiii, 4, 14–16, 21, 37–38, 47, 49–50, 56, 85–86, 88, 90, 92, 95, 114, 121, 122

Davar, 40, 168–169
Deity, definition of, 3–4, 36–37, 47–48
Divine beings/entities, 11, 13, 15, 31, 40, 47, 65, 72, 75, 76, 77, 80, 84, 91, 94, 95, 97, 98, 102, 107, 108, 113, 120, 138n40, 139n43
Divine identity, 19, 29, 30, 34, 43, 44, 50, 71–72, 87, 90, 93, 121, 122, 123
Dominion, 18, 42, 43, 81, 129, 133, 163

Enthronement, 41, 70
Equality with God, 9n14, 12, 13, 27, 51–53, 122, 148
Eschatology, eschatological, 6, 40, 52, 53, 70, 75, 91, 121, 156
Essence (divine) 47, 49, 50, 84
Eternal generation of the Son, 45, 49–50

INDEX OF SUBJECTS

Exaltation, xiii, 16–19, 33, 41–43, 50–51, 53–55, 66, 70, 71–72, 87, 93–94, 113, 128, 142–144, 148, 155, 163, 172
Exalted beings/angels, 47, 73, 89–91, 93–95

Forgive, Forgiveness of sins xiv, 9, 28–29, 34, 39–40, 77, 79, 91–92, 112, 118, 154, 179,
Fourth Gospel, 39, 41, 53, 101, 104, 139, 168, 173–175, 178
Function, Functional, Functioning, 6, 10, 11, 23, 66, 67, 77, 87, 92–94, 119, 131, 140, 145, 154–156, 179

God Almighty, 123, 84, 114
God of Israel, 19, 20, 65n1, 131
God-functioning, 94
Godhead, 21, 49, 56, 60, 61n15, 62
Godlike, 91, 92, 94
Gospels, Synoptic Gospels, 5, 6, 9, 17n32, 53, 61, 66, 87, 115, 139, 141, 150, 151, 154
Gospel of John, 6, 8, 9, 11, 19, 31, 39, 49, 102, 151, 177–179

High priest, 5, 18, 68, 74, 93, 130n10, 141, 143, 179
Holy Spirit, 24, 49, 82, 117, 134, 135, 152, 153
Homage, 43, 70, 89
Homoousios, 50

Iaoel, see Yahoel
Idolatry, 18, 51, 73, 96
Immortality, 45, 60–61, 115, 176
Incarnation viii, xiii, 4, 10–14, 16, 21, 30, 36, 54, 61, 87, 94, 96–98, 101, 107, 116, 120, 134, 135, 138n40, 139n43, 147, 153, 154, 168–171, 173, 175

Jesus Christ
  Angel, not an, xiv, 34, 94–95, 97, 113, 137
  Baptism of, 5, 7, 17n32, 24, 51, 141, 146, 151

Conception of xv, 82, 160
Crucifixion of, 5, 54, 61
Deity of, 3–4, 10, 15, 16, 36–37, 58, 60, 87, 93
Firstborn, 17, 19, 31, 106, 112, 162
Flesh, taking on, 10, 11–12, 17n32, 40, 66, 73n22, 84, 97, 101n8, 107, 135, 138, 147, 164, 168–169, 171, 172, 175
From heaven, 11, 40, 147–148, 160–161, 170–175
God's agent, 10, 33, 35, 59, 66, 71, 72n20, 84, 111–112, 128, 140–143, 145, 154–155, 164, 168, 178, 179
Humanity of viii, xiii, xiv, 4, 6, 17n32, 29, 41–43, 45–46, 54, 60–62, 62n16, 65, 82, 83, 84, 95, 97–98, 100–102, 104, 106, 113, 118–119, 127–145, 146–156, 157–164, 167–176
Image of God, 10, 29
Intermediary of creation, 14n25, 21, 33, 94, 95, 112, 114, 122
Judge, 9, 51–53, 70, 81, 119, 141, 144
Lamb, 19, 43, 104, 166
Lord, vii, xi–xii, 4, 7, 14, 17–19, 22, 25–26, 30, 33, 42, 80, 81, 105, 111–112, 117–118, 143, 164
Messiah, 4, 6–9, 21, 23–25, 26, 27, 29–30, 40, 43, 45, 46, 51, 80, 107, 111, 116, 118, 121, 122, 128, 140, 151, 156, 158, 163, 169, 172, 174
Messianic agent, 140, 142, 145, 179
Oneness with God, 27, 29, 123
Prophet, more than, 55, 154
Resurrection of, 13, 17, 33, 45, 87, 105, 106, 116, 117, 128, 143, 144, 148, 155, 156, 163, 167
Revealer of God/Father xiii, 10, 12, 29–30, 55, 87, 95, 117, 174
Savior, 20–22, 35, 46, 136
Second Adam, 62n16, 144, 145, 168
Self-consciousness of, 6, 8, 10, 93, 115, 123

INDEX OF SUBJECTS

Servant, 12, 45, 54, 118, 148, 150, 176
Son of God *passim*, but especially, 4–10, 23–30, 38–39, 45, 50, 51–53, 55, 86, 95, 115–116, 135, 137, 141, 151, 152, 154, 159, 163
Son of Man, 18, 30, 42, 51, 69–72, 78, 79, 81, 87–89, 92, 93, 94, 110, 120, 122, 132–133, 141–142, 149, 159, 163
Sovereignty of, xiii, 17, 33, 55, 93
Trial of, 5, 15, 33, 93, 118, 141
Virgin birth of xiv, xv, 4, 65n2, 84, 113, 151–154, 160
Word of God, 82, 84n1, 85
John the Baptist, 40, 164, 174
Judaism, 8, 13, 16, 39, 41, 42, 43, 52, 66, 78, 87, 94, 96, 110,120, 149, 155, 166n4, 167n6, 174

Kingdom of God, 40, 114, 128, 144, 156, 164

Lord of the Spirits, 69, 70n14, 88, 149n9
Logos, 11, 30, 32, 54, 56, 60, 61, 98–100, 113, 138, 161, 168–169

Mary, xiv, xv, 4, 38, 45, 82, 84, 95, 97, 98, 101, 134–135, 145, 152, 159–160, 166
Melchizedek, 66n3, 75–78, 79, 90–92, 93, 94, 113, 121–122
Messiah
  Human descendant, 26, 38, 97, 98, 118, 119, 122, 129–136, 138–139, 149, 158–159
  Jewish expectations of, 13, 120, 128–133, 135, 147, 149–150, 152, 153, 157, 158–159, 167
  Messianic claimant/pretender, 9, 33, 39, 51, 174
  Messianic prophecies, 130, 137, 139, 144, 158, 162–163, 163–164
  Office of, 81, 97–98, 153

Son/descendant of David, 6, 7, 24–26, 37, 38, 51, 122, 130–137, 139, 149, 152, 153, 156, 159
Modalism, 19, 20, 34
Monotheism, viii, xiv, 4, 13, 16, 18, 38, 40, 42, 46, 49–50, 53, 66–67, 70–72, 86–88, 93, 114, 142, 143, 155, 157
Moses, 41–42, 44, 68, 72n20, 81, 96, 100, 118, 121, 130, 136, 169n9

Name of God, 67, 74, 89, 96, 120, 140

Omniscience, 40, 60–61, 140
Oneness of God, 48
Ontological, xiii, 4, 11, 13–17, 19–21, 23, 25, 31–33, 40–42, 47–49, 51, 53, 55–60, 84–87, 93, 95, 122–123, 152, 155

Paul, xv, 5, 9, 10, 12–15, 17–19, 21, 30, 31, 38, 42, 45, 56, 80, 98, 105, 111, 112, 118, 121, 122, 136, 137, 142–144, 146, 148, 170, 171, 175–177
Personification, 12, 98–100, 106, 138, 161, 168, 169
Peter, 5, 24, 25, 30, 33, 43, 103, 117, 118, 136, 141, 155, 164
Polytheism, 16, 30, 34, 46
Prayer, 8, 11, 39, 56, 104, 117, 147
Preexistence viii, xiii, xiv, xv, 3, 4, 10–13, 14n25, 15–17, 18, 28–30, 36, 37, 40–41, 54, 56, 60, 70, 79, 80, 83, 84, 94–95, 97–98, 101–102, 104–105, 107–110, 113, 116, 120, 135, 138n40, 146–148, 149n9, 150–151, 153, 154, 158, 160, 161, 164, 165–177
Prolepsis, 79–80, 109, 147–148
Prologue of John, 11, 40n9, 98–101, 138, 161, 168–169
Prophet like Moses, 44, 118, 130, 136, 138, 140, 149, 158
Prostration, 18, 43, 88–89, 94, 120–121, 129
Psilanthropism, 146–148, 152, 154, 156

INDEX OF SUBJECTS

Qumran, 6n7, 76, 90–92, 122, 129–132, 137, 149, 159, 168

Racovian Catechism xv, 146
Right hand of God, xiii, 4, 9, 16, 17, 18, 19, 22, 25, 30, 36, 50, 51, 54, 93, 118, 143, 145, 158, 167, 168

Sabbath, 8, 27, 39, 53, 140
Salvation, 19, 21, 35, 83, 118, 132, 150, 156
Septuagint, 15, 18, 19, 32, 42n11, 43, 72–73, 89, 91, 106, 115, 121, 129, 130n10, 137, 151, 162, 170
Servant of YHWH, 89, 176
Shema, vii, 117, 142
Socinianism x, xiv–xv, 113, 146
Solomon, 24, 25, 44, 115
Subordination viii, xv, 50, 52, 92, 142, 143, 144, 155

Throne(s), xiv, 41, 72, 102, 103, 133
 of God, 43, 44, 67, 69–71, 87, 92, 94, 120
 of David, 129–132, 135, 156
Trinitarianism, x, xiii, xv, 30, 33, 38, 39, 46n15, 48, 52, 59n9, 60, 82n50, 83, 123, 124
Trinity, ix, 4, 31, 46, 48–50, 127, 176

Unitarianism, xiv, 3, 83

Worship
 of Jesus, xiii, xiv, 9, 18–19, 21, 22, 30, 34, 43, 54, 55, 93, 94, 155, 179
 of exalted beings, 66, 70–72, 79, 87–90, 92, 94, 96, 120–121, 154, 179

Yahoel, 44, 66n3, 73–74, 89–90, 92, 93, 94, 96, 121, 122
Yahweh-functioning, 66, 87, 93, 119

www.ingramcontent.com/pod-product-compliance
Lightning Source LLC
Chambersburg PA
CBHW070251230426
43664CB00014B/2496